DAY HIKING

Mount Adams
and Goat Rocks

Wildflowers display a quilt of seasonal color on the Cowiche Mountain Loop.

Previous page: Green hillsides make a stunning foreground near Tatoosh Peak as Mount Rainier looks on from afar.

Lupine thrive in the moist soil near Deer Lake.

A fly enjoys a meal
of nectar on a Sitka
valerian flower in
Bird Creek Meadows.

A sea of green along the trail in the Gifford Pinchot National Forest demonstrates a very healthy ecosystem.

With a keen eye and a quiet gait you may spot mountain bluebirds on the east side of the Cascade Crest.

From the rocky summit of Hamilton Buttes, hikers are treated to vast landscape views.

Above: Fall foliage adds a splash of mauve to trailside greens near Cougar Lake.

Left: Jeffrey shooting star flowers are common in the moist soils of Indian Heaven Wilderness.

Opposite: The short green-so-much-it-hurts trail to Camp Creek Falls presents a very Northwest landscape.

Sunlight through the trees in Indian Heaven gives a foggy morning a divine feeling.

DAY HIKING

Mount Adams
and Goat Rocks

Indian Heaven · Yakima Area · White Pass

by Tami Asars

MOUNTAINEERS
BOOKS

Mountaineers Books is the publishing division of The Mountaineers, an organization founded in 1906 and dedicated to the exploration, preservation, and enjoyment of outdoor and wilderness areas.

MOUNTAINEERS BOOKS

1001 SW Klickitat Way, Suite 201, Seattle, WA 98134
800.553.4453, www.mountaineersbooks.org

Printed in the United States of America
Distributed in the United Kingdom by Cordee, www.cordee.co.uk
First edition, 2014

Copy Editor: Julie Van Pelt
Layout: Jennifer Shontz, www.redshoedesign.com
Cartographer: Pease Press Cartography
Cover photograph: *Meadows bursting with wildflowers accompany hikers near Goat Lake in the Goat Rocks Wilderness.*
Frontispiece: *Red huckleberries add a vibrant hue to the ghost trees on Coal Creek Mountain.*

Library of Congress Cataloging-in-Publication Data
Asars, Tami.
    Day hiking : Mount Adams and Goat Rocks / by Tami Asars.
      pages   cm
    Includes index.
    ISBN 978-1-59485-764-5 (pbk.) — ISBN 978-1-59485-765-2 (ebook)
1. Hiking—Washington (State)—Mount Adams Wilderness—Guidebooks. 2. Hiking—Washington (State)—Goat Rocks Wilderness—Guidebooks. 3. Mount Adams Wilderness (Wash.)—Guidebooks. 4. Goat Rocks Wilderness (Wash.)—Guidebooks. I. Title.
    GV199.42.W22M639 2014
    796.5109797—dc23

2013048308

Maps shown in this book were produced using National Geographic TOPO!

♲ Printed on recycled paper

ISBN (paperback): 978-1-59485-764-5
ISBN (ebook): 978-1-59485-765-2

Table of Contents

Goat Rocks Wilderness

Bumping Lake Area

US 12/White Pass Area

US 12/Packwood Area

Yakima Area

FR 23/Cispus River Area

FR 23/Takhlakh Lake Area

Indian Heaven Wilderness

Mount Adams Wilderness/ Trout Lake Area

A California quail poses on the Yakima Skyline Trail.

LEGEND

84	Interstate Highway	▲	Campground/Campsite
197	US Highway	■	Building/Landmark
14	State Highway	⊼	Picnic Area
	Secondary Road	▲	Summit
======	Unpaved Road	) (	Pass
== 24 ==	Forest Road	~	River/Stream
--------	Hiking Route	~	Falls
••••••••	Off-Trail Route		Lake
- - - -	Other Trail	⚶	Wetland/Marsh
••••••••	Other Off-Trail Route	)(	Bridge
—•—•—	Wilderness Boundary	→←	Tunnel
1	Hike Number	⚲	Lookout
T	Trailhead		Ranger Station/ Entrance Station
Ⓣ	Alternate Trailhead		
P	Parking	⊷	Gate
			Dam

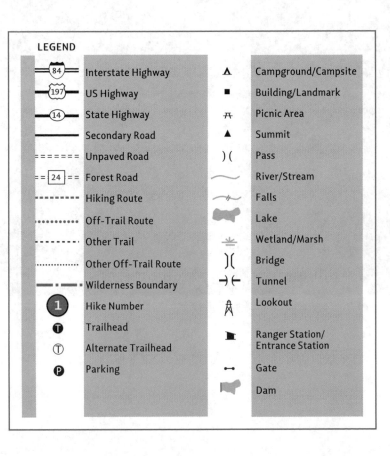

Hikes at a Glance

HIKE	DISTANCE (ROUNDTRIP)	DIFFICULTY	KID-FRIENDLY
GOAT ROCKS WILDERNESS			
1. Conrad Meadows and Surprise Lake	13 miles	4	
2. Bear Creek Mountain	7 miles	3	•
3. Round Mountain	5.2 miles	3	•
4. McCall Basin	14.6 miles	5	
5. Shoe Lake	15.4 miles	5	
6. Lost Hat Lake, Coyote Lake, and Lost Lake Lookout Site	12.2 miles	5	
7. Bluff Lake, Coal Creek Mountain, and Lost Lake Lookout Site	16 miles	5	
8. Lily Lake	3 miles	1	•
9. Three Peaks and Mosquito Lake	10.6 miles	4	
10. Packwood Lake	8.1 miles	2	•
11. Lily Basin and Heart Lake	14.2 miles	4	
12. Glacier Lake	5 miles	3	•
13. Snowgrass Flat	10.9 miles	5	
14. Goat Lake	10.6 miles	5	
15. Hawkeye Point	10.4 miles	5	
16. Nannie Peak and Sheep Lake	10.4 miles	5	
17. Cispus Pass	14 miles	5	
18. Walupt Lake and Walupt Creek	8.8 miles	3	•
BUMPING LAKE AREA			
19. Mount Aix	11.6 miles	5	
20. Twin Sisters Lakes	5 miles	4	•
21. Tumac Mountain	7.8 miles	3	•
22. Swamp Lake and Cougar Lakes	12.6 miles	4	
23. Goat Peak	6.4 miles	5	
US 12/WHITE PASS AREA			
24. Jug Lake	7.4 miles	3	•
25. Dumbbell Lake	14 miles	4	
26. Deer and Sand Lakes	5.2 miles	2	•
27. Spiral Butte	12.6 miles	5	
28. Shellrock Lake	10 miles	4	
29. Indian Creek	10 miles	4	

DOG-FRIENDLY	WILDFLOWERS	BIRD-WATCHING	HISTORICAL	WATERFALLS	CAR CAMP NEARBY
•					•
•	•		•		•
•			•		•
•	•				•
•	•				•
•	•		•		•
•			•		•
•		•			•
•					•
•			•		•
•	•				
•	•				
•	•				•
•	•				•
•	•		•		
•	•		•		
•	•				•
•					•
•					•
•	•				•
•	•		•		•
•					•
•			•		•
•	•		•		•
•					•
•					•
•					•
•					•
•					•

HIKE	DISTANCE (ROUNDTRIP)	DIFFICULTY	KID-FRIENDLY
US 12/PACKWOOD AREA			
30. Tatoosh Peak	11.4 miles	5	
31. High Rock Lookout	3.2 miles	3	•
32. Dry Creek Trail and Smith Point Lookout Site	7 miles	4	
YAKIMA AREA			
33. Umtanum Creek Canyon	6 miles	1	•
34. Yakima Skyline Trail	6–7 miles	3	•
35. Umtanum Creek Falls	2 miles	2	•
36. Black Canyon	7 miles	2	•
37. Waterworks Canyon	3.6 miles	2	•
38. Tieton Nature Trail	3.6 miles	1	•
39. Buck Lake	3 miles	2	•
40. Edgar Rock	2.2 miles	3	•
41. Boulder Cave	1.4 miles	1	•
42. Cowiche Canyon	5.8 miles	2	•
43. Uplands Trail to Winery Trail (Cowiche Canyon)	3.6 miles	3	•
44. Snow Mountain Ranch and Cowiche Mountain	6.1 miles	3	•
FR 23/ CISPUS RIVER AREA			
45. Sunrise Peak	3.2 miles	4	
46. Jumbo Peak Knoll	5.2 miles	3	•
47. Dark Meadow	8.4 miles	3	
48. Blue Lake	5.5 miles	4	
49. Wobbly Lake	2.8 miles	2	•
50. Camp Creek Falls	0.5 mile	1	•
51. Curtain and Angel Falls	3.75 miles	3	•
52. Tongue Mountain	3.1 miles	3	•
53. Juniper Peak	5.8 miles	3	
54. Layser Cave	0.4 mile	1	•
FR 23/TAKHLAKH LAKE AREA			
55. Hamilton Buttes	1.8 miles	2	•
56. Green Mountain	5.6 miles	3	•
57. Takhlakh Lake and Takh Takh Meadow	2.3 miles	2	•
58. Council Bluff	3.2 miles	3	•
INDIAN HEAVEN WILDERNESS			
59. Lake Wapiki	7 miles	3	•
60. East Crater and Bear and Elk Lakes	10.3 miles	3	•
61. Indian Race Track	6.8 miles	3	•

DOG-FRIENDLY	WILDFLOWERS	BIRD-WATCHING	HISTORICAL	WATERFALLS	CAR CAMP NEARBY
•	•		•		•
•			•		•
•			•		•
•	•	•	•		•
•	•	•			
•	•	•		•	
•	•	•	•		
•	•	•			•
•	•	•			•
•	•	•			•
•	•		•		•
					•
•	•		•		
•	•		•		
•	•		•		
•	•		•		•
•	•				•
•	•				•
•					•
•					•
•				•	•
•				•	•
•	•		•		•
•	•				•
•			•		•
•	•				•
•					•
•	•				•
•					•
•					•
•					•
•			•		•

HIKE	DISTANCE (ROUNDTRIP)	DIFFICULTY	KID-FRIENDLY
62. Thomas, Blue, and Tombstone Lakes	7 miles	4	•
63. Cultus Creek and Deep Lake	7.3 miles	3	
64. Placid and Chenamus Lakes	3.2 miles	2	•
65. Squaw Butte and Skookum Meadow	9.2 miles	3	
MOUNT ADAMS WILDERNESS/TROUT LAKE AREA			
66. Bird Creek Meadows and Hellroaring Viewpoint	3.3 miles	3	•
67. Heart Lake	2.2 miles	1	•
68. Shorthorn Trail	5.6 miles	3	
69. Mount Adams South Climb	11.6 miles	5	
70. Snipes Mountain and Crooked Creek Falls	12.8 miles	4	
71. Stagman Ridge, Horseshoe Meadow, and Lookingglass Lake	10.4 miles	4	
72. Salt Creek	6.2 miles	2	•
73. Crofton Ridge	5.2 miles	2	•
74. Pacific Crest Trail to Horseshoe Meadow	11 miles	4	
75. Riley Creek	9.4 miles	3	
76. Steamboat Mountain	1.4 miles	3	•
77. Langfield Falls	0.4 mile	1	•
78. Sleeping Beauty	2.6 miles	4	•
79. Killen Creek	6.2 miles	3	•
80. Divide Camp	6.8 miles	3	•
81. Muddy Meadows and Foggy Flat	11.6 miles	3	•

DOG-FRIENDLY	WILDFLOWERS	BIRD-WATCHING	HISTORICAL	WATERFALLS	CAR CAMP NEARBY
•	•				•
•					•
•					•
•	•				•
•	•				•
•	•				•
•					•
			•		•
•				•	•
•	•				•
•		•			•
•					•
•					•
•					•
•	•				•
•				•	•
•					•
•	•				•
•	•				•
•	•				•

Acknowledgments

There is no way the pages of this book could contain the amount of thankfulness I have for the people who have graced my life and helped me follow my dreams. First and foremost, I'd like to thank my husband, Vilnis, who, while I was away from home, spent an entire summer eating frozen meals, being a bachelor, caring for our aging dog, Summit, and suffering through my tales of backcountry bliss and challenges. A whole book could be written about the wild encounters and places I experienced while writing this guide, and he listened to every single story. This book and my dreams were fulfilled through his love and support.

The list of friends, family, and neighbors who support me and share my passions is too large to list, but you know who you are. I'm honored to have you in my life. I'd also like to thank the many people I met while researching this book, who went from complete strangers to trusted friends. Together we hiked the hills, bumped up forest roads to hidden trails, laughed endlessly, and connected our spirits through the love of wild places. Among these friends is hiking legend, gentle spirit, and inspiration Herb Schmidt, as well as hiking animal Jerry Kobes. Your hospitality meant the world to me.

Special thanks to the folks from the Naches, Cowlitz, and Mount Adams ranger districts, especially Doug Jenkins, Andrea Durham, and Gail Bouchard. Your wisdom helped me navigate the hinterlands and you provided insight on various locations and issues. Thanks also to Craig Romano, fellow guidebook author and friend, who spent hours over coffee sharing his words of wisdom. I'd be remiss to not thank Mountaineers Books editor in chief Kate Rogers, who has believed in me from the start and continues to support my career by cheering from the sidelines.

Those who are reading these acknowledgments, I'm grateful for you too. I hope you enjoy the words in these pages, which will lead to the beautiful places that free our spirits and lift our hearts.

Opposite: A trail of wildflowers shows hikers the way to Sheep Lake.

A golden-mantled ground squirrel shows off its lovely stripes near Edgar Rocks.

Introduction

One day, while researching this book on a trail near Mount Adams, I was struck by a ponderous thought. Why was I hiking? And why was I writing a hiking guide to direct others where to go hiking? In the course of my research, I'd learned that most trails were created as survival tools for shepherds, hunters, and gatherers. Why then, with a full belly and a warm home, was I wandering about on mountain flanks, huffing and puffing up hills without a vital purpose? As I crunched over a snow patch left over from a stubborn winter, it hit me. There *is* a vital purpose for me and for all of us who hike: Day hiking gives the soul an opportunity to rest, the mind an opportunity to expand, and the body an opportunity to be challenged. Feet, instead of wings, bring us to high places, where the cares of life are left behind and the modern conveniences we depend on are unavailable. Hiking is not just about getting off the grid, but about getting back to the very things that build our human character.

I spent an entire spring, summer, and fall hiking every trail in this book. Some of them inspire poetry high above the clouds, while others make for nice wooded walks and good places to get exercise. I've come to love them all—the vistas, the breath-takers, the unimpressive, and the riparian and wooded.

A trail through desert landscape invites you to follow near Cowiche Canyon.

A cut log makes a fantastic flowerpot for huckleberry starts near Indian Heaven.

Some of the trails in this book are among the most beautiful in Washington State, complete with subalpine views, stunning flora and fauna, and unbelievable places to rest the body and soul. Others are remote, wild, and somewhat forgotten but still have value and a need for your feet, an organic form of trail maintenance. Still other areas are so popular that, despite their vastness, you won't feel alone. You'll know which is which because I give opinions and facts and am up front in all of my descriptions. Each trail has its own feeling, and I do my best to put you there, on the dirt, with words.

This book covers many hikes—from State Route 410 out to Yakima and south all the way down toward the small town of Trout Lake. It primarily focuses on the wilderness areas of Goat Rocks and Mount Adams, but you'll also find hikes in the Indian Heaven Wilderness, near Yakima, Packwood, and around the Cispus River and Forest Road 23.

All of the trails in this book are worth exploring. The diversity of ecosystems—from the sagebrush and volcanic stones to the deep, drippy moss-laden forests—will be a treat for any wilderness buff. You'll find rich human history as well—people have long depended on these trails, some of them for centuries, and many routes follow ancient footsteps. Evidence of long-ago human use persists, as in the peeled cedar trees that signal tree bark harvest by Native tribes.

I've done my best to include a wide variety of trails, suitable for almost every skill level and age, from oldest to youngest, as well as for your four-legged companions. Some trails climb to heights and give even the most fit a physical challenge, while others meander among the canyons, making for a companionable and leisurely walk-n-talk. Whatever trail qualities you seek, you'll find a few good candidates here for a getaway.

There is no greater honor than being able to share these trails and wilderness wanderings with you. May you find solitude, beauty, and enjoyment out in the landscapes described here.

USING THIS BOOK

As I trekked the trails in this book, I did so with you in mind, taking my GPS, writing tablet, and camera as trusty companions. My goal was to collect data, document unique features, and photograph the areas to give you the most accurate and up-to-date information on each trail. Of course, it would be remiss of me not to say that I enjoyed every viewpoint along the way. Exploring is just plain fun.

What the Ratings Mean

Each hike in this book starts with detailed trail facts, some more subjective than others.

Birds such as cedar waxwings are abundant in Indian Heaven Wilderness.

The **rating** of 1 to 5 stars is based on the beauty of the surroundings, the trail's condition, unique trail features, and wildlife opportunities. I always do my best to judge a trail based on what I think the majority of people would agree with. I think of myself as an avid but average hiker. Sure, I spend summers on trails, but I get tired of climbing just like the next gal. There is no science to the hike ratings other than what I have felt with my feet, lungs, and heart. My guidelines are as follows:

    ***** Spectacular scenery, worthy of what might be a long drive, one of the most fantastic trails in this book

    **** Great trail experience, enjoyable scenery

    *** Trail offers a feature or vista worth enjoying

    ** Good place to explore or get exercise

    * Decent opportunity for hiking, but trail may not be in optimal shape or may be frequently shared with other trail users such as horses, mountain bikes, or dirt bikes

The **difficulty score** is based on a hike's overall challenge, elevation gain, and the trail conditions. Shorter hikes that are very steep and grueling may be rated just as difficult as hikes that are longer with just a few somewhat strenuous sections. Likewise, trails that are overgrown or have water-crossing challenges may also be rated higher. In general the difficulty ratings are as follows:

5 Very strenuous and steep/long, with challenging sections and/or routefinding or bushwhacking required

4 Steep, possibly with obstacles, poorly maintained tread, and/or grueling sections

3 A moderate workout and average physical challenge

2 A decent grade; straightforward route-finding

1 Easy, peasy! A walk in the park

Other trail details follow, to help you gather information and make decisions about your adventures. The **roundtrip distance** includes out-and-back or loop mileage based on GPS and map calculations. Mileage can be challenging to determine, as maps vary in point-to-point distances, as do random Internet reports. Heck, take two GPS units down the same trail and they'll give you different, albeit close, readings. My point is that the mileage in this book is as accurate as possible, given the averages of all of my data.

Elevation gain is also tricky to measure. Elevation gain and loss will never be spot-on unless you use a correctly calibrated barometric altimeter and no weather moves in over the Cascades. But that never happens, since the Northwest is a moving weather target. Elevation gain for these hikes is based on topographic maps, US Geological Survey benchmarks, and GPS barometric altimeter readings. Total elevation gain for each hike is calculated as the cumulative gain for the full out-and-back or loop trip.

A hike's **high point** is simply the highest elevation you'll encounter on the trip. While this seems straightforward, keep in mind that the high point may be encountered anywhere along the trail, not necessarily at the final destination.

You'll also find the recommended **season** for each hike. These seasons vary so much from year to year that it's hard for even the most savvy hikers to know when they might encounter snow or unfavorable trail conditions. The Northwest is so fickle! This seasonal recommendation is an average time frame for trail travel when snow conditions usually permit passage. One year, you might be able to hike up a peak in June, while in other years you might have to wait until August. To be certain of trail conditions, contact the appropriate ranger district or land management agency before you head out.

When it comes to **maps**, I generally rely on the topographic Green Trails maps. These maps are easy to use and are updated regularly. Occasionally, especially for the hikes located near Yakima, maps are limited to online versions primarily intended for land management. In those scenarios, you'll find relevant website addresses in Appendix I, and I've provided more detailed directions and descriptions to help you get where you need to go. (If any cartographers are reading this, ahem, I have a way for you to make a buck or two.)

Each hike also tells you what agency to **contact** for up-to-date information, and you'll find the associated websites and phone numbers in Appendix I. The folks at the agency offices are generally very knowledgeable about trail conditions, maintenance issues, and closures, as well as the forest roads leading to trailheads. Through the years I've had some great conversations about local history and current events related to our trail systems. Feel free to pick their brains and get some education as well as current information!

Important **notes**, if any, follow. Here you'll find useful details to help you plan your hike, including required permits, trail restrictions, and whether you'll need a high-clearance or four-wheel-drive vehicle to reach the trailhead.

The **GPS coordinates** listed for each trailhead might help you get to the trail—or get back to your car if you make a wrong turn on your outing.

Last but not least, I've included fun little **icons** to help guide you in selecting your hike. **Kid-friendly** hikes are trails that are shorter, not too steep, and provide something for kids to enjoy along the route or at the end. **Dog-friendly** hikes are those on which dogs are permitted, which is pretty much everywhere except national parks. A healthy concentration of seasonal **wildflowers** is also noted, as is exceptional **bird-watching**. While you'll likely see birds on almost every trail described here, on some hikes the bird-watching is particularly spectacular. **Historical** hikes offer a look back on an area's human story, often including features such as lookout towers or other evidence of past human use. Trails that are overgrown, unmaintained, or suffering from lack of attention are noted as **endangered**.

 Kid-friendly

 Dog-friendly

 Exceptional wildflowers in season

 Exceptional bird-watching

 Historical interest

 Endangered trail

The trail descriptions themselves tell you how to get to the trailhead and what to expect during your adventure, including any interesting features, plants, or wildlife you might encounter, as well as any obstacles such as creek crossings or road washouts. Of course, backcountry conditions change faster than teenage hairstyles, so always

check with the relevant agency for up-to-date information before you go.

PERMITS, REGULATIONS, AND FEES

It seems no matter where you go these days, there is a fee, and playing in the outdoors is no exception. Costs to maintain trails, roads, and backcountry areas for recreation take a backseat to other government projects and obligations. To overcome these budget shortfalls, many user-funded federal and state passes have been developed. So many passes are required throughout the country that in order to figure it out, you either need a good flow chart, complete with dancing arrows, a spokesperson, and animated icons—or a good guidebook.

Let's simplify things. Each hike clearly notes any required passes or other fees. Only a handful of hikes in this book require a trailhead pass. That pass will be either the Northwest Forest Pass (or substitute a federal Interagency Pass) or the Washington State Discover Pass. The Northwest Forest Pass costs either $5 for one day or $30 for one year. It allows entry to many developed parking areas with facilities, including US Forest Service trailheads in Washington and Oregon. The federal Interagency Pass is broader, allowing entry to all Forest Service areas, national parks, and various other federal sites. The cost is $80 a year for most users, $10 for senior citizens, and free for disabled persons or those with active military service. It may be used in lieu of the Northwest Forest Pass at signed trailheads. Lastly, the Washington State Discover Pass ($30 annual or $10 day pass) allows recreation on all state-managed lands, including state parks, water-access points, heritage sites, wildlife and natural areas, and other various trailheads. All of these passes can

WHOSE LAND IS THIS?

Most of the hikes in this book are on public land, which is to say land owned by you and me, the citizens. The question, then, is who manages the land that we own. Thankfully, that answer is pretty straightforward.

The majority of the hikes in this book are managed by the US Forest Service. The Forest Service in the Pacific Northwest oversees seventeen national forests, a national scenic area, a national grassland, and two national volcanic monuments. Nationwide, the agency manages a whopping 193 million acres of national forest and grasslands. The Forest Service, as stated on its website, is "dedicated to the improvement of water resources, development of climate change resiliency, creation of jobs that will sustain communities and restoration and enhancement of landscapes." No doubt that's a lot of work. Most of these lands, with the exception of wilderness areas, are managed for multiple use, which loosely means that people use the land for various purposes—among them timber sales, wildlife habitat, and motorized and nonmotorized recreation. With all of these uses on public lands, it's easy to see how some conflict with each other. Some uses may not exactly sustain the health of the land and water resources.

In the Gifford Pinchot National Forest, where many of the hikes in this book are located, timber sales have resulted in some eyesores and open areas across trails and hillsides. Fires have caused rerouting of streams and runoff and often, due to budget cutbacks, trails have been forgotten and left unattended. Thankfully, the three wilderness areas in this book— Indian Heaven Wilderness, Goat Rocks Wilderness, and Mount Adams Wilderness—are federally protected to ensure the health of their natural condition and retain the primeval character of these beautiful places.

Some lands described in this book are managed by the Washington Department of Fish and Wildlife. Hikes in these areas are clearly identified and are usually open to multiple uses, including hunting and fishing as well as hiking. When funds are lacking, some of these areas are left unkempt, with bullet holes peppering signage and trash strewn about from target practice. Nonprofits help to clean up the mess others leave behind, but the job is too big for just one or two days of volunteers on the trails.

Figuring out who manages the land you are enjoying is important because each agency has its own set of rules, fees, and recreational passes. While it can be confusing, it's our land and we should learn how it's managed on our behalf. As citizens, we have a say! Let the agencies know whether you approve or disapprove of their care for our property.

be purchased at select outdoor retailers, land management offices, or online (see Appendix I).

Some hikes are on conservancy land, a few others on Yakama Nation land. Yakama Nation allows the public access to their land on the east side of Mount Adams July through September. The day-use fees are $5 (good for five days from the date issued), and $5 for fishing ($10 for up to five days). Permits can be purchased using cash or check at self-serve kiosks on Yakama land.

Mount Adams itself has a couple of requirements if you plan to hike or climb above 7000 feet between June 1 and September 30. You'll need to purchase a Cascades Volcano Pass from the Mount Adams Ranger Station in Trout Lake or the Cowlitz Valley Ranger Station in Randle ($10 per person weekdays, $15 weekends, $30 annual unlimited) and also fill out the climbing register (free).

Finally, let's talk briefly about wilderness use permits. These permits are not park passes but rather are free permits self-issued at the trailhead, required by law to be in your possession. At the trailhead, you'll usually find a wooden box filled with blank carbon-copy-style permits and a dull golf pencil (if you're lucky). Bring a pen just in case. These permits help the US Forest Service track the number of people and stock using the trails, which provides valuable data to help with funding and other projects. The permits also serve as a safety net for you in the event of natural disasters, such as fires or landslides, or if a hiker goes missing. Please take the time to fill out this free permit and attach it to your pack.

WEATHER

One thing you can always count on is unpredictability in weather. The Cascades are famous for throwing down the challenge of variable weather, year-round. In the summertime, weather is generally good, with high-pressure systems creating sunny days and comfortable breezes. But low-pressure systems, with their accompanying rain and drizzle, can also move in, tossing into summer a few days that feel more like fall.

Locals in the Northwest live for summers, which are a welcome warm break from rain and harsh weather. Rarely is the sunshine too hot in the Cascades, as the cooling ocean breezes and mountain winds help to regulate air temperature. The mild climate makes for some great trail days, with light breezes keeping the climbs comfortable and the fresh air keeping the views crisp. Some of the hikes in this book, however, are farther on the eastern side of the Cascade Crest. Here, in the Yakima, Tieton, and Naches areas, the climate is semiarid, which creates almost perfect temperatures in spring and fall but can make summers very hot and winters very cold. Lack of shade and water also make hiking in the summer's dry heat downright unpleasant. The hike descriptions in this guide indicate which trips are best for spring and fall.

In winter, because of our proximity to the ocean, storms create substantial snow accumulations, even more than 58 feet in some areas! So your best weather bet for the hikes in this book are spring through fall. During the spring months, many eastern Washington and lowland hikes are usually snow-free. In the summer, depending on the year's snowpack and weather, the high country opens for enjoyment mid to late July. Most of the trails can be enjoyed all the way into late fall, although some have lingering snow patches well into September.

A few things to know about Northwest weather and variability: On the western side of the Cascade Crest, coastal fog can build over the Puget Sound, causing a marine layer of misty fog that socks in the mountain valleys. Marine layers generally burn off by afternoon but may be enough to discourage hikers from getting outside at first glance.

When high-pressure systems bring sunshine to the Northwest, there may be no better place on Earth to be hiking. But with weather so variable, always be prepared

SENSING THE STORM

Use all five senses for forecasting weather and impress your friends! First, stop and look. See those wispy clouds, known as mare's tails, that have started to increase in the sky? They are talking to you and trying to tell you that a weather change will happen within twenty-four hours.

Next, stop and listen. Do you hear a lot of birds? If so, are they flying and chattering low to the ground or high? Birds follow insects, which follow pressure systems. Low pressure, or crummy weather, will push birds lower to the ground to search for food; this phenomenon is particularly fun to watch with swallows near lakes.

Next, touch the pinecones and see if they are stiff or flexible. When pinecones absorb moisture from the air, they become very pliable and usually indicate that wet weather is nearing.

Finally, smell and taste the air. Notice anything? If you smell a slight odor of composting plants or dark woody earth, rain is on the way. When weather changes quickly, you can almost taste this strong smell. Plants release more gasses just before a storm and can be a great indicator of changing weather.

with layers of warmth and waterproofing. Clear summer days often lead to cold summer nights, not uncommonly below the freezing mark. During my research for this book, I hiked with a lightweight down jacket and an ultralight waterproof windbreaker in my pack, and I used both of these layers often. Thunderstorms can come up quickly, often without warning. I'll never forget the day I set out in sunny skies only to get stuck in a thunder and lightning storm that sparked several small smoldering wildfires near Sheep Lake and the Pacific Crest Trail. The morning forecast had no mention of mountain storms, and all indications had pointed to a clear day. Back down the muddy trail I went, sloshing as fast as possible back to the safety of my vehicle. While thunderstorm are somewhat rare, if one occurs, stay away from large, lone trees, fire towers, rocky outcroppings, or even caves. Instead, head for a thick grove of fairly small trees and wait it out, or get back to your vehicle if

safe to do so. Avoid swimming in mountain lakes or hanging out on their shores, as they are great conductors of electricity.

ROAD AND TRAIL CONDITIONS

One lesson that every hiker learns quickly is that just because a road line shows up on a map doesn't mean it exists in real life. Countless times I've lumbered my vehicle down poorly marked Forest Service roads only to find that a natural occurrence, such as a landslide or flooding creek, has wiped out the road. When this happens, the trail, only accessible by foot, ends up overgrown and in a sad state of disarray. With the quantity of rain the Northwest receives, it's not surprising that Mother Nature's water chisel is often working hard to rearrange the backcountry. The hikes in this book all note any road and trail challenges I encountered, but things can change quickly. Always contact an area's land management agency for the most up-to-date conditions.

Along those lines, it's worth mentioning that thousands of volunteers work tirelessly on trails to keep them open and maintained for your use. Nonprofits such as the Washington Trails Association, Student Conservation Association, EarthCorps, and the Cascadians, among others, together devote thousands of hours to maintaining some of the areas described in this book. These hardworking volunteers work in conjunction with the land management agencies to clear debris, improve drainage, and make necessary structure repairs in the name of devotion and love of the outdoors. If we all gave a day or two of labor per year, think of how much we could accomplish! Trail projects can always use another pair of hands, so please help out by getting involved with your favorite trail conservation organization.

TRAIL ETIQUETTE

Many of the trails in this book are open to multiple kinds of recreation, while others are in wilderness areas that only allow hikers and stock. Each hike specifies what uses are allowed on the trail.

Wilderness areas are designated to minimize human impact and to keep the areas wild and natural. Regulations prohibit motorized and mechanized equipment, from bicycles all the way to chain saws. Keep that in mind when you see huge trailside trees that have been manually cut by hand. If you prefer motor- and bicycle-free trails, sticking to the wilderness areas will limit your frustrations.

Multiple-use trails outside of wilderness areas are those where hikers, horses, mountain bikes, and dirt bikes share the trails. To most hikers, this is more than a nuisance—it can be downright dangerous. Dirt bikes flying downhill can't be expected to

stop quickly, so hikers need to use extreme caution and hop off the trail if they hear a buzzing motor approaching. Mountain bikes are much quieter, but they are thankfully easier to dodge than motorized traffic. Lastly, it can be frustrating to play poop roulette and suffer the stench of pile after pile of horse dung on the uphills.

User conflicts are as old as the hills and have been debated to exhaustion. Until legislation changes, all allowed users have a right to be there—everyone is trying to enjoy the outdoors and their sport. Before we get completely bent out of shape about it, let's remember that some of the trail user groups fund bridges and restoration projects, as well as assist in backcountry rescues or recoveries. A remote trail with many types of users might also be less prone to getting overgrown. Avoiding all multi-user trails does you a big disservice—there are so many beautiful places to see! Odds are that you won't see another person, let alone one enjoying a different activity. Of course, writing to your legislators is your best bet if you want to see a change.

Sharing the Trails

During your romp around the hills, a few tips can help you and others have an enjoyable experience. Most are common sense but serve as good reminders for all of us:

- **Stay on the trail** and don't cut switchbacks or take shortcuts, which can cause erosion and compromise safety.
- **Avoid walking off-trail in meadows** or delicate subalpine areas. Although tempting, avoid imitating Julie Andrews and her meadow twirls.
- **Stay to the right** if the paths are wide enough for passing. If you decide to pass someone, announce yourself to avoid

A feather shed from a Steller's jay makes a colorful sight on the trail in Indian Heaven Wilderness.

startling them by calling out a courtesy "on your left." On popular hikes, **hike single file to allow others to pass**. Otherwise, feel free to lock elbows and skip.

- **Give ascending hikers the right-of-way** if you're headed downhill. Hikers huffing up big hills are working hard. We've been there, we know that pain.
- **Yield to stock or horses by stepping off-trail to the downhill side**. Be sure the animal sees you and talk calmly so that it can identify you as a person.
- When encountering **dirt bikes or mountain bikes, step off-trail**. Moving yourself off the trail is easier and much faster than moving a speeding two-wheeled object.
- **Move yourself and your pack off the trail** when you stop for a break, so you're not in the way. It would be awkward if other hikers had to ascend your torso.
- That said, do assess your surroundings and **select a durable surface** such as a rock or log for parking your pack and your rear end.

- **Keep your voices to a minimum** to allow others to have a wilderness experience—unless you're a Juilliard graduate and are singing something uplifting. On second thought, that's too subjective. Stick with the first suggestion.
- **Keep dogs under control**. Use care to prevent your pooch from disturbing wildlife or other trail users. Keep your dog on a leash when that's required or otherwise under voice control at all times.
- **Know before you go and obey the rules**. Wilderness areas come with a special set of regulations designed to keep things pristine. Learn the rules of your trail and follow them. 'Nuf said.
- In subalpine areas, **piddle on pumice**. Mountain goats and deer love a fresh puddle of piddle because it contains salt. Gross, I know. They'll tear up meadows or hillsides to get at your waste, so save the pristine areas and find a rock to sprinkle.
- **Dispose of waste properly**. If you brought it in and didn't eat it, pack it out. If nature calls and there isn't a back-

country privy around, dig a cathole 6 to 8 inches deep at least 200 feet (100 big steps) from water, camps, and trails. Cover the cathole well afterward and pack out toilet tissue. If you smoke, pack out your cigarette butts. Use only biodegradable soap, if any, and keep all suds and anything else you might wash off yourself 200 feet from creeks, lakes, and rivers—pollutants such as bug spray can jeopardize the health of salamanders, frogs, and other water-dependent creatures (including you).

- **Leave what you find behind**. Others may want to enjoy those flowers and plants too. The only exception is packing out any trash you might find. Thanks for doing your part if others "forgot."
- **Respect wildlife**. Avoid jeopardizing natural behaviors such as foraging by *not* feeding animals. First, you might lose a limb; second, it's not good for the critter. Observe and photograph wildlife from a distance and allow even more space if the animal is with young. Keep food contained and odor-free in your pack and be sure to pick up crumbs and wrappers when you finish eating.
- Finally, **follow the Golden Rule** as you travel and realize that there may be situations where you need to lend a hand, give a wave, or share your gorp. Do your best to be a good steward of the land and a good citizen to your fellow trail user.

WATER

Experienced hikers know to carry more water than they think they will need, especially on hot days. Running out can lead to problematic dehydration, which can have you feeling dizzy, headachy, prematurely exhausted, or even worse. Tucking a few

Bitterroot thrives on the dry soils of Snow Mountain Ranch.

water-treatment tablets in your first-aid kit is not a bad idea, for "just in case" moments. Luckily, most of the hikes in this book have water somewhere along the trail, with a few exceptions. All backcountry water should be treated to avoid pathogenic microorganisms and parasites with names straight out of science-fiction horror movies, such as *Leptosporidium*, *Cryptosporidium*, and *Giardia*. Nothing says "bad day" like having a protozoa doing the breaststroke in your Nalgene. Treat your water by using either a chemical such as iodine or chlorine tablets, or by running it through a portable water filter. Treatment tablets and various water filters, including lightweight options using ultraviolet light, are available at your local outdoor retailer.

WILDLIFE

Those of us who enjoy the outdoors usually also get a kick out of seeing the wildlife that roams the deep ravines, high peaks, and forested thickets. The creatures that call these places home are, most often, mild mannered and rarely pose a threat unless startled or protecting their young or food sources. The two creatures that generally spark the predator/prey fear instinct in Northwest hikers are black bears and cougars (a.k.a. mountain lions.) To lessen your odds of a gnarly encounter with either beast, a few behavior tips can help.

Bear-Country Tips

Seeing a bear in the wild is a magical experience and one you'll never forget, especially if you're using common sense and a little bear-country know-how. Most of the bears in Washington State are black bears (*Ursus americanus*), whose healthy population is estimated at between 20,000 and 30,000 individuals. There are only an estimated 10 to 15 grizzly bears (*Ursus arctos horribilis*) in the state, mostly living in the North Cascades. The majority of the black bears I've seen have scattered before I even had a chance to grab my camera—a sign of a healthy bear behavior.

The following bear-country etiquette can help you have a safe and fun backcountry experience:

- **Sing, clap, or holler occasionally**, especially near blind corners or brushy overgrown basins. My signature shout is "Hey Bear," followed by clinking my trekking poles together.
- **Leave the area immediately** if you stumble upon a carcass or fresh kill.
- **Don't wear scented** perfumes, lotions, and delicious-smelling sunscreens in bear country.
- **Keep your eyes open for signs of fresh bear activity**, such as tracks, scat, small broken or scratched trees missing bark, and broken berry bushes. Use extra vigilance if you suspect a bear has recently been in the area.
- If you feel somewhat unnerved by hiking in bear country, you may want to use **bear deterrent spray**, kept in a harness on your hip. Only use this spray if a bear charges you, *not* to "repel" bears. A gentleman in one of the hiking classes I teach told me a horrible story of spraying the burning pepper solution all over his tent in an effort to keep bears at bay. It was a very painful lesson, which he now tells with humor.
- If a bear feels threatened, it may act distressed or agitated, and the signs will be very clear. Watch for jaw popping, huffing, vocalizing, or forcefully slamming paws to the ground. **Do not look**

the bear in the eye, as this is perceived as a challenge and sign of dominance. **Never turn your back on the bear**, but if safe to do so, slowly walk backward, giving the bear as much space as possible. **Talk calmly and identify yourself as a human**. If the situation escalates and the bear charges, find every ounce of courage possible to **stand your ground and do not run**. Usually the charge is a bluff and the bear will run right past you. Once the bear is gone and it's safe, leave the area immediately and change your soiled drawers.

Cougar-Country Tips

While they walk among us on our trails, these great beasts seldom want anything to do with hikers, and encounters are very rare. Thankfully, their food source in the Northwest is plentiful and humans are not on the menu. I'm guessing we just don't taste as good as venison! That said, having heightened awareness in cougar country is a good idea:

- **Keep your eyes open for their distinguishable paw prints**, which are almost always showstoppers given their sheer size, lack of claw marks, and unusual heel pad.
- Cougars are silent hunters and can move through a forest with nary a broken stick. **Listen for loud birds** instead, such as gray or Steller's jays, who will sound alarms if a predator is around.
- **Never let small children or small dogs run in front of you** and out of view.
- **Leave the area immediately** if you encounter a carcass or fresh kill.
- If you do encounter a curious cougar, whatever you do, **don't run**. Tell the cougar you see it by **making and retaining**

While cougar sightings are rare, a keen eye will catch their footprints in remote areas, such as this one near White Pass.

eye contact (opposite of what to do with a bear). Do your best to **appear as large and formidable as possible** by yelling and waving your arms over your head or moving your jacket up high. The cougar may assess the situation and decide you are too intimidating to challenge. **Pick up small children** or place them up on a stump where they appear larger. If safe to do so, back away slowly and do not turn your back. If all efforts fail and the cougar attacks, **fight back and fight dirty. Do not play dead!** Throw punches, poke eyeballs, throw rocks, and use every bit of energy you have to fight it off. When it's over, go write your best-selling novel of the event or post your wide-eyed, arm-waving tale on YouTube.

HUNTING

Hunting is permitted on most public lands, except for in national and state parks. Bear season starts on August 1 in Washington, followed by elk and deer season, which lasts into December in certain areas. Unfortunately, this timing coincides with precisely some of the best weather and accessibility for hiking backcountry trails. Many of the trails in this book are remote, get little use, and are exactly where wildlife hang out. In researching this book, I came across many hunters. Most were very friendly and less than intimidating, but encountering me on their trail shouting "Hey Bear" and clacking trekking poles made them less than thrilled.

To avoid misidentification, it is very important that hikers wear bright orange during hunting season. If the pooch is along for the hike, be sure to pick up an orange dog vest at your local pet shop or outdoor retailer before hitting the hills. I myself have a giant ugly orange vest that fits over my torso as well as my backpack. Add to the chic ensemble my bright orange ball cap and I look like a giant Dorito with legs. Vanity aside, the orange keeps me safe and charmingly brings out the beta-carotene in my skin.

Ticks and Snakes

Oh yes, the creepy crawlies and the parasites. What joy it is that we have to deal with both of them on trails. The good news is that they are primarily seasonal and usually only found on the east side of the Cascade Crest.

Ticks on these trails are primarily Rocky Mountain wood ticks, but other types do exist in the state. Most are found in sagebrush-type landscapes, but occasionally they make their way to the transition zones. These small parasites perch on brushy foliage waiting to hop onto unsuspecting hikers or animals. From there, they bury their ugly mouth into the skin layer, where they can feed for days and transmit deadly diseases if not detected. Thankfully, Washington State has relatively few reports of tick-borne diseases, but prevention is the best way to avoid the problem altogether. The most prominent time for ticks in the Yakima-, Tieton-, and Naches-area hikes is spring through early summer. When hiking in tick-prone areas, use a DEET-based insect repellent on skin and treat your clothing with the chemical permethrin. Wear light-colored clothing so that you can spot ticks easily. And wear long sleeves and long pants tucked into boots. When you stop for breaks, check yourself, your hiking partners, and your pooch for tiny hitchhikers. When you return to your car, do a thorough search for ticks everywhere, including your neck, underarms, ears, legs, and backs of the knees. Inspect anything that looks suspect—sometimes ticks are hard to see. When you get home, hop in a warm shower and do a triple check before declaring a tick-free victory.

As for **snakes**, the trails in this book near Yakima, Tieton, and Naches are home to several types that are commonly seen in summer months. Before you cancel your plans and avoid these trails altogether, know that most encounters are more interesting than frightening. Snakes in drier climates are on the menu of large birds of prey, and they try to make themselves scarce by hiding under rocky ledges or in thick grass.

The two most common snakes you may see are Pacific gopher snakes (also called bull snakes) and western rattlesnakes. Because of similar coloration, size, and coiling behaviors, Pacific gopher snakes (*Pituophis catenifer catenifer*) are often the victims of mistaken identity, taken for the more threatening western rattlesnake. The lack of a tail rattle on the gopher snake is the easiest way to tell the difference. Gopher snakes are constrictors and are nonvenomous but can be cantankerous and strike if agitated. Most times, they'll slither off the trail and get out of your way.

Rattlesnakes are the gentlemen (or ladies) of the viper world and are kind enough to give you a courtesy tail shake to let you know they are near. Western rattlesnakes (*Crotalus viridis*) are most active in late spring and hot summer months, and in general they fear people as much as we fear them. When threatened, they rapidly move the thick rattle on their tail creating a *ch-ch-ch-ch-ch* sound that, to me, sounds a lot like an oscillating lawn sprinkler. As a cruel trick of nature, grasshoppers and dried grass in wind also make similar sounds. Learning the exact noise of a rattlesnake might help—do an online search for "rattlesnake rattling" to get an onslaught of YouTube videos with rattlers doing their thing, and the occasional dumb behavior of people who are antagonizing the poor things. Remember, rattlesnakes are just animals, like us, trying to survive, and they do keep the population of mice and gophers balanced.

Everyone will have a great day if you follow a few simple tips when hiking in snake country:

- View snakes **from a distance**.
- **Keep your dogs leashed** and close by.
- **Use caution** when crossing fallen logs, scree fields, and rocky outcroppings.
- **Instruct kids to stay close**, and teach them about snakes.
- **Use trekking poles to probe** the ground as you hike.
- **Don't reach blindly under rocks** or ledges.
- **Wear boots** instead of sneakers.

BEWARE OF BEFUDDLED ELK

While hiking the trails, I can't count the times I have almost jumped out of my skin because of a wayward elk thundering out of a forest glade, startled by my footsteps. Seriously, the rush of adrenaline rivals a good day skydiving.

Perhaps my most humorous elk moment came when I was hiking near Edgar Rock and a young bull came flying out of a dark conifer patch, running in my direction as if confused by what he had heard. When he realized his mistake, he stopped, stood there for a few minutes staring at me, and then let out a loud bugle in my direction. In a flash, he turned and ran back from where he'd come. "Well you showed me!" I comically shouted as I tried to calm my racing heart.

Elk rarely show aggression toward hikers, and trust me, that's not only textbook knowledge, but comes from firsthand experience hiking in their midst. However, bulls are definitely moodier in the fall rut, and it's always a good idea to make noise as you move about the forest. Unless, of course, you like dealing with bull.

Rattlesnake bites are very rare in Washington but can occur if you accidentally step on a snake or happen to startle one at close range. The good news is that bites are rarely fatal, but it's important to render first aid immediately. First, retreat from the snake as quickly as possible and remain calm. Contact emergency personnel immediately. Remove restrictive clothing such as jewelry, watches, socks, et cetera, and immobilize the limb, keeping it below the heart. Cleanse the wound but don't flush it with water. Cover the area with a dry dressing and do not apply ice. If possible, place a lightly constricting band (with a finger's worth of wiggle room for blood flow) above the bite to help prevent the spread of venom. Keep the victim calm and reassured until medical personnel arrives.

APPAREL AND GEAR

One of my favorite pastimes is shopping online for outdoor equipment deals and cruising the aisles of my local outdoor retailer. You could call me a gear junkie with well-worn credit card, but it's money well spent. Being comfortable on the trails is no crime. And if something unforeseen happens, you need to be able to survive for a few days with enough provisions to meet your basic needs. Telling you the entire contents of my pack might require another book, but a few key things are a must.

First, get a good pair of hiking boots or trail-running shoes that fit well, not too snug, not too loose. You should be able to wiggle your toes up and down and side to side comfortably without them jamming into the shoe's sidewalls. Blisters are not your friend! The three things that cause blisters are heat, moisture, and friction. Eliminate these and you'll have happy hiking heels. I highly recommend waterproof hiking shoes or boots. If the rain doesn't wet your socks, the creek crossings, leftover snowfields, or damp dew in meadows might.

The layering technique for clothing works well in the Northwest climate. Cotton is comfy but should be avoided because it retains moisture, which zaps heat quickly.

BLISTERS

Nothing can ruin a good day faster than getting a blister, except maybe *Giardia*. For blisters, first off, learn to recognize when you might be getting a "hot spot" and stop and treat it with a bandage immediately. A hot spot is simply the feeling that something is rubbing or not feeling "right" in your shoe. It can result from any number of things, such as an ill-fitting shoe, a sock seam, or simply a small friction irritation such as a pine needle.

The three things that cause blisters are moisture, friction, and heat. Folks who perspire a lot may want to try sock liners to help wick away moisture. Another trick is to stop once an hour and change socks, or at least take your feet completely out of your shoes. Just a little air on those piggies goes a long way toward your overall comfort. While I generally recommend waterproof, breathable hiking shoes, for people who have "hot feet" I recommend foregoing the waterproofing and opting for a more breathable fabric. If you're ond of those folks, buy yourself a pair of Gore-Tex socks and slide your feet into them when you need to cross a snowfield, deal with a rain shower, or balance on stones to cross a stream.

There are few places more beautiful than Snowgrass Flat in the peak of wildflower season.

Choose synthetic or natural fabrics, such as silk or wool, which wick moisture from your body (never underestimate the power of wicking undies and a good base layer). Be sure to bring a warm layer such as a polar fleece or other type of insulated jacket, even on warm days. You never know when a mountain wind will whip into your bones, or when you may need to hunker down in an emergency.

For rain, choose waterproof/breathable jackets with good ventilation, such as under-arm or side zippers. Soft-shell material can prevent that clammy feeling you get when hiking in the rain. My raingear lives at the bottom of my pack and comes out whenever the bugs get bad or the sky clouds up for a squall. A waterproof backpack cover will keep your lunch and other essentials dry. It can also double as an emergency shelter or sit pad. A sturdy pair of trekking poles is also nice in wet weather, for preventing slips and slides over slick tree roots or rocky tread.

The Ten Essentials

Never leave home without the Ten Essentials, even if you're just going for a short hike. Small mistakes, such as leaving your firestarter at home, can add up to serious consequences in emergencies. I purchased a lightweight stuff sack for my Ten Essentials, which helps keep them together. When I change packs, say from my day hiking pack to my winter ski pack, I just move the stuff sack and I'm assured that I never forget anything.

1. **Navigation (map and compass):** Always bring a map in a waterproof case and a compass, and know how to use them. I find topographic maps that clearly show elevation using contour lines the best for navigation.

2. **Sun protection (sunglasses and sunscreen):** Sun, though a most welcome sight, can also spell trouble at elevation. Wearing sunglasses, sunscreen, and a hat can shield you from the summer heat, preventing serious health issues such as snow blindness, heat exhaustion, and heat stroke.

3. **Insulation (extra clothing):** Even if the weather is warm, one stiff breeze can bring on chills for a sweaty hiker. Always pack a layer of insulated and waterproof clothing to ward off cold and to use in case of emergency.

4. **Illumination (flashlight/headlamp):** Even if you intend to hike only during daylight hours, always bring a flashlight or headlamp. You never know when a missed turn or great day of exploring may keep you out after dark.

5. **First-aid supplies:** While it's impossible to be completely prepared for all emergencies, bring enough supplies to treat the basics. Bandages, moleskin (for blisters), pain relievers, and Ace wraps top my personal list.

6. **Fire tools (firestarter and matches):** Waterproof matches and firestarter should come on your day hike just in case you need to spend the night. I once experienced this unpleasantness at the trailhead when I locked my keys in my car. You never know when you'll need a warm fire.

7. **Repair kit and tools (including a knife):** Having a small amount of "what-if" goodies is key to successfully dealing with backcountry mishaps. Safety pins, a mini roll of duct tape, or a shoelace or small amount of cord can be incredibly useful in a pinch. More important, carry a knife or multitool.

8. **Nutrition (extra food):** No one expects the unexpected! Bring extra food in case you get lost or have to hunker down. I keep a few packets of energy gel (which has a lengthy expiration date) in my Ten Essentials kit for a just-in-case situation; they're lightweight and bring decent nutritional value to a hungry body.

9. **Hydration (extra water):** Water sources are often unreliable in hot summer months, so plan on bringing more than you'll need. I generally carry 64 ounces of water, but this varies depending on the length of the hike. Trailside water is a nice bonus but should always be treated with either chemical tablets or a water filter to eliminate waterborne pathogens.

10. **Emergency shelter:** Carry something that can double as a small tarp if you need to hide from the elements. A waterproof backpack cover, a large garbage bag, a bivy sack, or an emergency space blanket can all serve this purpose.

There is magic to be found in the tiniest of details, such as this smiling grasshopper near Umtanum Creek.

TRAIL SAFETY

Whether you intend to hike solo, with a partner, or with a group, it's important to give a few seconds' thought to the "what-ifs" of heading into the wilderness. Statistically, if you follow a few tips, you'll have a safe, enjoyable day of hiking. Remember, no matter what gadgets, devices, or gear you have in your pack, the gray matter between your ears is the single-most important piece of equipment you own. Keep it sharp and focused as you plan and hike.

If You're Lost or Injured

Getting lost, disoriented, or injured doesn't have to mean horrible consequences if you've thought ahead.

- **Let someone know where you're headed**. If possible, purchase or print two maps, both marked with your planned route. Take one with you and leave the other one with a trusted friend, along with when you intend to return, the contact information of the relevant land management agency, and a firm time to contact the agency if you're late coming home. You may want to give yourself some buffer time, in case your hike takes more time than expected. You may also want to indicate the number of people in your party and any health conditions they may have, to prepare search teams. I know, I know, it seems like overkill, but taking a few extra minutes can potentially save a life.

- **If you do find yourself lost or injured, stay put!** It is much easier for search teams to locate a fixed target than a moving one. Be patient and stay positive. Search and Rescue does a great job moving quickly, but it does take time to round up volunteers and get the mission organized. Use your waiting time to gather downed firewood, filter water, and assess your food situation. With any luck, you'll be in your warm bed by evening.

- Cell phone coverage is often spotty in the mountains. You may want to purchase a **personal locator beacon**, which connects to a private satellite network and alerts emergency personnel if triggered. The device itself costs roughly $100, and the subscription service costs around $100 annually. It will be the best money you've spent if you have a true backcountry emergency.

Trail/Trailhead Crime

Thankfully, trail and trailhead crime is fairly infrequent. Use common sense, maintain situational awareness, and follow these simple tips:

- **Never leave valuables in your vehicle**. When I hike, I ditch my fancy wallet at home in exchange for a small plastic baggie that contains my driver's license, medical card, and cash/credit card. My pack is lighter and my mind relieved that nothing will be stolen, even if my car is vandalized. I also leave a small laminated sign on my front seat that reads "no valuables in vehicle." I haven't interviewed any would-be thieves lately to see if this has been a deterrent, but with all the hiking I do, I have yet (knock on wood) to be a victim of trailhead vandalism.
- When you arrive at the trailhead and before you exit your car, **drive around and get a feel for anyone who may seem out of place**. Be sure to look for anyone sitting in their cars as if waiting. Instincts are rarely wrong, so if you get a

bad vibe, find a different trail or postpone your hike.

- Speaking of instincts, if you meet someone on the trail, **trust your red-flag feelings**. If the creep factor is sliding upward, allow yourself to be guarded, firm, and rude if necessary.
- **Never tell anyone you meet on-trail where you're going, even if he/she seems harmless**. You may have to be vague. For example, instead of saying "I'm headed to the lake," say "I'm hiking until I get tired." Keeping your plans private may deter a criminal with ill intentions from knowing where to find you.
- **Never mention party size, especially if you're alone**. When you meet others on the trail, say "we" instead of "I" to mask party size. If you really get the willies about someone, shouting off into the bushes things like "Would you hurry up?" or "Are you done yet?" may cause the criminal to be even more befuddled about how many are in your group.
- **Avoid hiking with headphones**. While I love rocking as much as the next gal, avoiding headphones is sensible, especially since many of the hikes in this book are remote. Keeping your wits about you is key for navigating wildlife and natural challenges too, such as creek crossings.

ENJOY THE TRAILS

Many of the trails in this book are in need of footprints to keep them in good shape. Enjoy the beautiful places they lead to and the blissful feelings that hiking brings to the soul. As we continue to explore the great Pacific Northwest, remember to get involved with the protection of these lands

THE FIRES OF 2012

On September 8 and 9, 2012, a large thunderstorm came through the William O. Douglas Wilderness and Gifford Pinchot National Forest, setting off wildfires over a huge stretch of the Cascades. One of the hardest-hit regions was the Mount Adams Wilderness, where several pocket fires quickly merged and spread to 20,038 acres before firefighters, along with autumn rains, finally fizzled the smoldering mess.

The research for this book was completed just before the fires closed the trails and overwhelmed the area for the remainder of that summer. Some trails in this book have been altered by the burn: Hike 68, Shorthorn Trail; Hike 69, Mount Adams South Climb; Hike 70, Snipes Mountain and Crooked Creek Falls; Hike 71, Stagman Ridge, Horseshoe Meadow, and Lookingglass Lake; Hike 72, Salt Creek; Hike 73, Crofton Ridge; Hike 74, Pacific Crest Trail to Horseshoe Meadow.

During the Cascade Creek Fire of 2012 many firefighters like these worked tirelessly to protect the landscape.

All fire-affected trips are noted in the hike descriptions themselves. Be sure to use caution when hiking on trails that have charred, dead-standing trees and loose, loamy soil, as trees may become unstable, especially in high winds. Do check with the land managers for updated conditions, but don't be scared off completely! Nature is full of lessons and is a fantastic teacher.

A burned area can be fascinating to walk through. The creaking trees sway back and forth, keeping cadence with the wind in the midst of the eerie feeling of destruction all around. In the burn zones I've visited, the longer I've wandered in and out of blackened trees, smelling the wafts of charred bark and loamy, darkened soils, the more the landscape has become familiar, almost serene. In these areas I am not alone, for the forest is full of life, and at times I can almost make out words in the high-pitched whine of the leftover limbs. I find myself witnessing nature's new birth.

Bees and hummingbirds flirt with the vibrant purple fireweed that grows with strength and fervor in the nutrient-rich soil, a vision against the black background. Underbrush previously limited by light is flush with new life instead of woody forest debris. Beetles and ants race around logs, carrying on their important mission of finding sustenance in the scorched bark. Above, the drumming of the black-backed woodpecker can't be ignored. Many of the burned trees were dead on their feet before the fire—a perfect opportunity for Mother Nature to do some housecleaning. In these fire-scorched zones, you can gain a new appreciation of the living, breathing, regenerating ecosystem. Somewhere in the distance, listen for a slow creak that says "welcome."

by putting pressure on Congress to preserve our open spaces. You may also want to volunteer for trail maintenance. Volunteers are constantly needed to help cut blowdowns, reroute water drainage, and cut back overgrown shrubs. When it's all said and done, we are all responsible for caretaking our wild places.

A NOTE ABOUT SAFETY

Safety is an important concern in all outdoor activities. No guidebook can alert you to every hazard or anticipate the limitations of every reader. Therefore, the descriptions of roads, trails, routes, and natural features in this book are not representations that a particular place or excursion will be safe for your party. When you follow any of the routes described in this book, you assume responsibility for your own safety. Under normal conditions, such excursions require the usual attention to traffic, road and trail conditions, weather, terrain, the capabilities of your party, and other factors. Because many of the lands in this book are subject to development and/or change of ownership, conditions may have changed since this book was written that make your use of some of these routes unwise. Always check for current conditions, obey posted private property signs, and avoid confrontations with property owners or managers. Keeping informed on current conditions and exercising common sense are the keys to a safe, enjoyable outing.

—*Mountaineers Books*

Opposite: Those who work to get here are rewarded with grand views of wildflowers lighting up the hillsides of Coal Creek Mountain.

goat rocks wilderness

Ask any Pacific Crest Trail through-hiker which sections of the PCT they enjoyed most, and they'll almost always include the 31.1 miles of pure eye candy through the Goat Rocks Wilderness. Luckily for day hikers, the PCT is only one of the many trails through this beautiful area. The vast rocky spine and peaks are remnants of an old stratovolcano, which has eroded away and left awe-inspiring peaks filled with pockets of glaciers and snowfields. Add the copious wildflowers bursting in almost every meadow, and the Goat Rocks is a poet's dream. Congress designated the Goat Rocks Wilderness in 1964—108,096 acres of wild country sitting between the two towering volcanoes of Mount Rainier and Mount Adams. The trails along the ridgelines and through the subalpine cirques are among some of the most beautiful in the country, while others in the deep forested valleys are desolate and somewhat abandoned. To each there is a feeling and a purpose. Enjoy your exploration!

1 Conrad Meadows and Surprise Lake

RATING/ DIFFICULTY	ROUNDTRIP	ELEV GAIN/ HIGH POINT	SEASON
*/4	13 miles	1505 feet/ 5260 feet	July–Oct

Maps: Green Trails Walupt Lake No. 335, White Pass No. 303; **Contact:** Okanogan-Wenatchee National Forest, Naches Ranger District; **Notes:** Free wilderness use permit at trailhead. Trail open to horses; **GPS:** N 46 30.471, W 121 16.926

This is perhaps one of the weirdest trails in this book. When I first set foot into this area, I thought someone had dropped me onto the set of Bonanza, complete with cowboys on horses, roaming cattle, and rumors of roundups. The cattle allotment agreement between private landowners and the Forest Service allows for grazing between late June and early October. The bovines have decimated the trails, made enough dust to start the next Dust Bowl, and lessened the chances of seeing wildlife. But we can't complain too loudly. The private land owners are nice enough to let us walk through their pastures to get to the Goat Rocks Wilderness and enjoy beautiful Surprise Lake. Those with extra motivation and off-trail skills can make the cross-country trek to Warm Lake, not far from Surprise Lake.

GETTING THERE

From Packwood, drive northeast on US 12 for approximately 36 miles to the east end of Rimrock Lake. Look for a sign that says "Rimrock Lake Rec. Area" at a road known as the Tieton Road. Set your odometer to 0 and turn right (south) here. Drive around the the lake for 4.5 miles and turn left (south) on Forest Road 1000 (signed "South Fork Tieton"). Follow the road past the pavement's end at 10.3 miles. At 11.4 miles, bear left at the Y, remaining on FR 1000. At 16.5 miles, bear right, again staying on FR 1000. At 17 miles from US 12, pit toilets and Conrad Campground show up to the left (southeast). Park just beyond at the pullouts on either side of the road.

ON THE TRAIL

Not only is this a weird trail, it's also very confusing. For this trip I made the most meticulous notes and GPS notations of any hike in this book, to keep you from scratching your head and wondering about every intersection.

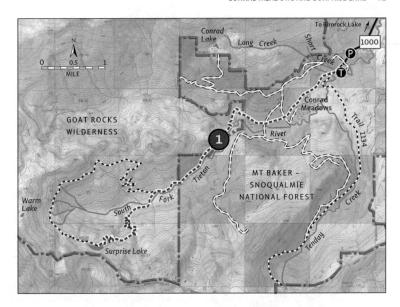

Start by walking from the parking lot, up the closed road past the Bear Creek Mountain Trail, until the road winds around to the right and is blocked by a red gate. To the gate's left (southwest) the trail is signed for South Fork Tieton Trail No. 1120—your trail! After following it a short distance, come to a couple of creek crossings, absent bridges. Makeshift logs and boards allow you to avoid wet shoes in late season.

After the second creek, the trail opens up at a Y junction in a meadow. Tenday Meadows Trail No. 1134 goes left (south) here, while South Fork Tieton Trail No. 1120 goes right (southwest). Look around for cows in the summer. They are big and love to stare. If you haven't been around them, they are somewhat intimidating and will stand right in the middle of the trail. Good thing they are mostly harmless and seem scared to death of people when you get close. Shouting "get along little doggies" worked like a charm for me. Keep the pooch leashed up to avoid creating a mob of mooing madness or having him get kicked.

At the junction, go right (southwest) and follow the sign directing you toward South Fork Tieton Trail No. 1120. From here the trail becomes a road, presumably for the ranchers, before it turns back into a trail. Several cow trails try to confuse you, but staying straight ahead and not veering much to the left or right will take you where you need to go. Most of these smaller trails lead back to the main trail eventually, so it's hard to get lost, but it feels like a maze. Eventually the dusty trail (start humming Aaron Copland's hoedown music here) crosses a fairly substantial dirt road 1.5 miles from where you parked.

Cross the road and BOOM, what's there? An actual trailhead complete with wilderness permits! Fill out your permit and continue following the trail toward Conrad Meadows, where you might see (you guessed it) more cows who have wandered off to greener pastures. Chattering Douglas squirrels warn you away from their food supply or their young in the pines. Through the trees, there are cabins and a few outbuildings on the private lands nearby. The Goat Rocks Wilderness boundary is up ahead almost 0.5 mile farther, announced by a trailside sign. Just past this is an unnamed trail junction, signed only with an arrow pointing left.

Stay left and continue on Trail No. 1120, which descends about 100 feet to cross

In late September, fall colors create earth-toned grasslands near Conrad Meadows.

Conrad Creek on a sturdy bridge made with log beams; there's no handrail, so watch your footing. More meadows come and go, giving the trail an open, airy feeling as you weave between private land and wilderness area. The South Fork Tieton River provides a good soundtrack to the southeast, while the grassy meadows continue to guide you along.

At 4.1 miles past where you parked, come to a fork in the trail, signed "Surprise Lake Loop, Trail 1120." This is actually the start and end of a loop that can be done in either direction. The trail description here is to Surprise Lake and back, but you can continue past the lake and do the whole loop, adding 2.5 miles to your day and an additional elevation gain of 370 feet.

To reach Surprise Lake, go left, which is the southern fork of the loop. Until now, you've only gained 420 feet, so prepare to climb up, up, and up to gain roughly 1000 feet in 2.4 miles. Thankfully, the switchbacks are under the forest canopy and stay mostly shaded in the warm summer months. Occasionally, views of the valley and neighboring peaks pop up through the trees to the trail's north.

In 6.5 miles from the parking area, arrive at teal-colored Surprise Lake. This area is popular with horsemen, so don't be surprised if you're greeted by some *neighs*. Hold your horses and don't let the neighsayers get to you; there is plenty of room for everyone. The best views of the Goat Rocks Wilderness, including Gilbert Peak, are along the lakeshore's unofficial path, around to the southeast. There are several places to sit and have lunch before heading back toward cow town, the same way you came.

To do the loop, or to navigate the subalpine terrain to Warm Lake, continue heading west on the main trail. After Surprise Lake the terrain quickly changes to alpine meadows filled with wildflowers and great views of the Goat Rocks. The cairn, marking the beginning of the cross-country trek up and over the ridge to Warm Lake, is 1.2 miles past Surprise Lake, almost halfway around the loop. Remember, there is no trail, so only set off to find Warm Lake if you're good at navigating and daylight is on your side.

2 Bear Creek Mountain

RATING/ DIFFICULTY	ROUNDTRIP	ELEV GAIN/ HIGH POINT	SEASON
****/3	7 miles	1635 feet/ 7330 feet	early Aug– early Oct

Map: Green Trails White Pass No. 303; **Contact:** Okanogan-Wenatchee National Forest, Naches Ranger District; **Notes:** Free wilderness use permit at trailhead. High-clearance vehicle required, four-wheel or all-wheel drive recommended. Trail open to horses; **GPS:** N 46 33.343, W 121 18.721

Bear Creek Mountain is a classic Goat Rocks hike complete with everything you'd expect from a beautiful subalpine area. As the site of a former lookout tower, it boasts huge views of Tieton Peak, Old Snowy, and McCall Glacier. I highly recommend this popular trail, but make sure you have a high-clearance vehicle, or even better, four-wheel or all-wheel-drive, to get to the trailhead—this puppy's rough!

GETTING THERE
From Packwood, follow US 12 northeast for 26.9 miles to the Clear Lake Recreation Area. Set your odometer to 0 and head south on the Clear Lake/Tieton Road. At 5.2 miles, turn right on Forest Road 1205. At 7.9 miles, turn left on a road marked "742." In 8.1 miles, at the road fork, go right on FR 1204. At 10.4 miles, stay left at the road fork and continue on FR 1204. At 11.8 miles, turn right at an unsigned road fork. This road is a doozie; take your time and make sure you have a good spare tire. At 14.2 miles from where you left US 12, find the Bear Creek Mountain trailhead.

ON THE TRAIL
The trail starts out gently climbing in and out of a light and airy forest filled with pines and firs. Look closely as you climb for a sneak preview of coming attractions—the peak! Gentle climbing continues as you pass through several subalpine meadows frequented by deer, elk, and occasionally the mountain's namesake, bear. In roughly 2 miles, cross Bear Creek, a small ravine filled with seasonal flowers such as lupine, buttercup, daisy, and monkey flower. Most of the forest is behind you now as you break into subalpine scenery and increasing talus.

At 2.5 miles, arrive at a junction with Trail No. 1130S, also marked "Bear Cr. Mtn. L.O." (lookout). This is the beginning of the climb to the summit of Bear Creek Mountain. Turn right (southwest) and pick your way up the steep rocky slopes that sport various hues of gray, tan, and pink, dotted by patches of low-growing greenery struggling to survive the short growing season.

Once you've huffed and puffed for a bit, crest the ridgeline filled with juniper, lupine, and pine, and then break out onto the actual summit plateau at 3.5 miles. Watch your footing, because all you want to do is walk and gawk! To the south stands Mount Adams; to the north, Mount Rainier; to the southwest,

Benchmarks, such as this one on Bear Creek Mountain, are fun to find.

the Goat Rocks spine, McCall Glacier, Gilbert Peak, Conrad Glacier, Meade Glacier, and the list goes on and on. Two survey markers live in these rocks, both dated 1961. An L4-style lookout tower—the iconic windowed structures with wraparound decks and thick shutters—stood watch over these peaks from the 1930s to the 1960s, although it

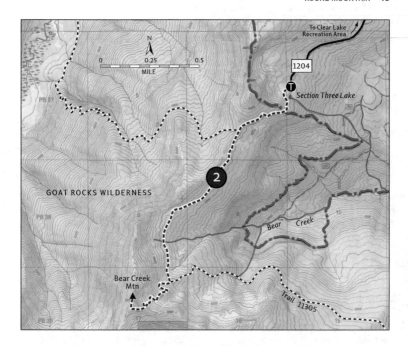

was last staffed in 1945, so it was desolate for years. It's now simply a dot on history's timeline, as nothing remains. On a warm day, find a perch on a rock to suck in the fresh air and supreme views and to grab lunch, a nap, or both, before heading back.

3 Round Mountain

RATING/ DIFFICULTY	ROUNDTRIP	ELEV GAIN/ HIGH POINT	SEASON
***/3	5.2 miles	1700 feet/ 5970 feet	July–Oct

Maps: Green Trails Goat Rocks/William O. Douglas No. 303S, or White Pass No. 303; **Contact:** Okanogan-Wenatchee National Forest, Naches Ranger District; **Notes:** Free

wilderness use permit at trailhead. Trail open to horses; **GPS:** N 46 38.174, W 121 18.162

While some lookout tower sites hold no evidence of their former buildings, Round Mountain's rusty posts and cement pillars stand testament to a forgotten time in history. The remains of the foundation allow you to visualize the tower's location while nature works hard to take it back. From the mountaintop, enjoy great views of Rimrock Lake to the east and the Goat Rocks peaks to the south.

GETTING THERE

From Packwood, drive northeast on US 12 for 26.9 miles to the Clear Lake Recreation

The lookout tower is gone, but the remnants of it still remain along with a grand view on Round Mountain.

Area. Set your odometer to 0 and head south on Clear Lake/Tieton Road. Drive 2.9 miles and turn right on Forest Road 530 (marked "1200530/Round Mountain TH 4/Trail 1144"). Follow the road to its dead end at the trailhead, 7.2 miles from the highway.

ON THE TRAIL

This trail gets a fair amount of horse traffic and can be very dusty. But dust does mean a drier climate, so if it's raining just to the west, you may have a dry day here! The trail begins in a transition zone between the east and west, and the landscape can't seem to pick a side. Warm-climate whitebark pines scent the air, while Steller's jays fight for attention in hillside Douglas firs. The climbing is steep from the get-go and stays that way until the end, when it *really* starts climbing. The reward is the view of Rimrock Lake that starts popping up behind you as you travel through the light and airy forest.

At 2.2 miles, arrive at a junction with a spur trail (signed "Round Mtn. L.O. 1144A"). Head left (south) and climb the steeply

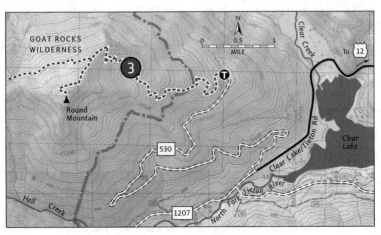

pitched 0.4 mile to the top. An L4-style lookout tower, with its wraparound windows and deck, stood here from 1936 to 1976, when it was destroyed. From the summit, Mount Adams's top pops up behind Bear Creek Mountain, Old Snowy, and the Goat Rocks spine. To the south are great views of Clear Lake, Rimrock Lake, Kloochman Rock, and the Yakima hills. Be sure to walk west (right) and follow a lightly used pathway leading to more views and a rocky outcropping. From this vista, the silver forest runs from the valley to the ridge of the western peaks, testament to past forest fires, and Mount Rainier even joins the view party.

4 McCall Basin

RATING/ DIFFICULTY	ROUNDTRIP	ELEV GAIN/ HIGH POINT	SEASON
****/5	14.6 miles	2585 feet/ 5200 feet	Aug–Oct

Maps: Green Trails Goat Rocks/William O. Douglas No. 303S, or White Pass No. 303; **Contact:** Okanogan-Wenatchee National Forest, Naches Ranger District; **Notes:** Free wilderness use permit at trailhead. Trail open to horses. Mountain bikes permitted on defunct roadway only. Road closure adds 8 miles roundtrip; **GPS:** N 46 34.638, W 121 21.502

Call it a backward duathlon for those who are determined and tough! Until the bridge on Forest Road 1207 is repaired, a road walk of 8 miles round trip is required to access the trailhead. Luckily, mountain biking the road is a great alternative to shave off some time. Let's face it: this is a long, tough day and not for everyone. The reward, however, is worth the effort.

When you arrive in McCall Basin, you'll find plenty of solitude and will likely have the wildflower meadows and views all to yourself.

GETTING THERE

From Packwood, drive northeast on US 12 for 26.9 miles to Clear Lake Recreation Area. Head south on the Clear Lake/Tieton Road for approximately 3 miles to the west end of Clear Lake to the junction with FR 1207. Follow FR 1207 to its closure, park, and hop on your bike or walk to the road's end approximately 4 miles farther.

ON THE TRAIL

If you bike the road, lock up your ride, as bikes are not permitted in the wilderness area. Start by following the fairly level North Fork Tieton Trail No. 1118 for less than 0.25 mile before arriving at a junction with Trail No. 1128. Stay right and continue on Trail No. 1118, toward Tieton Pass. The trail climbs up and away from the river at a moderate pace and arrives at a junction with the Hidden Springs Trail No. 1117 in just over 1 mile from the trailhead.

Continue straight and keep climbing on Trail No. 1118 through deep forest canopy and green Northwest foliage, such as vanilla leaf and twinflower. A few seasonal stream crossings break up the climb, allowing for good water-filtering opportunities and requiring a hop, skip, and a jump to get across. After gaining 1500 feet of elevation roughly 5 miles from the trail's start, intersect the Pacific Crest Trail and the Clear Fork Trail at Tieton Pass.

Turn left (south) on the PCT. A gentle grade climbs to a small saddle in 0.8 mile near small Lutz Lake. While the lake isn't big on views, it's pretty and peaceful. In 0.5 mile from the lake, look closely for a trail

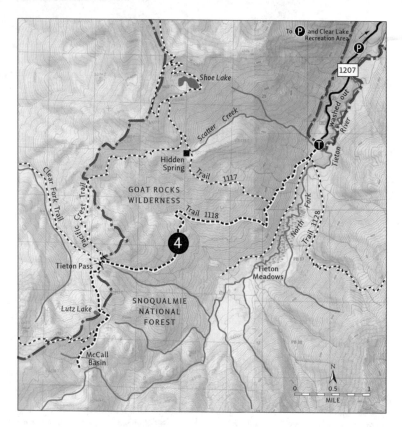

forking left (south). This is the trail to McCall Basin; follow it and begin your descent into the valley. Bugs love this meadow in early season, so waiting to enjoy this area until later in the summer will save you some bites. Bears frequent this area too and you may see "piles" of their visits, so watch your step. Surrounding you in these subalpine meadows are rainbows of seasonal wildflowers such as mountain daisy, indigo paintbrush, mountain bistort, and lupine. Tieton Peak stands proudly and prominently, begging for attention as the other peaks of the Goat Rocks spine hide behind its girth.

If time permits, a few side trips are worth exploring. The paths through the basin converge on a well-worn trail that leads to a gap and good view of the valley far below. Farther down, the well-worn trail leads to an impressive waterfall at the headwaters of the North Fork Tieton River. This same trail used to make a loop back to FR 1207, but it gets little use and is now very difficult to navigate; only attempt it if you are an expert

Wildflowers abound in the areas around McCall Basin.

with map and compass and can find your way out of a rugged landscape. Whatever you do, gobble up the views and take plenty of photos for lasting memories, and then head back the way you came.

5 Shoe Lake

RATING/ DIFFICULTY	ROUNDTRIP	ELEV GAIN/ HIGH POINT	SEASON
****/5	15.4 miles	3610 feet/ 6600 feet	late July– Oct

Map: Green Trails White Pass No. 303; **Contact:** Gifford Pinchot National Forest, Cowlitz Valley Ranger District; **Notes:** NW Forest Pass required. Free wilderness use permit at trailhead. Trail open to horses; **GPS:** N 46 38.612, W 121 22.782

Shoe Lake is one of the most popular hikes in the Goat Rocks Wilderness, complete with everything you'd expect from this spectacular area. Like many hikes in Goat Rocks, this one makes for a long day, but it features open subalpine terrain and great

views of snowy peaks, wildflower hillsides to indulge the senses, and the grassy shoreline of Shoe Lake, a fine destination for a picnic. Despite the lake's reputation of popularity, the vastness of the area absorbs people and offers a surprising amount of solitude. You'll probably see only a handful of people on a sunny weekend and will find plenty of quiet places to enjoy the backcountry. Additionally, you'll have a chance to sample the Pacific Crest Trail, Goat Rocks–style!

GETTING THERE

From Packwood, drive northeast on US 12 for 20.3 miles to just past the summit of White Pass. Look for a parking area to the south (right), just beyond the ski area, signed "Pacific Crest Trail South." There is ample room for parking.

ON THE TRAIL

The trail starts off climbing steeply in the forest through lichen-laden hemlocks and Douglas firs, close to the ski area, but never actually on the runs. Instead, the trail keeps you in the woods, only briefly popping out to

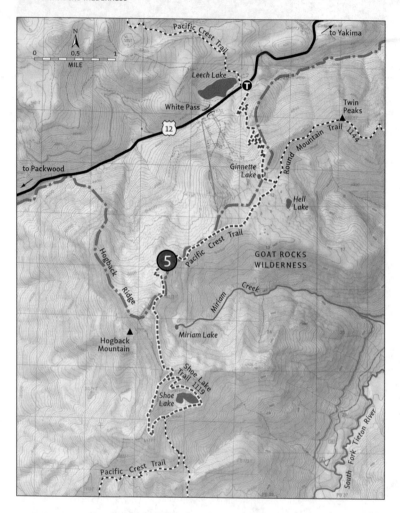

an open area near Ginnette Lake, which feels more like a muddy pond or mosquito's dream come true in late summer.

After 900 feet and 2.4 miles of climbing from the trailhead, arrive at a junction with Round Mountain Trail No. 1144. The landscape changes slightly now, opening up with more meadows and views to the north of White Pass and the peaks beyond. Keep your boots heading south on the PCT, which continues climbing and reaches another junction, this time with Chair Lift Trail No.

The Shoe Lake basin welcomes hikers with ample meadows for exploring.

1112, heading to the right (north) 1 mile beyond the Round Mountain Trail junction.

Continue up the PCT to a saddle at 6300 feet, which makes a fine place to stop and enjoy the views! The rocky Hogback Mountain in front of you gives way to a big alpine cirque, one that you will soon cross. Seasonal wildflowers of lupine, aster, and paintbrush provide a visual treat, while Miriam Creek and the lake basin below provide good habitat for wildlife. Keep your ears open and an eye out for hoary marmots, who whistle their alarms as hikers walk above.

The trail beckons you to continue, so follow its call and traverse the subalpine hillside of the east shoulder of Hogback Mountain to a high point just shy of 6600 feet and roughly 6.5 miles from the trailhead. Beneath you now is the Shoe Lake basin, showing off its high heel, 700 feet below. In the distance to the south are the beautiful peaks of the Goat Rocks Wilderness, among them Bear Creek Mountain, Tieton Peak, and Old Snowy.

Just after the high point, find a junction with Shoe Lake Trail No. 1119 located to the east. From here, you can make a full loop into the basin by following the Shoe Lake Trail

and heading back on the PCT, or by following the PCT first and then heading back on the Shoe Lake Trail. Or, you can just drop into the basin on the Shoe Lake Trail and hike back out the same way to save yourself 0.3 mile. So many options! No matter which way you go, there is much to see and enjoy.

6 Lost Hat Lake, Coyote Lake, and Lost Lake Lookout Site

RATING/ DIFFICULTY	ROUNDTRIP	ELEV GAIN/ HIGH POINT	SEASON
***/5	12.2 miles	4270 feet/ 6340 feet	Aug–Oct

Map: Green Trails Goat Rocks/William O. Douglas No. 303S; **Contact:** Gifford Pinchot National Forest, Cowlitz Valley Ranger District; **Notes:** Free wilderness use permit at trailhead. Trail open to horses; **GPS:** N 46 37.507, W 121 26.718

There certainly seems to be a lot of "lost" things in this area, so hold on tight to your hat and keep your eyes out for the lake! Sure, you'll have to wade across the Clear Fork River, but this very thing may just be the reason why you'll find such solitude. The huff-and-puff climbing through forest is worth it to reach the meadowy hillsides of Lost Hat Lake. Beyond that lie the rewarding views from the former site of the Lost Lake Lookout.

GETTING THERE

From the Packwood Shell gas station, drive northeast on US 12 for 16.5 miles. Look very closely for a wide-shoulder pullout on a sharp left-hand turn of the highway, found at around 3750 feet.

ON THE TRAIL

Scratch your head and wonder where in the world the trailhead is located. Walk to the right of the freeway barrier and find the start of the trail tucked down on a steep

hillside. Crazy, right? Fill out your wilderness use permit, and then start your descent to the Clear Fork crossing. Drop 560 feet in 0.8 mile before getting out your wading shoes and trekking poles to ford the river. In late summer, the river is a manageable height, just below the knee, and not too swift. If it looks too high, table the hike for another day or head back and approach the trail via the Lily Lake trailhead (Hike 8). After safely getting across, hop back on the trail and start your climb through fir and cedar, crossing a couple of tumbling creeks on logs. Horses have damaged the trail in places, so watch your footing and your ankles.

In just under 2 miles from the trailhead, arrive at a junction with Clear Fork Trail No. 61 and the remains of a forest shelter (still holding the nickname "Skeeter Shelter,"

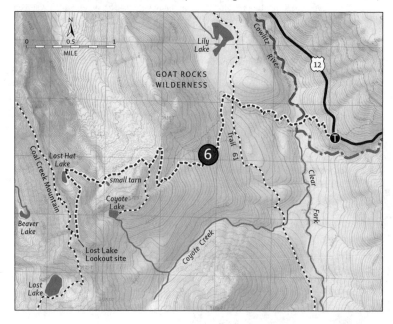

presumably due to its large population of biting bugs), which bit the dust several years ago and is now a curious pile of logs with a roof. Continue straight and climb another 3.3 miles in what feels like endless forest, with thick berries near your knees, before the way opens up to meadows and crests a pass at 5200 feet.

From here, unofficial trails lead off in different directions. One very well-used path goes left (south); it's the unofficial trail to Coyote Lake which lies less than 1 mile from this junction. Make a note to check it out on the way back if time allows, because it's a lovely spot. For now, continue heading straight (southwest) and find yourself losing a little elevation before gaining it again to arrive at a tarn filled with Northwest salamanders. The scenery is now much more subalpine as you walk the trail through meadows and continue winding up to Lost Hat Lake at 5 miles.

From the lake, curve back to the south before making the final huffy-and-puffy

Don't forget to swing into Coyote Lake on your way to Lost Lake Lookout.

push to the ridgeline and the site of the former Lost Lake Lookout, 6.1 miles from the trailhead. The lookout tower watched for wildfires from 1934 to the mid-1960s before being destroyed. The views are spectacular. Coyote Lake is directly below you to the east, peaks of the Goat Rocks are to the south, and Mount Rainier is to the north. Fantastic, right?

---

7 Bluff Lake, Coal Creek Mountain, and Lost Lake Lookout Site

RATING/ DIFFICULTY	ROUNDTRIP	ELEV GAIN/ HIGH POINT	SEASON
**/5	16 miles	4440 feet/ 6340 feet	Aug–Oct

Maps: Green Trails Goat Rocks/William O. Douglas No. 303S, or Packwood No. 302; **Contact:** Gifford Pinchot National Forest, Cowlitz Valley Ranger District; **Notes:** Free wilderness use permit at trailhead. Trail open to horses. Roundtrip includes road walk; **GPS:** N 46 39.238, W 121 34.699

This hike is for the crazy adventurer who likes navigational, distance, and vertical challenges. It's for those who want to get away from everything and everyone and don't mind working for it. Because of the washed-out road to the trailhead, the odds of seeing another pulse that isn't covered in fur is very slim. Don't expect a pristine trail. Wear long pants to avoid getting scratched by brush. Expect to climb over many blowdowns and to challenge yourself with routefinding in places. Why is this trail in this guidebook then? Simple really: The end is worth it. At the top, I sat on a rock and watched a beautiful, healthy black bear eating huckleberries surrounded by wildflowers. I enjoyed complete solitude with breathtaking views and little evidence of the human race, except the faint trail I followed. The effort equals reward!

GETTING THERE

From Packwood, drive northeast on US 12 for 4.5 miles and turn right (east) on Forest Road 46. In 1.5 miles, go right at an unsigned four-way intersection. In another 1.5 miles, turn left on FR 4612 and travel to the end, where the road is washed out. Park on the side of the road, located 4.2 miles from US 12, and walk to the actual trailhead.

ON THE TRAIL

Several years ago Purcell Creek threw a tantrum and obliterated the road to the trailhead. Now, you'll have to walk 1.3 miles to reach the actual, easy-to-miss trailhead located to the right (south) on a hairpin turn. Once there, fill out your wilderness permit and hit the trail, which starts out looking well used under a canopy of timber. Before long, the Goat Rocks Wilderness welcomes you with a tree placard.

After climbing 500 feet in 1.3 miles, arrive at the tree-lined shores of Bluff Lake. This small lake is a good place to get water if you or the pooch need to stock up. From here, things get interesting and the true climbing begins.

In just over 0.5 mile and another 380 feet of elevation gain, the area opens up a bit and Mount Rainier shows up behind you through the trees, a sneak preview of better views to come. This area, and the hillsides above it, is referred to as the Huntington Berry Patch and produces fruit in the warmer summer months. Look for mountain goats on the cliffs of Coal Creek Bluff, which start to appear to the trail's right (southwest). This

Fungus adds visual interest to a downed log near Bluff Lake.

very trail you are following was used by Native American goat hunters to access the ridge back in the day.

The trail levels off a little and passes by a small grassy meadow before it begins climbing again, with huckleberries crowding your legs. Blowdowns and small detours around them abound, and it's easy to lose track of the trail. If you think you're lost, stop and go back to where you were last sure you were on the path. Stand on the trail and study the brush for signs of broken branches or depressions of a pathway. Usually, it's visible. If not, get out the map and compass and navigate your way through it. The trail goes through phases of obvious and not so obvious, but eventually obvious wins and the way becomes easy to follow.

In about 3.5 miles from Bluff Lake, the trail alternates between meadow and forest as it approaches the ridge. Here you are treated to views of Johnson Peak to the south and Beargrass Butte to the west. Finally, you get the feeling you're getting somewhere! A silver forest shows up and guides you through dwarf huckleberries galore, while Mount Rainier is a pillar on the skyline behind you. The trail crests hillsides of wildflowers—western anemone, mountain daisy, and Sitka valerian—before entering the corner of a small flowered meadow, the closest thing to level since the lake more than 4.4 miles back. If you're spent, this is a fine place to have lunch before turning back. But you're pretty close to the old Lost Lake Lookout site, and it's well worth it!

Continue onward, and watch your footing on these crazy, hard-to-follow, sidehill trails. In 0.8 mile beyond the meadow, arrive at a junction with Packwood Lake Trail No. 78 and Clear Lost Trail No. 76. The sign here has tipped over and is doing nothing at this point but causing confusion. Take the uphill trail (No. 76), which is straight ahead. It reaches

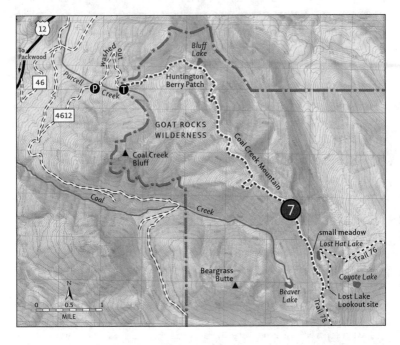

the ridgeline before continuing down the valley to a trailhead off of US 12 (see Hike 6).

In about 1 mile from the meadow, arrive at the very top of the world, or so it feels, as you stand on the rocky top, site of the old lookout. The Lost Lake Lookout stood here from 1934 until the 1960s. Before that, in the 1920s, there was an old tent cabin that consisted of a wooden floor and sidewalls holding up a seasonal canvas structure, all of which was bolted to the stone. Bits and pieces of history still remain, mostly in the form of concrete and bent metal anchors.

The views from here will melt you! Below are the inviting subalpine shores of Coyote Lake, with White Pass far in the distance. To the north is Mount Rainier and to the south the jagged peaks of Goat Rocks. When it's

time to head back, you might find, as I did, that it feels much faster going home.

8 Lily Lake

RATING/ DIFFICULTY	ROUNDTRIP	ELEV GAIN/ HIGH POINT	SEASON
*/1	3 miles	205 feet/ 3665 feet	May–Oct

Maps: Green Trails Goat Rocks/William O. Douglas No. 303S, or White Pass No. 303; **Contact:** Gifford Pinchot National Forest, Cowlitz Valley Ranger District; **Notes:** Free wilderness use permit at trailhead. Very rough road to trailhead, high-clearance vehicle required. Trail open to horses; **GPS:** N 46 39.337, W 121 29.172

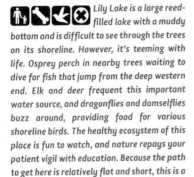 Lily Lake is a large reed-filled lake with a muddy bottom and is difficult to see through the trees on its shoreline. However, it's teeming with life. Osprey perch in nearby trees waiting to dive for fish that jump from the deep western end. Elk and deer frequent this important water source, and dragonflies and damselflies buzz around, providing food for various shoreline birds. The healthy ecosystem of this place is fun to watch, and nature repays your patient vigil with education. Because the path to get here is relatively flat and short, this is a good adventure for kids or for those unable to do steep or difficult hikes.

GETTING THERE

From Packwood, drive northeast on US 12 for 4.5 miles and turn right (east) on Forest Road 46. In 1.5 miles, arrive at an unsigned four-way intersection. Continue straight on FR 46 for another 7.3 miles to the trailhead at the road's end.

ON THE TRAIL

The trail starts off wide but before long narrows, escorting you through seasonal oval-leafed blueberries. Continue on the level trail and notice the large cedars popping up trailside. These old giants have stood watch here for hundreds of years—oh the things they must have seen!

In 1.5 miles, Lily Lake shows itself through the trees on the right side of the trail. Several small, faint trails head into the woods to access the very swampy shoreline. Because these trails are so underused, the shrubs have taken over the lake, and finding a shoreline spot for lunch can be tricky. Locate a good log and balance your way out to a view, or simply find a tall shoreline tree to peek around for a snapshot of the lake. The

The marshy Lily Lake teams with wildlife.

This hike will not knock your socks off with views. In fact, you might curse my name if I didn't give you the facts here. This trail doesn't get a lot of use or maintenance, and it climbs steeply in deep forest to a mediocre, small forested lake. Why include it in this guidebook? Simple. The woods here have beauty and solitude. Good money says you won't see a single soul, but you will find some company in songbirds, knocking woodpeckers, and large conifers. It's a nice place to clear your head and work out your body. The description here is an out-and-back, but you can make a more scenic trip by using two cars and swinging down on Packwood Lake Trail No. 78 to the Packwood Lake trailhead.

lake's water level changes with snowmelt, so in early summer watch out so you don't get your feet wet.

The lake makes a fine turnaround spot, or you may wish to continue onward. In 0.8 mile, the trail arrives at a junction with Clear Lost Trail No. 76, and from there many more hiking opportunities abound.

9 Three Peaks and Mosquito Lake

RATING/ DIFFICULTY	ROUNDTRIP	ELEV GAIN/ HIGH POINT	SEASON
**/4	10.6 miles	4105 feet/ 5080 feet	July–Aug

Maps: Green Trails Goat Rocks/William O. Douglas No. 303S, or Packwood No. 302; **Contact:** Gifford Pinchot National Forest, Cowlitz Valley Ranger District; **Notes:** Free wilderness use permit at trailhead. Four-wheel drive required, or add 0.6-mile road walk to roundtrip. Trail open to horses; **GPS:** N 46 37.473, W 121 35.340

GETTING THERE

From Packwood, head northeast on US 12 for 1.5 miles. Turn right (east) on Thompson Road. In 2.4 miles from Packwood, turn right (east) onto Forest Road 1266. In 8.3 miles from Packwood, the road turns steeply to the right and becomes manageable only by four-wheel drive. If you don't have a capable vehicle, park in the wide area directly in front of you. If you have four-wheel drive, crank up the rough roadway to find the trailhead on your left in 0.3 mile. The road is narrow, so pull off as much as possible to park on the shoulder.

ON THE TRAIL

The well-marked trailhead comes as a bit of a surprise, considering how isolated the place feels. Once you've written up your wilderness permit, hit the trail and begin climbing very steeply, almost mercilessly, until you pop out onto a defunct forest road-turned-trail. In fall, brightly colored foliage on the hillsides almost makes you forget you are walking on something man-made. The

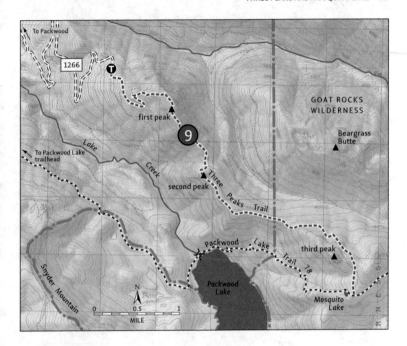

old roadbed also offers up views behind you (north) of Mount Rainier, a welcome sight.

In a few hundred feet the roadway gets narrower, resembling a trail more than a road and luring you to continue. Watch closely for white, diamond-shaped tin markers on trees guiding the way. It's easy to miss the next turn, a hard right, just after the road-bed turns back to trail at 0.8 mile from the trailhead. Once you've found it, the climbing begins again, and in 0.7 mile from the old roadbed, climb 720 feet to the top of the first forested peak.

Once on top, descend steeply, losing 480 feet in 0.8 mile down the backside. Look-ing at the map or an elevation profile on a GPS unit, you can clearly see that there are three peaks on this hike; however, the slight

variations in topography make the first peak the only one that is distinctly directly up and then directly down. Before you attain the next peak, a series of ups and downs keep you rolling along, wondering what constitutes the top. An open area allows you a sneak peak across the valley to the north, with views of Beargrass Butte.

Gain the ridgeline and wander through the trees with cliffs not far below. The Goat Rocks Wilderness boundary welcomes you at 3.5 miles into the trip, just before you ascend the final peak. Instead of going straight up and over, the trail hugs the peak's eastern flank and rolls gently along the mountain-side, gaining moderate elevation. Mount Rainier flirts with you through the trees, as do the silver forests of Coal Creek Mountain,

If you are looking for complete solitude, there may be no better place to find it than Three Peaks Trail.

before you reach an unfortunate section I call "blowdown mania." Wind and saturated soil caused this chaos of downed trees a couple of years ago, and now navigating is tricky. Hop up, hop over, hop around, and keep your eyes fixed on where the trail should be. You'll find it, just keep looking. Under all of that duff it's still there and eventually shows up a couple of hundred feet away on the other side of the downed-tree jungle.

One last small section of blowdowns shows up just before the trail intersects with Packwood Lake Trail No. 78, 5.1 miles from the Three Peaks trailhead. Turn right (west) at this junction and find Mosquito Lake tucked into the forest only 0.2 mile from the intersection. A forested campsite to the north of the trail makes a fine place to sit and have lunch before turning back. Or, if you left a car at the Packwood Lake trailhead, you have about 6.6 miles to go, for a through-hike of 11.9 miles in total.

10 Packwood Lake

RATING/ DIFFICULTY	ROUNDTRIP	ELEV GAIN/ HIGH POINT	SEASON
****/2	8.1 miles	1105 feet/ 3300 feet	May–Oct

Map: Green Trails Packwood No. 302; **Contact:** Gifford Pinchot National Forest, Cowlitz Valley Ranger District; **Notes:** NW Forest Pass required. Free wilderness use permit at trailhead; **GPS:** N 46 36.527, W 121 37.625

The Packwood Lake area was popular long before the official trail construction in 1910. The Native Taidnapam people used the lake for fishing, hunting, and picking berries centuries before the Valley Development Company constructed the trail with the intent of building a hydroelectric project. Today, the large lake sits nestled in the trees with great views of the surrounding mountains and, in all honesty, the destination is far more exciting than the forested trail to get there. But you needn't be bored—eating seasonal trailside berries can provide a treat for the taste buds, while identifying the abundant Northwest plants helps pass the time. The game of "I spy" works well too, provided it's not "something green"! The trail is cool under evergreen boughs for most of the way, but a sprinkling of boulder fields helps break the monotony and offers some views of hillside peaks.

GETTING THERE

From Packwood, locate Snyder Road (Forest Road 1260) off of US 12 near the center of town, and head south for 5.5 miles to the road's end at the trailhead and very large parking area and well-kept pit toilets. Watch for elk on the road, especially on the blind corners.

ON THE TRAIL

Mount Rainier's summit beams from across the valley before you set foot on the trail. Moss, berries, salal, and Oregon grape make

The gentle grade of Packwood Lake Trail makes this gorgeous place a great choice for those with vertical challenges.

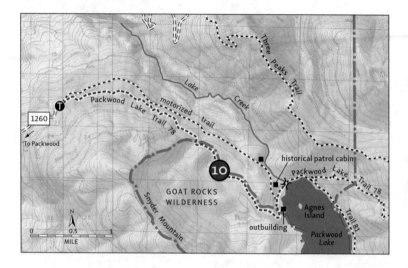

up a sea of green near your feet while above a young forest canopy sways from once-harvested land. In approximately 0.75 mile, a recovering clear-cut affords views of the Cowlitz Valley, with your first decent peek of Mount Rainier since the trailhead. From there the trail hops back under the forest canopy and before long a sign announces that you are officially entering the Goat Rocks Wilderness.

Seasonal creeks drip down hillsides but are often dry by summer, so bring plenty of water for trail breaks. A couple of large, mossy boulder fields show up as you continue onward. If you've prepared yourself for a long hike, you'll think your eyes are playing tricks when you spy the lake through the trees—it shows up quicker than expected! Descend a couple of hundred feet to the lakeshore at 3.8 miles and, if the day is warm, jump in for a swim. The 452-acre lake was created over twelve thousand years ago when Snyder Mountain to the southwest

broke off and slid into the former Lake Creek valley, creating a natural dam and plugging the lake.

Notice several outbuildings to the left (northwest), which seem oddly out of place. These structures are part of the hydroelectric power plant that began operation here in 1964. Still in use today, the plant averages 94 million kilowatt-hours of electricity annually. Roughly 100 feet ahead to the left (northwest) is a beautiful historical patrol cabin, one of the oldest in the Gifford Pinchot National Forest. In its day, it was staffed by rangers who kept a close eye out for fires during the dry season and patrolled the Goat Rocks area on horseback. At present, the old structure is getting a much-needed restoration, so tread lightly around its perimeter.

After the patrol cabin, cross a sturdy bridge and at 4 miles arrive at a good vista for gawking and for photographing Agnes Island, backdropped by Johnson Peak. The land you are standing on was once a resort complete with boat rentals, fishing outfitters, and even a general store, but it was dismantled in 1992 at the request of the Forest Service to protect and preserve this sensitive area.

From here, trails go in many directions and you may want to continue on Trail No. 78 to visit Mosquito Lake (Hike 9). Or just continue around the lakeshore (on Trail No. 81) for plenty of great campsites where you can enjoy some R&R. When you're done exploring, head back to the trailhead the way you came.

11 Lily Basin and Heart Lake

RATING/ DIFFICULTY	ROUNDTRIP	ELEV GAIN/ HIGH POINT	SEASON
*****/4	14.2 miles	3530 feet/ 6120 feet	Aug–Oct

Maps: Green Trails Goat Rocks/William O. Douglas No. 303S, or Packwood No. 302; **Contact:** Gifford Pinchot National Forest, Cowlitz Valley Ranger District; **Notes:** Free wilderness use permit at trailhead. High-clearance vehicle required. Trail open to horses; **GPS:** N 46 33.851, W 121 35.998

If you want to experience some of the most stunning subalpine beauty in the Goat Rocks, take this trail! Two alpine cirques dotted with dancing creeks and wildflowers await. At the end of the breathtaking journey is one of the most perfect little subalpine lakes in the state.

GETTING THERE
From Packwood, head south on US 12 for 1.5 miles and turn left (east) on unsigned Forest Road 48, which looks like a gravel road through a meadow. Travel 9.6 rough miles and stay left at the road fork. After another 1.2 miles, find the trailhead on the right and park on the roadside.

ON THE TRAIL
The trail begins in deep forest and in just under 0.5 mile the Goat Rocks Wilderness sign shows up, followed by a junction with

The appropriately named Heart Lake will make you fall in love with the wild country.

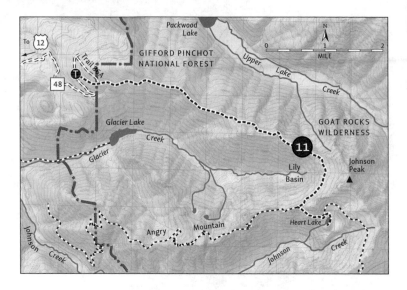

Trail No. 86A, an equestrian spur trail. From there, the trail starts climbing through beargrass, huckleberries, Oregon grape, and twinflower while gaining a wooded ridgeline. Views of surrounding peaks start tempting you to look through the trees. The trail climbs steadily before showing off a good view to the north of Packwood Lake and Mount Rainier.

The forest transitions into subalpine terrain, the trail traversing a couple of talus fields that open up to heather-dotted hillside meadows before you reach a rocky saddle at 4.2 miles. Look for little pikas in the talus yelling their warning. The trail flirts with the north and south sides of the ridgeline before making up its mind and planting you directly on the south side and well on your way into Lily Basin and the cirque under the broad shoulders of Johnson Peak. The at-times skinny trail cuts into the hillside and is filled with small playful creeks and colorful

wildflowers, giving the eyes a feast in every direction. Don't attempt to cross this section if snow is present, since the creeks create hazardous conditions underneath delicate snow bridges.

Cross several scree fields before gently climbing out of the cirque and heading southwest. At the far side, a trailside campsite at about 5.7 miles makes a fine place for lunch, with views of Mount Rainier, rocks for sitting, and a level surface to spread out cheese and crackers. Or make your rumbling tummy wait—you aren't far from Heart Lake, the final destination.

The last bit of climbing delivers you to a junction with Angry Mountain Trail No. 90 to the right (west), 6 miles from the trailhead and the highest point so far at 6110 feet. The emerald-green Heart Lake is below you to the left (southeast), although you can't see it from this vista. Continue on Trail No. 86, dropping 275 feet in 0.4 mile.

Turn right at the unsigned intersection, and continue descending to reach Heart Lake basin 0.4 mile below the unsigned junction. Look for mountain goats in the high country above and listen for marmots whistling from marshy meadows in all directions. Is this as close to paradise as we can get on Earth? Perhaps.

12 Glacier Lake

RATING/ DIFFICULTY	ROUNDTRIP	ELEV GAIN/ HIGH POINT	SEASON
***/3	5 miles	1435 feet/ 2970 feet	May–Oct

Map: Green Trails Packwood No. 302; **Contact:** Gifford Pinchot National Forest, Cowlitz Valley Ranger District; **Notes:** Free wilderness use permit at trailhead. Trail open to horses. Roundtrip includes road walk; **GPS:** N 46 32.735, W 121 37.448

When you want peace and a place to enjoy nature, look no further than Glacier Lake. The hike in is through mossy Northwest forest, with a side of playful creek, babbling as you travel. At the end, picnic at a large alpine lake with views of several forested peaks. The lakeshore is rather loggy and not ideal for swimming, but this is a tranquil place to enjoy mountain scenery. The relatively short hike makes for a perfect day trip, too, with plenty of time to spare for grabbing a burger and exploring the sights back in Packwood.

GETTING THERE
From Packwood, drive south on US 12 for 3 miles and turn left (east) on Forest Road 21. Follow FR 21 for just over 5 miles to FR 2110, located on the left (northeast). This spur road was badly damaged in late 2008 and is closed, and there are no plans for repairs. Park your vehicle off of FR 21 and walk 0.5 mile up the spur road to the official trailhead.

ON THE TRAIL
As you walk up the washed-out road you'll realize why you can't drive up it. A huge chunk of road is simply missing and at one point looks like a giant make-believe creature took a big bite. There is little room for more than walking around the disaster. After that, the walk up the road is gentle, switching back a couple of times before the official trailhead sign appears straight ahead.

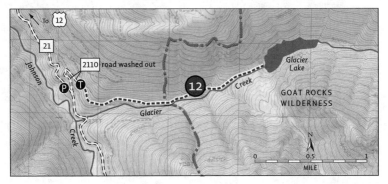

A hiker explores the conifer forest on the way to Glacier Lake.

The trail begins in a deep and beautiful forest, a sea of green at your feet and above your head. It's evident that this area gets a lot of rain and as a result, moss encases the edges of the trail like a thick Berber carpet. In roughly 1 mile from where you parked, drop down to Glacier Creek, the lowest spot on the trail and a good place to splash your face on a hot day or to let the pup get a drink. In very short sections, the trail leading away from the creek is steep and has been rerouted around obstacles such as downed trees and washed-out hillsides. The detours are manageable and no navigation skills are required.

About 0.5 mile after leaving the creek, encounter a sign on the left that announces the Goat Rocks Wilderness boundary. The ancient forests around these parts are more than beautiful; they provide shelter for native animals and plants, such as the rare calypso orchid. From late May to mid-June, these extraordinarily delicate flowers can be found trailside just under 0.5 mile beyond the wilderness boundary. Calypso orchids live no more than five years and are extremely susceptible to being disturbed, touched, or picked. The plant thrives on the fungus from the roots of the ancient trees around them, and for this reason does not transplant. Finding just one growing alone is a treat, but finding mossy meadows of them is almost surreal and this hike does not disappoint. Take plenty of pictures and tread gently.

Climb onward and before long, at about 2.3 miles from where you parked, a huge mossy boulder field surrounds you. These stone giants are the result of a massive landslide that took place more than six hundred years ago, damming Glacier Creek and forming the lake. The trail eventually spits you out at the lake's shoreline, where a couple of nice campsites make for a good picnic and turnaround spot. Logs in large quantities surround the lake, so swimming and fishing can be tough, but there is adventure to be found by bushwhacking the faint trail along the lake's north shoreline. This trail was likely made by fishermen looking for a window through the logs to cast a line and land one of the lunker rainbow trout that are rumored to live deep in the cold waters.

13 Snowgrass Flat

RATING/ DIFFICULTY	ROUNDTRIP	ELEV GAIN/ HIGH POINT	SEASON
*****/5	10.9 miles	2370 feet/ 6400 feet	Aug–Oct

Map: Green Trails Goat Rocks/William O. Douglas No. 303S; **Contact:** Gifford Pinchot National Forest, Cowlitz Valley Ranger District; **Notes:** NW Forest Pass required. Free wilderness use permit at trailhead. Trail open to horses; **GPS:** N 46 27.838, W 121 31.131

Snowgrass Flat is a spectacular 10+-acre subalpine wildflower meadow located near the headwaters of Snowgrass Creek. Its reputation for beauty has made this area one of the heaviest used in Goat Rocks, so expect company, even on weekdays. Aside from seeing wildlife of the human variety, the wildflower show that Mother Nature displays in the summer is arguably one of the best in the state. A colorful loop near the crest allows hikers to see all sides of the exquisite displays. The wildflower season depends on snowpack and weather but often peaks by early to mid-August.

GETTING THERE

From Packwood, drive south on US 12 for 3 miles and turn left (east) on Forest Road 21. Follow FR 21 for 13 miles and turn left at a sign for Snowgrass Trail No. 96/Chambers Lake. After 1 mile, bear left at a small road

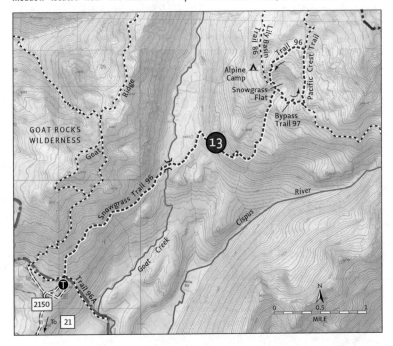

fork; there is no sign but this is FR 2150. After 2 miles, and after passing a sign marked "Chambers Lake/Snowgrass Flat Trail No. 96," turn right at a sign pointing toward Snowgrass Flat Trail; you will find yourself in a turnaround loop. Follow the loop roughly 0.3 mile to the trailhead located to the right (north) and parking on the left (south).

ON THE TRAIL

The trail starts off at the trailhead signed "Snowgrass 96A," the hikers-only trailhead. In just 0.1 mile, the trail reaches a junction with Trail No. 96 that comes in from the Berry Patch trailhead, which is suitable for equestrian traffic. Snowgrass Trail No. 96A now becomes Trail No. 96 and heads northeast, crossing seasonal streams and traversing a nearly level forested hillside.

In 1.8 miles from the trailhead, and after gaining only 160 feet, cross Goat Creek on a sturdy, well-constructed bridge. The creek is loud and swift beneath your feet; be grateful for the efforts of those who built this crossing! Just beyond the bridge is a trailside campsite with large logs for sitting if you need a break or a snack. The trail then cruises by a small pond, which dries up in the later summer months but provides a pop of green grass and sparse seasonal flowers year-round.

The climbing begins just after the pond, but thankfully the moderate steepness is mostly under a coniferous canopy, keeping you shaded and comfortable as you huff and puff. The climbing begins to offer up rewards, and the trail opens up to a talus field and a view of Mount St. Helens to the southwest. Grassy meadows with beargrass, lupine, and arnica punctuate the forest as you get higher up the slope.

At 3.8 miles and after gaining 1215 feet, arrive at a trail junction with Bypass Trail No. 97. This is the beginning of the loop, which

Mother Nature's garden blossoms during peak season near Snowgrass Flat.

can be done in either direction. Turn right on the Bypass Trail to enjoy the appetizer of lupine fields, saving the main course of Snowgrass Flat for later. Begin walking through alternating firs and meadows filled with lupine, indigo paintbrush, arnica, Sitka valerian, dwarf huckleberry, and grasses.

In less than 0.5 mile, cross a stream with a makeshift bridge of downed logs and prepare to be confused. Trails go everywhere here and several dead-end at campsites. In an effort to avoid confusion, the Forest Service has posted two signs, both saying "Bypass Trail No. 97" with arrows. The sign that's directing traffic in our direction is incorrectly pointing straight ahead to a campsite. Instead, go right (east) on the most-used trail.

More colorful meadows follow before the trail climbs to a junction with the Pacific Crest Trail, 1 mile beyond the Snowgrass Trail junction. Someone has constructed a towering cairn of shale at the PCT junction—a masterpiece! Turn left (north) on the PCT and hike through more of the same enchanting scenery. Large boulders are strewn about in places, adding some depth to the colorful fields.

In just over 0.5 mile from meeting up with the PCT, the trail opens up to giant flowered meadows and views of the Goat Rocks peaks, complete with the colorful geological layers that make up the interesting rock on their flanks. Wander through this paradise before the trail levels out at a junction with Snowgrass Flat Trail No. 96 (the return portion of the loop). If you haven't had enough of these views, or you're looking for a great place to eat lunch, stay on the PCT until you discover a few boulders located on the left (west) side of the trail—a fantastic place to perch. Otherwise, turn left (west) on

Snowgrass Flat Trail No. 96 for your gradual descent back to the loop's start.

In 0.6 mile, intersect Lily Basin Trail No. 86. While it's tempting to head over to Goat Lake (Hike 14), Hawkeye Point (Hike 15), and Lily Basin (Hike 11), save that for another day and continue on Trail No. 96 amid the explosions of colorful sights, buzzing bug sounds, and wafting scents of floral hills. The trail you're enjoying was named for a type of plant that stockmen, in the olden days, referred to as "snowgrass." It's unknown exactly what plant they meant, because "snowgrass" is a nickname for tussock, a plant native to New Zealand and not found in the Northwest's alpine climates. The plant that most closely resembles tussock here is beargrass. This trail is also part of an ancient path used by Native Americans to access the Klickitat drainage, located to the east of Cispus Pass.

Let your mind wander back in history, and then arrive at the junction with Bypass Trail No. 97, just 1.4 miles from turning off the PCT. Stay on Trail No. 96, descending through familiar scenery and tracing your steps back to your waiting vehicle.

14 Goat Lake

RATING/ DIFFICULTY	ROUNDTRIP	ELEV GAIN/ HIGH POINT	SEASON
*****/5	10.6 miles	3045 feet/ 6665 feet	Aug–Oct

Map: Green Trails Goat Rocks/William O. Douglas No. 303S; **Contact:** Gifford Pinchot National Forest, Cowlitz Valley Ranger District; **Notes:** NW Forest Pass required. Free wilderness use permit at trailhead. Trail open to horses; **GPS:** N 46 28.025, W 121 31.678

Wildflowers guide your feet toward Goat Lake.

This place will knock your Thorlos off! There may be no place in the Goat Rocks Wilderness as stunning as this spectacular lake, tucked deep into flower-filled subalpine cirques. It's the kind of scenery found in calendars, postcards, and storybooks. It has, however, been discovered by throngs of other hikers, who, like us, seek this kind of surreal beauty. Give them a smile, a nod, or a wave as you pass and expect to share. We all come here to bathe our souls in mountain grandeur and to melt away any mind noise that hums through our busy brains.

GETTING THERE

From Packwood, drive south on US 12 for 3 miles and turn left (east) on Forest Road 21. Follow FR 21 for 13 miles and turn left at a sign for Snowgrass Trail No. 96/Chambers Lake. Drive 1 mile and then bear left at a small road fork; this unsigned road is FR2150. After another 2.3 miles, find the Berry Patch trailhead to the north and parking to the south.

ON THE TRAIL

This whole area, from the trailhead up the trail for a few miles, is called Berry Patch. Long ago the Yakama and Taidnapam tribes harvested huckleberries here in the summer. After that, from 1910 to the mid-1930s, a ranger cabin stood not far from the parking area, a base camp for patrolling the Goat Rocks high country.

Head up Goat Ridge Trail No. 95 and prepare for a moderate climb. Just beyond the trailhead is a junction with Snowgrass Flat Trail No. 96 to the right (southeast) (Hike 13). If you're motivated and have the gumption, you can make a loop out of this trip by continuing past Goat Lake to the Snowgrass Flat Trail and hiking down to this spot. Those not wishing for the extra miles will be more than content sitting on the shores of Goat Lake and enjoying the day.

As you climb, pass through huckleberries and beargrass that enjoy the acidic soil at the base of the many trees, which are covered by a layer of lichen referred to as witch's hair. The long green stringy strands definitely get the imagination going wild, and you can almost hear the cackling! Up, up, up you go, gaining almost 900 feet in 1.2 miles before arriving at a junction with Trail No. 95A. If time permits, this is an interesting side loop that leads to the site of a former lookout tower. The Goat Ridge tower, a classic L4 construction, complete with a basement, stood in this area from the 1930s to the 1960s, enabling fire personnel to watch for blazes in the dry summer months.

If time is limited, skip the side loop and continue heading up toward Goat Lake. In 0.7 mile beyond the junction, the top portion of Trail No. 95A loops back to the main trail. Continue straight as the path begins to open up to meadows and grasslands as well as views across the Goat Creek valley to the peaks of the Goat Rocks beyond. Traverse an open hillside before reaching another junction, this one with Jordan Creek Trail No. 94, 2.2 miles from the trailhead.

From this point on, the views get better and better, with subalpine splendor around every corner. To the south, Mount Adams creeps in and out of view, and ahead to the northwest, snowcapped Mount Rainier shows itself. At roughly 3 miles, the trail opens up into Jordan Basin, a glacial cirque teeming with colorful flowers, playful marmots, and trickling creeks. Beyond, Hawkeye

Point's jagged peak comes into view and the trail seems to come alive with wonder. Keep your eyes open for mountain goats, often seen in herds of thirty or more throughout these rocky hills—so much so that many things in this place are named after them. There are a couple of decent campsites in the basin near Jordan Creek, which make lovely places to grab snacks or take a sit break.

The trail switches back as it climbs steeply out of Jordan Basin and hooks up with Lily Basin Trail No. 86, 4.5 miles from the trailhead. Go right (east) and find yourself in yet another eye-popping subalpine cirque. The trail hugs the mountain's flanks and remains fairly level before it drops into the rocky talus surrounding Goat Lake. Take advantage of the views from above the lake as this vista is every bit as good as, if not better than, standing next to its shore.

Goat Lake is large and often has snow or icebergs floating around in it well into October. Marmots are often crashed out on rocks near the lake's edge and campers of the human variety usually fill every available flat spot with tents, even in midweek. Leave No Trace practices are important on every trail, but with this kind of traffic they must be followed to the letter. Find a good rock to sprawl out and enjoy the view. Pretend you're a marmot, lethargically resting and sunning yourself before heading back the way you came.

Alternatively, those who eat their fill of energy bars may want to continue hiking around the cirque on Lily Basin Trail No. 86, which is a fantastic place to wander. A full loop can be made by following the Lily Basin Trail to Snowgrass Flat Trail No. 96, making for a wonderfully exhausting but mind-blowingly beautiful long day.

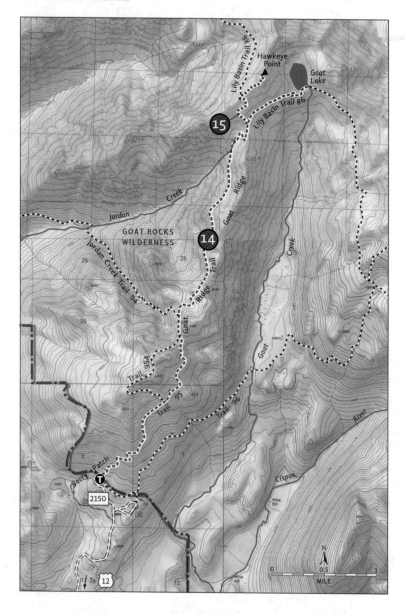

15 Hawkeye Point

RATING/ DIFFICULTY	ROUNDTRIP	ELEV GAIN/ HIGH POINT	SEASON
*****/5	10.4 miles	3315 feet/ 7430 feet	Aug–Oct

Maps: Green Trails Blue Lake No. 334, Packwood No. 302, White Pass No. 303; **Contact:** Gifford Pinchot National Forest, Cowlitz Valley Ranger District; **Notes:** NW Forest Pass required. Free wilderness use permit at trailhead. Trail open to horses. Snow lasting long into summer can make for hazardous slope crossings; **GPS:** N 46 28.025, W 121 31.678

⚙🏠 *Interested in standing on the top of the world, looking down on mountains, lakes, and meadows? One* of the highest and most remote peaks in the Goat Rocks Wilderness begs for your footprints. Years ago, a fire tower stood watch here, looking out in almost every single direction. The tower is long gone, but the remnants of history remain in the form of rusted metal brackets and a flat spot large enough to sit and ponder the glory of this amazing scenery. This is truly one of the most memorable places to visit in all of Washington State.

GETTING THERE

From Packwood, drive south on US 12 for 3 miles and turn left (east) on Forest Road 21. Follow FR 21 for 13 miles and turn left at a sign for Snowgrass Trail No. 96/Chambers Lake. Drive 1 mile and then bear left at a small road fork; this unsigned road is FR 2150. After another 2.3 miles, find the Berry Patch trailhead to the north and parking to the south.

One might feel like a hawk from the very high perch of Hawkeye Point high above Goat Lake.

ON THE TRAIL

The trail starts out in what is known as the Berry Patch. This area was once important to the Yakama and Taidnapam tribes for harvesting seasonal huckleberries. From 1910 to the 1930s, a ranger cabin stood in this area, a jumping-off point for patrols of the Goat Rocks backcountry. Long gone are any signs of such history—instead, a decent-sized parking area and well-marked trailhead are here in their place.

Locate Goat Ridge Trail No. 95 and begin your ascent toward Jordan Basin and Hawkeye Point. In a very short distance, arrive at a junction with Snowgrass Trail No. 96 (Hike 13). Bear left and proceed on the Goat Ridge Trail, climbing moderately through huckleberries, beargrass, and forest. In 1.2 miles, after nearly 900 feet of climbing, arrive at a junction with Trail No. 95A. This trail is a side loop, taking you to yet another old lookout spot, on Goat Ridge. If time permits, it's a neat way to see two interesting former lookout sites in one day. If not, save your time and vigor for Hawkeye Point, the best view of the two.

In another 0.7 mile, the top portion of the loop from Trail No. 95A hooks back into your main route. Stay on the Goat Ridge Trail and continue heading up, through vegetation that begins to open up a little, revealing more meadows and open areas in between the trees. Traverse a hillside that pleads with you to stop and look across the Goat Creek valley to the peaks beyond. On a clear day, the view is breathtaking and teases with a sample of what's to come.

In 2.2 miles from the trailhead, Jordan Creek Trail No. 94 arrives on your left (west). From here the scenery really starts to change and the views just keep getting better. Mount Adams glows to the south while ahead,

to the northwest, Mount Rainier appears like a dream. Meadowy hillsides filled with seasonal wildflowers—such as lupine, Solomon's seal, and mountain bistort—guide you as you start your subalpine journey into Jordan Basin, a vision in green with so much scenery it's hard to know which way to look. Small waterfalls trickle down the hillsides. Cliffs and unnamed peaks in all directions entice you to stop, look, and listen for the clicking hoofs of mountain goats. Whistling marmots scurry around rocks, gathering greens to prepare for a long winter of hibernation. It's as if someone dropped you into a storybook and as you travel along, it just keeps getting better.

A couple of campsites near Jordan Creek make fine places to stop if you need a break. Otherwise, switchback up and out of the basin and arrive on a ridge and a junction with Lily Basin Trail No. 86, 4.5 miles from the trailhead. The view from here is so stunning it might spoil you for hiking anywhere else. And there's more scenery to come, so head left (north) on the Lily Basin Trail and begin climbing toward Hawkeye Point.

The landscape changes from subalpine to alpine, and soon you'll find yourself climbing higher and higher in stone, with little vegetation. Creative folks have set up campsites here by clearing rocks and building walls for wind blocks. Imagine the stars on a clear night! Keep a close eye out for weather as you move up the slope—a lightning storm would spell danger for sure. At roughly 7000 feet, immediately before you crest the ridge, notice a curious trail heading up to the right (northeast). This is the trail to Hawkeye Point, although it's not marked.

Several trails exist here and are fairly faint until they converge into one—a main and well-used trail that climbs almost 400 feet in roughly 0.5 mile to the summit of Hawk-eye Point. In 1927, a four-sided cabin with a cupola, or lookout dome, was constructed here and stood until it was removed in 1966. Large eyebolts remain, as well as some rusty relics such as old nails, dinner bowls, and other antique pieces. What a perspective from this vista! Below you is Goat Lake and all around you are mountains such as Egg Butte, Johnson Peak, and Old Snowy. The contrast between the high peaks, glaciers, green cirques, and lake below provides enough soul food to feed you for years. Play the game "glimpse the goats," and see who can find the goats first. Herds, often of more than thirty animals, live on these peaks and are frequently seen grazing and resting below. When time is up, trace your steps back to your waiting vehicle and enjoy the memories of this place for years to come.

16 Nannie Peak and Sheep Lake

RATING/ DIFFICULTY	ROUNDTRIP	ELEV GAIN/ HIGH POINT	SEASON
***/5	10.4 miles	3040 feet/ 6110 feet	Aug–Oct

Map: Green Trails Goat Rocks/William O. Douglas 303S; **Contact:** Gifford Pinchot National Forest, Cowlitz Valley Ranger District; **Notes:** NW Forest Pass required. Free wilderness use permit at trailhead. Trail open to horses; **GPS:** N 46 25.377, W 121 28.271

Like many trails in the Goat Rocks Wilderness, this one has scenery galore! As a bonus it ends in a sparkling subalpine lake engulfed in seasonal wildflowers and filled with Northwest sala-manders, which are fun to watch. On the way to the lake, bop up to Nannie Peak and the site of a former fire lookout. Like so many of these old fire tower sites, nothing remains but bits and pieces of steel and views to melt your soul.

GETTING THERE

From Packwood, drive south on US 12 for 3 miles and turn left (east) on Forest Road 21. Follow FR 21 for 15.9 miles and turn left (east) on FR 2160. Continue on FR 2160 for 4.6 miles, staying left at the fork for Horse-shoe Lake. Follow the signs to Walupt Lake trailheads and park in the day-use areas. The trail is to the east of the parking lot.

ON THE TRAIL

Hop onto Walupt Lake Trail No. 101 and follow it for about 70 yards before arriving at a junction with Nannie Ridge Trail No. 98 to your left (north). Head up the Nannie Ridge Trail, climbing steadily in thick forest, with plants such as Oregon grape accompanying you near your feet. Several small seasonal creeks trickle across the trail but dry up in midsummer after the snow melts out in the high country.

In just under 2 miles, the conifers thin out and huckleberry and beargrass patches take their place, opening up some views. Mount St. Helens displays its blown top through the trees to the southwest. At 2.5 miles from the trailhead (around 5820 feet elevation), gain the ridge and come to a flat spot to stop for a breather. To the trail's left (north) is the well-used unofficial trail to Nannie Peak.

Turn left and traverse an open slope with views to the south of Mount Adams. The way turns rocky and opens up more distant views under the big shoulders of Nannie Peak, just above you. The trail pops back into the trees

The Sheep Lake area in Goat Rocks is a meadowy vision.

before turning back to the west and coming to lupine meadows, which guide you up to a ridgeline, elevation 6080 feet. The trail splits into a T here, going both north and south.

Head south (left) to the summit of Nannie Peak—rumor has it that it was named not after a goat but a mule named Nannie. The official summit (elevation 6100 feet) was once home to a traditional L4-style lookout tower, complete with wraparound deck, that stood guard from 1934 to the mid-1960s. Concrete footers and a couple of steel bolts are all that remain. The views from here are breathtaking, with Mount Adams stealing the show and Mount St. Helens flirting with the skyline.

Once you've had your fill, you have a couple of options. You can either go back down to the T on the ridgeline and head back the way you came or you can go straight (north) at the T for another spectacular view—this ridgeline trail north will lead you through larch and subalpine fir to a rocky outcropping looking out to the Goat Rocks peaks. Once you've enjoyed this view, trace your steps back to Nannie Ridge Trail No. 98. A side note: After the rocky outcropping, the trail continues and eventually loops back to the Nannie Ridge Trail, but this route is not recommended; the stone is loose in places and the route requires downclimbing a cliff face, with fall hazards.

Once back on the Nannie Ridge Trail, descend a gradual 245 feet before starting gentle ups and downs toward Sheep Lake. Large cliffs rise above your head as you

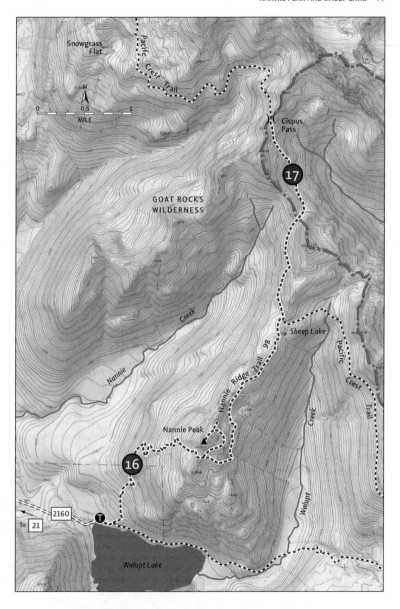

Snowgrass Flat

Pacific Crest Trail

0   0.5   1
MILE

Cispus Pass

17

GOAT ROCKS WILDERNESS

Creek

Nannie

Sheep Lake

Nannie Ridge Trail 98

Pacific Crest Trail

Nannie Peak

16

Creek

Walupt

2160

To 21

T

Walupt Lake

traverse the rocky pathway. A curious side trail comes in from the left in less than 0.5 mile from the Nannie Peak Trail junction. This is the end of the hazardous loop described above.

A little less than 0.5 mile farther, pass a pond to the east at around 5600 feet. Continue onward in primarily open flower-filled meadows, with teasing Goat Rocks views. In just shy of 2 miles from the Nannie Peak Trail, arrive on the shores of Sheep Lake, elevation 5710 feet.

This beautiful little subalpine lake is very popular, so take care to stay on main trails and practice Leave No Trace principles. If you're tempted to swim, look closely. The lake is teeming, and I mean teeming, with Northwest salamanders in summer months. The amphibians, as well as the animals of the human variety camping and hiking on the nearby Pacific Crest Trail, depend on this lake to be a clean water source. Please keep contaminants such as sunscreen, bug spray, and sweat away from the lake. When you've enjoyed all the beauty the place has to offer, follow your footsteps back to where you started.

17 Cispus Pass

RATING/ DIFFICULTY	ROUNDTRIP	ELEV GAIN/ HIGH POINT	SEASON
*****/5	14 miles	4500 feet/ 6500 feet	Aug–Oct

Maps: Green Trails No. 303S Goat Rocks/ William O. Douglas, or Walupt Lake No. 335; **Contact:** Okanogan-Wenatchee National Forest, Naches Ranger District; **Notes:** NW Forest Pass required. Free wilderness use permit at trailhead. Trail open to horses; **GPS:** N 46 25.377, W 121 28.271

Craving wildflowers, subalpine cirques, and views with a "Wow" factor? Then this is your trail! Yep, it's a challenging hike with a lot of huffing and puffing, but the views from Cispus Pass and beyond will more than compensate for the push to get there. Some of the best scenery in the Goat Rocks Wilderness awaits you.

GETTING THERE

From Packwood, drive south on US 12 for 3 miles and turn left (east) on Forest Road 21. Follow FR 21 for 15.9 miles and turn left (east) on FR 2160. Continue on FR 2160 for 4.6 miles, staying left at the fork for Horseshoe Lake, and follow the signs to Walupt Lake trailheads and park in the day-use areas. The trail is to the east of the parking area.

ON THE TRAIL

Follow Walupt Lake Trail No. 101 around the wooded shores of the lake for about 70 yards and turn left (north) on Nannie Ridge Trail No. 98. The climbing begins in thick forest, with Oregon grape near your feet and towering Douglas firs overhead. Several seasonal creeks cross the trail but dry up as the summer progresses.

In less than 2 miles, the trees get sparser, handing the torch to huckleberries, beargrass, and grassy meadows. Mount St. Helens shows off its rim through the trees to the southwest. After 1930 feet of climbing and 2.5 miles from the trailhead, gain the ridge and arrive at an unofficial but well-used trail to the main trail's left (north). This is the unofficial trail leading to Nannie Peak (Hike 16). Make a mental note to come back and check it out another day.

For now, enjoy the climbing reprieve as you descend a gradual 245 feet and start

Cispus Pass is an alpine paradise and a wanderer's dream come true.

gentle ups and downs with teasing views of the Goat Rocks spine. In just shy of 2 miles from the unofficial Nannie Peak trail, arrive at the spectacularly scenic shores of Sheep Lake, a popular camping and hang-out spot for day hikers and Pacific Crest Trail hikers alike. Before you decide to take a swim, look closely. The lake is teeming, and I mean teeming, with Northwest salamanders, which live in harmony (or try) with the folks who come here to enjoy their home. Please think twice before introducing what might be on your skin (bug spray, sunscreen, lotions, sweat, etc.) to their habitat. Enjoy the place, then move on—you have a lot of fantastic scenery to enjoy up ahead!

Several trails have been established in this area, making it a bit confusing to find the main trail, which is located to the northwest of the lake. Once back on track, arrive at a junction with the PCT and head left (north). This is the beginning of your hike up to Cispus Pass, and from here on the views keep getting better. Subalpine meadows of grass and lupine expose views of unnamed peaks as you climb the remaining 600 feet toward the tundra-like open ridges of the pass.

Look for a small sign on a tree announcing Cispus Pass, elevation 6470 feet, about 6.3 miles from the trailhead. This is the high country, elevating both your body and soul.

Few people in the Northwest ever get to see all of this towering mountain grandeur, so take it all in. Why stop here, though? A giant alpine cirque awaits exploration and offers more sights as you wander its circumference. Walk about halfway around for more views, or simply turn back when you've seen enough.

18 Walupt Lake and Walupt Creek

RATING/ DIFFICULTY	LOOP	ELEV GAIN/ HIGH POINT	SEASON
**/3	8.8 miles	1525 feet/ 4980 feet	July–Oct

Map: Green Trails Walupt Lake No. 335; **Contact:** Okanogan-Wenatchee National Forest, Naches Ranger District; **Notes:** NW

Forest Pass required. Free wilderness use permit at trailhead. Trail open to horses; **GPS:** N 46 25.377, W 121 28.271

Since this trail gains less than 500 feet of elevation in the first 2.5 miles, it makes for a fine family outing or walk in the woods for those unable to climb big hills. In addition to the shaded forest, a few short, steep side trails lead downhill to the lake's shoreline, where there are good places to picnic, swim, or just enjoy some quiet time.

GETTING THERE

From Packwood, drive south on US 12 for 3 miles and turn left (east) on Forest Road 21. Follow FR 21 for 15.9 miles and turn left (east) on FR 2160. Continue on FR 2160 for 4.6 miles, staying left at the fork for Horseshoe Lake, and follow the signs to

Water quietly laps the shoreline of peaceful Walput Lake.

Walupt Lake trailheads and park in the day-use areas. The trail is to the east of the parking area.

ON THE TRAIL

Follow Walupt Lake Trail No. 101 east along the north side of Walupt Lake. Gentle ups and downs guide you along a wide trail, with several side trails leading to the lake's shoreline below. Take mental notes about which one will be best for a swim break on the way back. For now, enjoy the shaded path through towering firs above your head and Oregon grape growing near your feet.

In 1.2 miles from the trailhead, the trail rounds the eastern tip of the lake before continuing on under the swaying conifer canopy. A faint trail turns off the main one here and heads south toward the lake's shoreline. If the kids are feeling tired, this makes a good place to stop for lunch before turning back, making this a 2.4-mile hike with a gain of 220 feet. Those who want to continue will find that the trail now becomes a bit narrower and slightly more rugged.

The old-growth forest continues to keep you cool in the summer heat before it gives way to a wetland, 2 miles from the trailhead. In early summer, mosquitoes in this area might carry you away, so bring plenty of

Signs direct you along the trail inviting you to wander to your heart's content.

bug goop. In 2.5 miles from the trailhead, arrive at the crossing of Walupt Creek, which requires tricky wading in early season but is easily crossed in mid- to late summer by playing rock hopscotch. From the creek, the trail begins its steeper climb toward the Pacific Crest Trail through brushy riparian vegetation.

In 1.5 miles beyond the creek (4 miles from the trailhead), the path levels out slightly to reveal an unsigned trail junction. Your trail goes right and continues southeast,

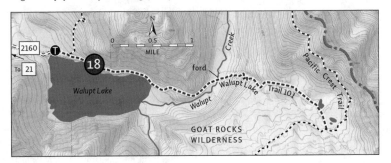

while the other little branch heads off to a small pond with a couple of campsites. In 4.4 miles from the trailhead, and after 1280 feet of climbing, arrive at the trail's end at a junction with the Pacific Crest Trail.

You may want to continue north on the PCT for some good views of several unnamed nearby peaks and some gorgeous subalpine terrain. A full loop can be made by taking the PCT north, turning south on Nannie Ridge Trail No. 98 (Hike 16), and eventually looping to the Walupt Lake Trail, for a trail day of 13.7 miles with an elevation gain of 3040 feet.

Opposite: In late summer and early fall bugling elk can be heard in the many meadows near Tumac Mountain.

bumping lake area

The area around Bumping Lake is rugged, rough, and isolated, the perfect place to enjoy hiking in complete solitude. That said, most of the forest roads that lead to the trailheads could be also be named "bumping" due to the twisting and jarring your vehicle will take to arrive at them. Most of these trailheads require high-clearance vehicles, patience, and time. Don't let rough roads and remoteness stop you, however; just make it a great weekend by grabbing a car-camping spot and enjoying all that this spectacular area has to offer. Camping is available both in the Okanogan-Wenatchee National Forest Bumping Lake Campground and in dispersed camping spots off Forest Service roads near the trailheads.

19 Mount Aix

RATING/ DIFFICULTY	LOOP	ELEV GAIN/ HIGH POINT	SEASON
*****/5	11.6 miles	4280 feet/ 7766 feet	Aug–Oct

Map: Green Trails Bumping Lake No. 271; **Contact:** Okanogan-Wenatchee National Forest, Naches Ranger District; **Notes:** Free wilderness use permit at trailhead. Trail open to horses; **GPS:** N 46 48.836, W 121 18.326

Perhaps it's called Mount Aix (pronounced "aches") because of how your body feels after huffing it up here. Crossing the talus fields near the top requires strong, steady legs and might be considered a bit dangerous due to the exposure. Getting to the actual summit of Mount Aix is precarious and might make you woozy if you're not familiar with alpine scrambles. But oh the views! The good news is, if you aren't feeling up for the summit, you don't have to go to the very top to enjoy this hike. Sure, this is the toughest trip in this book, but the scenery from even Nelson Ridge will make you misty and will blow your mind. The barren talus and stone landscape provides ample opportunities to see far east into the scablands of eastern Washington; to the west lie Mount Rainier and so many other peaks beyond. Bring plenty of water on this one, as the top is exposed and dry.

GETTING THERE

From Chinook Pass, drive east on State Route 410 for 22.4 miles. Turn right (south) on Bumping Lake Road (signed for Bumping Lake/Camp Fife/Goose Prairie). In 11 miles, the road turns to gravel. Stay straight, following the very rough gravel road for 2.3 miles, then bear left on Forest Road 1808 (signed "Deep Creek"). Continue another 3.8 miles to find the trailhead on the left (east). If you don't have four-wheel drive, you can park just off the road and walk to the trailhead a couple hundred feet away.

ON THE TRAIL

If you think you've seen switchbacks, just wait until you see these! From the start, Mount Aix Trail No. 982 swings back and forth, climbing through forest mixed with peekaboo views of neighboring hills. Up, up, up you go, losing count of how many times you've gone back and forth, some switchbacks long, others short. Look for red-tailed hawks and Douglas squirrels in the trees above when you stop to catch your breath. The narrow trail cut into the hillside could cause a nasty ankle twist, so keep your focus on your feet and drink plenty of water as you go.

In about 2.5 miles from the trailhead, the switchbacks become a more consistent

Travelers should use caution with footing on the last stretch of Mount Aix.

length and your visual rewards begin. To the west, Mount Rainier pops up and begs you to keep climbing for a better view. An unnamed peak to the south of Nelson Ridge begins to show you its permanent snow fields and gets your mind wondering where, exactly, you are headed. The climb to Nelson Ridge ends with one long switchback, which heads southeast before reaching the junction with Nelson Ridge Trail No. 984 at 4.3 miles.

With the majority of the climbing out of the way, pat yourself on your sweaty back for a serious accomplishment. For a sit break, or if you don't want to go much farther, head north on the Nelson Ridge Trail and find a rock perch where you can swoon over the views. You can't see Mount Aix from the trail junction, so you may want to follow

the Mount Aix Trail a bit farther southeast and around the bend to at least glimpse the behemoth before you leave.

To obtain the summit, head south at the junction on the Mount Aix Trail, watching your step through the rocky scree and loose dirt. The trail turns to the southeast and in a few moments, you'll see what you came to climb. There in front of you is a giant mountain of stone with a very distinct peak that once sported a cupola cabin fire lookout on its summit.

The trail drops and follows the ridge before continuing on the southern shoulders of Mount Aix. Use extreme caution from this point on, as one slip could really hurt! Several trails lead to the true summit, but none of them is official. The best and least hazardous route is also the longest, wrapping its

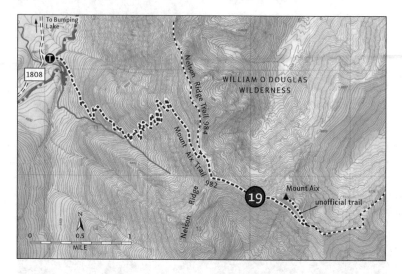

way around the southern side of the peak before climbing the eastern flank. From the top, the views on a clear day are some of the best in the state. Look for the mountain goats that are almost always within view on neighboring peaks or grazing in valleys below. When you've enjoyed the beauty, give your quads a pep talk and start the steep descent back to the trailhead.

20 Twin Sisters Lakes

RATING/ DIFFICULTY	ROUNDTRIP	ELEV GAIN/ HIGH POINT	SEASON
****/4	5 miles	1060 feet/ 5210 feet	late July– Oct

Map: Green Trails White Pass No. 303; **Contact:** Okanogan-Wenatchee National Forest, Naches Ranger District; **Notes:** Free wilderness use permit at trailhead. Trail open to horses; **GPS:** N 46 45.158, W 121 21.690

This scenic pair of lakes has long been a fantastic place to enjoy some peace and quiet and take a time-out from the buzz of daily life. What's more, elk find the meadows around the lakes a perfect place for grazing and raising young, so if you travel quietly, you may have an opportunity to walk away with a few wildlife photo souvenirs. Kids and those with physical limitations will enjoy the fairly short trail length leading to ample visual rewards.

GETTING THERE

From Chinook Pass, drive east on State Route 410 for 22.4 miles. Turn right (south) on Bumping Lake Road (signed for Bumping Lake/Camp Fife/Goose Prairie). In 11 miles, the road turns to gravel. Stay straight, following the very rough gravel road for 2.3 miles, then bear left onto Forest Road 1808 (signed "Deep Creek"). Follow FR 1808 until it ends at Deep Creek Campground and the trailhead on the road's right.

ON THE TRAIL

Head up the path and enter the William O. Douglas Wilderness, gaining moderate elevation under a canopy of fir trees as you make your way south toward the lakes. In about 1.3 miles, a small gorge appears to the trail's left (east), showing off the headwaters of Deep Creek and giving you a trickling white noise soundtrack. The path levels out a bit just before the lake, giving you a reprieve from climbing and letting you know you're getting close.

The first of the Twin Sisters Lakes arrives at 1.7 miles from the trailhead, with good shoreline access to dip your feet or just to sit and watch for rising rainbow trout. But don't linger too long; the bigger and more private of the two lakes awaits. Head right (south-west) and follow the shoreline through several small wildflower meadows dotted with conifers. The lake plays peekaboo to the trail's right (north) through the sparse trees, and in 0.6 mile arrive at an easy-to-miss junction with Trail No. 980A. While it's tempting to duck down to the lake's shoreline well before this junction, following this side trail is the best way to find beautiful lakeside nooks and crannies without twisting ankles or bushwhacking.

Trail No. 980A starts branching off into many side trails and it becomes harder and harder to figure out which one is considered the main path. Almost all of the smaller paths will lead you to lakeside camp spots, sit logs, and great views of the larger Twin

Scenic lake views abound from shoreline access at Twin Sisters.

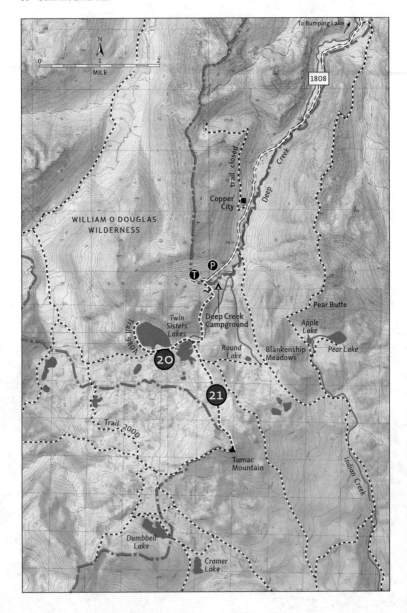

Sisters Lake. Please respect the trail restoration signs and avoid walking where the short growing season is trying to repopulate the vegetation. In fall, keep a close ear out for the hollow sounds of bugling bull elk that call these meadows and hills home. Trace your steps back to the trailhead when you've enjoyed the beauty and serenity these gorgeous lakes have to offer.

21 Tumac Mountain

RATING/ DIFFICULTY	ROUNDTRIP	ELEV GAIN/ HIGH POINT	SEASON
****/3	7.8 miles	2130 feet/ 6340 feet	late July– Oct

Map: Green Trails White Pass No. 303; **Contact:** Okanogan-Wenatchee National Forest, Naches Ranger District; **Notes:** Free wilderness use permit at trailhead. Trail open to horses; **GPS:** N 46 45.158, W 121 21.690

Like so many summits in this area, Tumac Mountain once held a lookout tower that stood guard over the area, providing a perfect perch for firewatchers. Today, the tower is gone, but the views remain. A gentle, forested climb leads to the first of the Twin Sister Lakes followed by several seasonal wildflower meadows and eventually the scree-covered peak itself. Don't forget the camera as elk call the landscape around Tumac's shapely shoulders their home.

GETTING THERE
From Chinook Pass, drive east on State Route 410 for 22.4 miles. Turn right (south) on Bumping Lake Road (signed for Bumping Lake/Camp Fife/Goose Prairie). In 11 miles,

the road turns to gravel. Stay straight, following the very rough gravel road for 2.3 miles, then bear left onto Forest Road 1808 (signed "Deep Creek"). Follow FR 1808 until it ends at Deep Creek Campground and the trailhead on the road's right.

ON THE TRAIL
The trail starts off climbing gently through the open forest, entering the William O. Douglas Wilderness in 0.1 mile. The way is shaded and comfortable even in the warm summer sun. At about 1.3 miles, the path starts to level out a bit, giving you some reprieve from your climb and showing off the small gorge of the Deep Creek headwaters to the east.

Arrive at the smallest of the Twin Sisters Lakes at 1.7 miles, having gained 965 feet from the trailhead. The lake is serene and a great place to stop for a snack or to just enjoy the peace and quiet of the wilderness. From here, head left (southeast) and follow Sand Ridge Trail No. 1104 through several meadows filled with huckleberries, beargrass, and seasonal wildflowers. If you brought your bug goop, you will no doubt be hosing yourself in copious quantities in early season; these bugs show no mercy!

In 0.4 mile from the lake, arrive at a trail junction with Trail No. 44 (confusingly marked No. 944 on some maps, No. 44 on others). Follow Trail No. 44 southeast through more meadows and picturesque little rock gardens that almost look like they were designed by a landscape architect. In fall, you'll likely encounter elk bugling for mates and fattening up in the meadows before they have to survive a cold winter. The meadows are exchanged for views as you climb higher. Below your vista lie Blankenship Meadows and the Twin Sisters,

Meadows like this attract herds of elk near Tumac Mountain—keep your eyes and ears open!

as well as Mount Aix and distant peaks beyond.

The path narrows as you traverse several switchbacks, edging closer to the top of the extinct volcanic cinder cone now known as Tumac Mountain. Like so many of these great "top of the world" views, Tumac Mountain's summit once held an L4-style fire lookout, with its classic wraparound deck; it was built in 1937 and was used for years before being removed by 1968. Once you've enjoyed gawking at all there is to see, head back the way you came.

22 Swamp Lake and Cougar Lakes

RATING/ DIFFICULTY	LOOP	ELEV GAIN/ HIGH POINT	SEASON
****/4	12.6 miles	2635 feet/ 5441 feet	Aug–Oct

Map: Green Trails Bumping Lake No. 271; **Contact:** Okanogan-Wenatchee National Forest, Naches Ranger District; **Notes:** NW Forest Pass required. Free wilderness use permit at trailhead. Very rough road to trailhead, high-clearance vehicle required. Trail open to horses; **GPS:** N 46 49.931, W 121 22.214

Those who work to get here are amply rewarded! Some of the roughest dirt roads in the state lead to the trailhead, and once on the trail, you need to ford the Bumping River. But don't let these obstacles get in your way. The trail to Swamp and Cougar lakes leads to alpine scenery worthy of your footprints. The meadows surrounding these gorgeous hills are filled with resident elk herds and wildflowers. Fish rise out of the lake's depths, while birds call from trees above. The quiet solitude of this place, void of the hustle and bustle of human activity, gives the soul a place to rest and the mind a place to relax.

GETTING THERE

From Chinook Pass drive east on State Route 410 for 22.4 miles. Turn right (south) on Bumping Lake Road (signed for Bumping

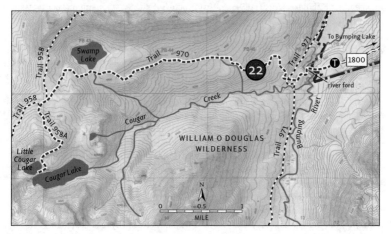

A pristine lake, not a swamp, makes Swamp Lake a fine day hiking destination.

Lake/Camp Fife/Goose Prairie). In 11 miles, the road turns to gravel. Continue 2.3 miles on the gravel road and then turn right onto Forest Road 1800, which you'll stay on for another 3.5 miles. Stay straight when the road forks in 0.7 miles and drive past the trailhead for Fish Lake Way (Trail No. 971A) to reach the end of FR 1800 to find Swamp Lake Trail No. 970.

ON THE TRAIL

The trail welcomes you with a small bridge crossing over a creek before wandering through evergreens such as western red cedar, lodgepole pines, and Douglas fir. Glimpse meadows through the trees, which give the pathway an open feel. In fall, listen for bugling elk that cause a noisy ruckus, parading around looking for mates. The white noise of the Bumping River becomes the background soundtrack, and before long a small rocky outcropping gives you views that show the river not too far below.

Begin a descent of about 90 feet on several small switchbacks and find yourself faced with crossing the river, 0.5 mile from the trailhead. In late summer, the wide river of snowmelt is rarely higher than your knees, making for a simple but chilly crossing. Once across, find a log to warm up your tootsies, making sure they are completely dry before hiding them again in your socks.

In a short 0.2 mile past the river crossing, the trail crosses Bumping Lake Trail No. 971 before continuing on Swamp Lake Trail No. 970, ducking back into the forest again. From this point, almost all the way to Swamp Lake, you'll be surrounded by a sea of green and will experience a gentle to moderate trail grade. Deep beneath the evergreen boughs it's easy to get lost in thought, as the consistency makes it easy for the brain to wander, providing time for reflection and purging of life's mind noise. A small creek breaks the monotony at 2.2 miles from the trailhead and is easily crossed by rock hopping.

Swamp Lake arrives almost unexpectedly to the trail's right (north), 4 miles from the trailhead, with campsites dotting the shoreline, providing plenty of places to sit for a break and enjoy the tranquility of this quiet body of water. A swamp it is not; it's rather a large shallow lake at the base of the proud American Ridge. When you're rested, there is more to see up ahead; onward to Cougar Lakes! The trail continues past Swamp Lake's southern edge and wanders in and out of bucolic meadows filled with seasonal wildflowers and sparse Douglas and subalpine fir.

In less than 1 mile from Swamp Lake, some confusing trail junctions meet up with the Swamp Lake Trail. First to join is American Ridge Trail No. 958, which shows up without any fanfare and causes you to stop and scratch your head. Technically, you're at the end of Swamp Lake Trail No. 970 and are going to be joining the American Ridge Trail for a short distance. Go forward on the main trail you've been following, which now curves to the left (south). Cross a big meadow, then a small bridge, and find yourself facing another trail junction with a curious sign post missing its sign for direction—yikes! Good thing you have a guidebook and a good map.

If you head right at the post, you'll hit American Lake and follow the American Ridge Trail until it ends at the Pacific Crest Trail. Head left (south) instead, since your goal is Cougar Lakes. Even though the trail isn't signed, you are now on Cougar Lake Trail No. 958A. The trail continues climbing through meadows and dwarf evergreens, heading south around a small summit area before dropping into the Cougar Lakes basin, 6.3 miles from the trailhead. Cougar and Little Cougar lakes are nestled beneath

rocky peaks, with plenty of places to sit and enjoy them. In fall, the changing reds and oranges on the hillside pair with the brilliant emerald green of the water and create a color spectacle. Since all good things must end, head back the way you came when it's time to call it a day.

23 Goat Peak

RATING/ DIFFICULTY	LOOP	ELEV GAIN/ HIGH POINT	SEASON
****/5	6.4 miles	3205 feet/ 6473 feet	July–Oct

Map: Green Trails Goat Rocks/William O. Douglas No. 303S; **Contact:** Okanogan-Wenatchee National Forest, Naches Ranger District; **Notes:** Free wilderness use permit at trailhead. Trail open to horses; **GPS:** N 46 57.896, W 121 15.934

A strenuous hike leads up, up, and away to a crossing with the American Ridge Trail and onward to the summit of Goat Peak, with its expansive views. You'll feel like you are standing on the top of the world, looking down on the Bumping River valley and out toward the towering volcanoes lining the skyline.

GETTING THERE
From Chinook Pass, drive east on State Route 410 for approximately 17.9 miles to a small, easy-to-miss parking area on the south side of the roadway, across from Hells Crossing Campground.

ON THE TRAIL
This trailhead supports Pleasant Valley Trail No. 999 and Goat Peak Trail No. 958C, so once you've filled out your free permit, turn

Fifes Peak stands proud across the valley on the climb up to Goat Peak.

left and start your climb toward Goat Peak on Trail No. 958C. A moderate climb through the conifers kicks things off, delivering you to the William O. Douglas Wilderness before the way turns much steeper.

Just when you want to stop and grab your water bottle, a seasonal creek shows up at your feet, roughly 0.5 mile from the trailhead. This is the only water on the hike, so make sure you chug-a-lug and resupply if necessary. Then continue cranking up the steep grade, climbing east for a short distance before following the trail south and gaining more and more elevation as you travel.

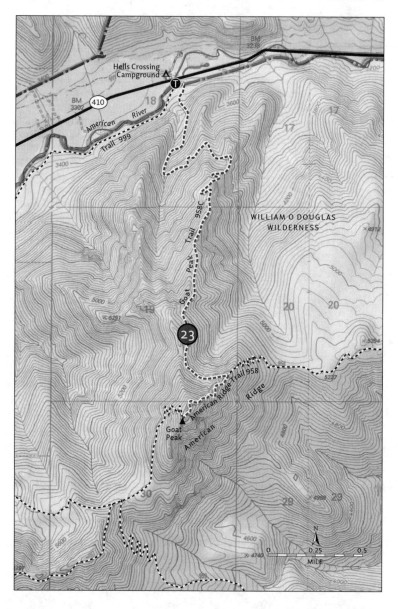

Before long, cross an open slope that gives way to great views of Fifes Peak across the valley—a reward for the hard huff and puff!

At around 4050 feet and 1.2 miles from the trailhead, the trail cuts across a ridgeline and then keeps on climbing through hemlocks, lodgepole pines, and other evergreens before spitting you out onto a rocky slope with decent views of the American River valley. Trail erosion caused by steepness is evident in places, so watch your feet and avoid doing a triple toe loop. The trail dances with the ridgeline, playing with both east and west sides before the scenery becomes more subalpine in nature and the grade a bit gentler as you reach the top of American Ridge and a junction with American Ridge Trail No. 958.

If you need a break, a rocky vista northeast of the junction makes a fine perch for a snack, with great surrounding views of many Cascades peaks. From the trail junction, head right (southwest) for the last strenuous push to the Goat Peak summit, climbing 575 feet in a scant 0.5 mile—feel the burn! From the main trail, a short spur climbs to the very tippy-top of Goat Peak, where an L4-style fire tower, with its classic wraparound windows and deck, once kept watch from 1933 to 1968. Now, what remains are just great views of Mount Aix, Fifes Peak, Mount Stewart, Mount Rainier, and Mount Adams.

Opposite: Gentle trails with wildflowers and lakes make the area north of White Pass a great place to visit.

us 12/white pass area

US 12 is a roadway through the Cascade Mountains connecting west-side towns such as Packwood with east-side ones like Naches and Tieton. Being a scenic highway, the road provides travelers amazing views of Goat Rocks to the south, Mount Rainier to the west, and interesting features such as Rimrock Lake farther east. Naturally, when hikers venture off the main highway to explore the backcountry, they are treated to up-close and personal views equally as spectacular. The backcountry north of White Pass is known for its abundance of small marshy lakes and gentle climbs winding around the bodies of water. You can almost lose count of the number of lakes, ponds, and tarns in the area, and you will definitely lose count of the copious seasonal mosquitoes! Bring plenty of bug spray in the warmer summer months. By late August and early September, most of the biting battalions have petered out, and you can enjoy the area without constant swatting. Despite the bugs, this is the perfect place for hopping onto a trail and "getting lost" along the many tranquil shorelines.

24 Jug Lake

RATING/ DIFFICULTY	LOOP	ELEV GAIN/ HIGH POINT	SEASON
***/3	7.4 miles	1485 feet/ 4480 feet	late July– Oct

Map: Green Trails White Pass No. 303; **Contact:** Gifford Pinchot National Forest, Cowlitz Valley Ranger District; **Notes:** Free wilderness use permit at trailhead. Trail open to horses; **GPS:** N 46 42.253, W 121 28.856

If you happen to find yourself at Jug Lake when it's windy, listen closely for the sound of the wind blowing across the lake, which some have claimed is identical to that of a person blowing into a jug, hence the lake's name. Whether or not you hear that hollow sound, you're sure to hear plenty of singing birds in the summer and bugling elk in the fall. Additionally, the meadow just beyond the lake attracts a lot of wildlife and puts on a display of seasonal wildflowers among the tall grasses.

GETTING THERE

From Packwood, drive northeast on US 12 just shy of 9 miles to Forest Road 45. Turn left (north) off the highway and continue 0.3 mile and take the left at a fork in the road. Continue 4.2 miles, then go right toward Soda Springs Campground. You will find the trailhead for Cowlitz Trail No. 44 on the right in 0.6 mile. Parking is just beyond the trailhead to the left.

ON THE TRAIL

The route to Jug Lake starts off on Cowlitz Trail No. 44, which is historically significant as it was a main artery of travel across the mountains for Native American tribes. The trail connected the people of the Cowlitz Valley with those of the Yakama River area and assisted them in crossing the Cascades to trade goods. These days, hikers like you and me can enjoy this gently graded trail, which almost immediately enters the William O. Douglas Wilderness and then begins climbing through dense forest of Douglas fir as the white noise of Summit Creek flows nearby.

In just 0.5 mile from the trailhead, Trail No. 44A, a connecting horse trail from the horse camp, meets up with your trail. Continue in forest, with seasonal huckleberries and vanilla leaf at your feet, rock hopping

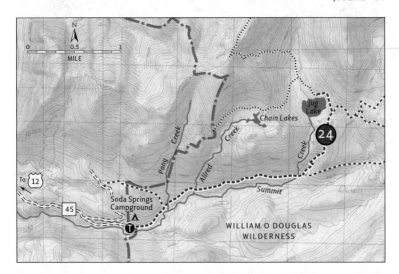

N
0   0.5   1
MILE

Jug Lake

Chain Lakes

Pony Creek

Allred Creek

Creek

24

To 12

Soda Springs Campground

45

Summit

WILLIAM O DOUGLAS
WILDERNESS

across several small seasonal creeks. Before long, traverse a rocky scree slope that opens up views to the adjacent hillside and the Summit Creek valley below.

In about 2 miles from the trailhead, a very rocky creek crosses the trail, an outlet from Jug Lake above. This creek can prove challenging and hazardous in early season, so proceed with caution and look for the safest way across, which usually means balancing on a log just downstream. Luckily, by late summer and into fall, the creek is just a trickle. Be sure to stop and gawk at the giant cliffs to the creek's north, colored by minerals of reds, pinks, yellows, oranges, and tans—a rainbow in stone!

Shortly after the creek, 2.2 miles from the trailhead, arrive at a junction with Jug Lake Trail No. 43. Turn left (northeast) on it and begin climbing more steeply now, switching back as you go. Beargrass shows up on the hillside, hinting that the landscape is changing as you get closer to the lakes above. In

under 1 mile, the trail crests the hill and your exertion is over; from here to the lakes it's smooth sailing on a mostly level grade.

In 1.2 miles from the Jug Lake Trail junction, arrive at a junction with Judkin Trail No. 47, which is also signed for Jug Lake with an arrow pointing in the same direction. Oddly, the Jug Lake Trail ends here before the lake and the Judkin Trail actually takes you to it. Someone probably should have thought that through, but it's easy enough to navigate, so we'll cut them some slack. Proceed on the Judkin Trail for 0.3 mile to find the beautiful shores of Jug Lake to the trail's left (southwest). Find a log, call it a picnic bench, and spread out your lunch.

Just beyond Jug Lake is a giant meadow, which is home to elk and deer as well as wildflowers such as green false hellebore. If you're here in fall, be sure to sport your bright orange shirt, as it's a popular area for hunters who sit in blinds nearby waiting to bag bucks and bulls. In midsummer you're

If the wind blows just right the sound is reminiscent of a person blowing on a jug—Jug Lake's namesake.

likely to see not only deer and elk but also plenty of mosquitoes, so hose yourself with bug goop and be prepared. Every map of this area has very clear trail lines drawn through this meadow, but be forewarned—the trails are anything but easy to find and follow, more like nonexistent! Only experienced navigators should attempt to pick their way through the waist-high field to locate the lightly used trails on the opposite side. Whatever you do, don't get lost! Elk are horrible at giving directions.

25 Dumbbell Lake

RATING/ DIFFICULTY	ROUNDTRIP	ELEV GAIN/ HIGH POINT	SEASON
***/4	14 miles	2210 feet/ 5150 feet	late July– Oct

Map: Green Trails White Pass No. 303; **Contact:** Okanogan-Wenatchee National Forest, Naches Ranger District; **Notes:** NW Forest Pass required. Free wilderness use permit at trailhead. Trail open to horses; **GPS:** N 46 38.703, W 121 22.942

Dumbbell Lake supposedly got its name from its shape, which reminded someone of a free weight—a serious stretch of the imagination. Regardless of the shape, or perhaps because of it, the lake's arms—or water peninsulas—make great places to sit and relax by these remote, quiet waters.

GETTING THERE
From Packwood, drive northeast on US 12 for 20.3 miles to just past the summit of White Pass. Look for a small dirt road signed "Pacific Crest Trail North." Follow the narrow dirt road north for 0.2 mile, passing Leech Lake, and locate the Pacific Crest Trail parking area to the right (northeast).

ON THE TRAIL
Begin on the Pacific Crest Trail under a canopy of evergreens that mostly consist of lichen-covered hemlocks and Douglas fir. In

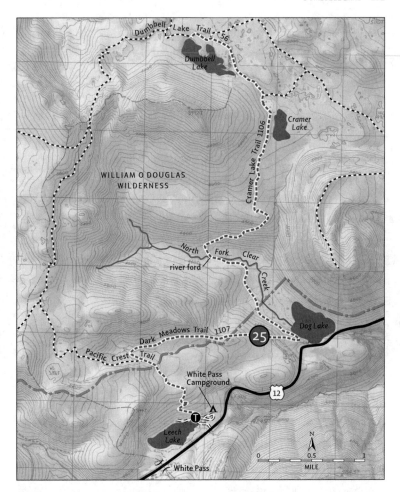

0.4 mile, cross a defunct Forest Service road. While it seems out of place in the summer, the road is actually a key connector to a series of groomed Nordic trails in the winter. Continue climbing several switchbacks before the trail eases up a bit past the William O. Douglas Wilderness boundary.

Shortly after the boundary, 1 mile from the trailhead, arrive at a junction with Dark Meadows Trail No. 1107 to your right. Follow the Dark Meadows Trail through dense timber and keep your ears and eyes open for elk and deer—these woods are full of them and they can easily scare the heck out of you

The many peninsulas of Dumbbell Lake make for great lunch spots.

as you quietly walk through the thick forest! Descend through conifers past a couple of peekaboo meadows, which ironically are not dark or too meadowy, but are filled with sunlight filtered through the trees.

In 1.8 miles from leaving the PCT, arrive at another trail junction, this time with Cramer Lake Trail No. 1106. In front of you is Dog Lake, which is mostly hidden by the trees, a popular summer camping and fishing spot. Head left on the Cramer Lake Trail, which begins climbing gently to the northwest, and in roughly 1 mile from Dog Lake, drop to a crossing of North Fork Clear Creek. Unfortunately, the moody creek swept the

bridge away long ago and you must either wade across or find another way to get to the opposite shore. In early season, the creek runs high and can be hazardous, but later in the summer you might be inclined to splish-splash your way through the cool, refreshing water. For those with more coordination than an elephant on roller skates, a log has come to rest to the west of the trail, which makes for a balance-y crossing, keeping shoes dry.

Once across, follow the trail as it makes a long turn back to the east and steeply crosses an open scree and talus slope, providing views down to Dog Lake in the valley below. Listen for the *eeeeep* squeals of pika living in the rocks near the trail. After the steep slope, the trail levels off a bit and turns north, climbing through forest until the shores of Cramer Lake are seen through the trees, 1.9 miles beyond the creek crossing. Cramer Lake is one of the largest of the White Pass backcountry lakes, with several ample campsites where day hikers can sit and relax.

In 2.3 miles from the creek crossing, arrive at a junction with Dumbbell Lake Trail No. 56, which heads northwest. Follow this trail as it rolls through gentle terrain dotted with huckleberries, open meadows, and marshlands until the shores of Dumbbell Lake come into view on the trail's left (southwest). In roughly 1 mile beyond the Cramer Lake Trail junction, an unsigned trail heads left toward Dumbbell Lake.

Follow that trail to the shoreline to arrive at your destination, 7 miles from the trailhead. The trails around Dumbbell Lake are a maze of small and wide pathways that lead to campsites. It's easy to wander and get confused about which way is back, so be sure you're a good navigator before you set off to explore the surroundings.

26 Deer and Sand Lakes

RATING/ DIFFICULTY	ROUNDTRIP	ELEV GAIN/ HIGH POINT	SEASON
***/2	5.2 miles	960 feet/ 5315 feet	late July– Oct

Map: Green Trails White Pass No. 303; **Contact:** Okanogan-Wenatchee National Forest, Naches Ranger District; **Notes:** NW Forest Pass required. Free wilderness use permit at trailhead. Trail open to horses; **GPS:** N 46 38.703, W 121 22.942

Pack up the kids, the dogs, and the extended family for this hike along *a gentle grade through the forest to two shallow lakes, perfect for wading and a picnic. If you walk quietly, you may even see the deer or elk that call these lakes home!*

GETTING THERE
From Packwood, drive northeast on US 12 for 20.3 miles to just past the summit of White Pass. Look for a small dirt road signed "Pacific Crest Trail North." Follow the narrow dirt road north for 0.2 mile, passing Leech Lake, and locate the Pacific Crest Trail parking area to the right (northeast).

ON THE TRAIL
The trail to the lakes follows a small piece of the Pacific Crest Trail, one of the longest continuous trails in the United States, and gives the day hiker a sample of its well-used and well-maintained pathway. Duck into the woods under the swaying hemlocks and Douglas firs, and in 0.4 mile cross a forest road. This road seems oddly out of place in the summer, but in winter it sees lots of cross-country skiers who use it as part of the Nordic trail system. After the road crossing, a few switchbacks guide you higher before the grade becomes more gentle and you pass into the William O. Douglas Wilderness.

At 1 mile from the trailhead, arrive at a junction with Dark Meadows Trail No. 1107 (Hike 25). Stay left at the junction and continue on the PCT. Trail volunteers work tirelessly in these parts keeping blowdowns cut back, improving rough trail sections, and rerouting water. One of those volunteers is likely to blame for spreading some joy by drawing a smiley face into the cut end of a log that faces the trail. When you see it, you can't help but feel cheery and grin right

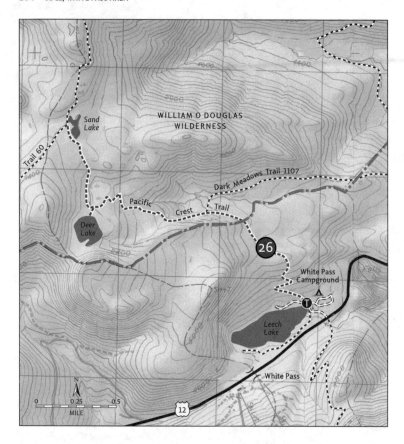

back. Despite the volunteers' best efforts, the trail is still mucky in a couple of spots, but it's only a slight inconvenience and besides, we all know that hiking boots really enjoy being muddy—it's what they live for!

Just shy of 2 miles from the trailhead, pass a beautiful meadow that shows up to the trail's right. The lake's namesake, blacktail deer, may be found eating grasses or seasonal flowers in this area, so keep a close eye and ear out for them. To the trail's left is a small spur that leads to Deer Lake's shoreline, the perfect place to stop and play. If you have small kids who are tired, they'll no doubt be revived by sticking their feet in the sandy bottom of this shallow, wooded lake. Campsites provide a few spots to sit in the shade for a break or to spread out the picnic blankets and dig in.

Back on the PCT heading north, you're only a hop, skip, and a jump away from Sand Lake, which is a mostly level 0.6 mile

You just can't help but smile back at this animated log near Deer Lake.

beyond Deer Lake. Sand Lake has a much different feel, as it's more open, its shoreline partially exposed near the trail, sporting grasses and seasonal wildflowers such as lupine and aster. Captain Obvious was at it again, probably giggling when naming this sandy-bottomed lake that's completely fed by snowmelt and rain.

If you decide to continue to Sand Lake's northern shore, you'll pass a junction with Sand Lake Trail No. 60. Those who enjoy exploring will want to take that trail a very short distance to the southwest to find an old three-sided shelter, now on its last legs, that was built by the Civilian Conservation Corps eons ago. When you've enjoyed the lakes and backcountry, trace your steps back to the trailhead.

27 Spiral Butte

RATING/ DIFFICULTY	ROUNDTRIP	ELEV GAIN/ HIGH POINT	SEASON
**/5	12.6 miles	3225 feet/ 5870 feet	mid-July– Oct

Map: Green Trails White Pass No. 303; **Contact:** Okanogan-Wenatchee National Forest, Naches Ranger District; **Notes:** NW Forest Pass required. Free wilderness use permit at trailhead. Trail open to horses; **GPS:** N 46 39.046, W 121 16.767

In all honesty, I wouldn't include this hike except for two reasons: First is the view. Though it doesn't open up into an unobstructed mountaintop—the butte is a forested peak with a small stony cliff face—the peekaboo view gives an interesting look at White Pass, Dog Lake, and the peaks of Goat Rocks. Second is the solitude. The odds of seeing other people are slim, making for an exceedingly peaceful, quiet hike where the mind can wander and purge any unnecessary brain chatter. This hike is not, however, for everyone. Blowdowns and brush on the butte trail have not been cleared in some time, causing a backcountry obstacle course. Horses outnumber hikers, and you'll be playing dung hopscotch to avoid the piles. Near the views, the loose soil and stone can make those with a fear of heights somewhat edgy. But for hikers who can hack it, there is reward to be found in this quiet wilderness—a great workout and decent views.

GETTING THERE

From Packwood, drive northeast on US 12 for approximately 26 miles to Forest Road 488, signed for the Sand Ridge trailhead. Turn left (north) and find the trailhead at the west end of the parking area.

ON THE TRAIL

Locate the trail by following an old roadbed a very short distance before it narrows and becomes Sand Ridge Trail No. 1104. Hit the dusty trail and follow several switchbacks as they carry you up through a transitional forest of Douglas firs and ponderosa pines. At 0.7 mile, notice an easy-to-miss junction on the right with Little Buck Trail No. 1147, which heads toward Indian Creek (Hike 29). Continue on Sand Ridge, climbing steeply now to gain more than 1000 feet in less than 2 miles in very fine, powdery dirt. Much of this soil is Mount St. Helens ash, which came to rest here after she blew her top on May 18, 1980; the rest is dirt that has been ground into fluff by horse hooves and hiker boots. Get into your climbing groove and

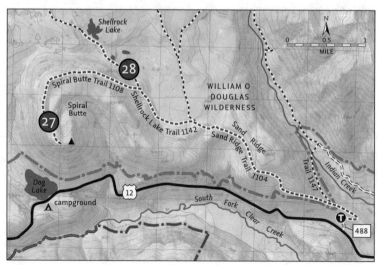

Ponderosa pines flourish in the dry climate near Spiral Butte.

smile about how dirty you'll be by the end of the day.

At around 4500 feet, the trail levels out and gives you a little reprieve from the huff and puff. At your feet, the kinnikinnick ground cover happily grows in the acidic soil, while ponderosa pines show up sparsely, allowing for views of unnamed surrounding peaks. At 2.8 miles from the trailhead, arrive at a junction with Shellrock Lake Trail No. 1142, which heads west (straight). Follow this trail, climbing more gently now toward Shellrock Lake (Hike 28) on rocky tread.

In 1.3 miles past the last junction, keep your eyes open to the left (west) for unsigned Spiral Butte Trail No. 1108. The only clue that you're close is a sign on the main trail saying "Shellrock Lake Trail." Once you locate the unsigned trail toward the butte, you'll start second-guessing that you're actually on it because it's so overgrown with huckleberries in spots. Rest assured, you've found it. The trail climbs steeply to the west through a brushy understory, gaining 520 feet in a

short 0.4 mile wrought with intermittent blowdowns before it levels out at a plateau at around 5300 feet, giving your lungs and quads a rest. Wander the plateau through continued huckleberry brambles, which sadly don't get enough sun to produce much fruit.

In 0.8 mile, the trail turns sharply south and finalizes the climb toward Spiral Butte. This place is so isolated that it might be a good place to hike and hide from paparazzi, if you were a celebrity. Seriously, I think I saw John Malkovich here once, but I didn't ask for an autograph so I'll forever be wondering. If you need to rest before the final push, plenty of blowdowns offer fine places to park and catch your breath.

You'll gain 545 feet in 1 last mile before arriving at the rocky cliff and the window to the surrounding area. Directly below you are the teal waters of Dog Lake. To the west is the ribbon of US 12 and the ski slopes of White Pass. Beyond the slopes lie the jagged and barren peaks of the Goat Rocks Wilderness. Don't get so caught up in gawking that you forget that loose soil could put an end to a good day. Watch your footing, enjoy the vista, and when enough is enough, head back the way you came.

28 Shellrock Lake

RATING/ DIFFICULTY	ROUNDTRIP	ELEV GAIN/ HIGH POINT	SEASON
***/4	10 miles	1900 feet/ 5930 feet	mid-July– Oct

Map: Green Trails White Pass No. 303; **Contact:** Okanogan-Wenatchee National Forest, Naches Ranger District; **Notes:** NW Forest Pass required. Free wilderness use permit at trailhead. Trail open to horses; **GPS:** N 46 39.046, W 121 16.767

While the trail to Shellrock Lake is a little uneventful, the lake itself is gorgeous. Sit on one of the small peninsulas jutting into the lake and watch rainbow trout rise for bugs or observe red-tailed hawks soaring through the skies above. Elk also live in the meadows and forests here, and their hollow bugles come fall add a touch of wilderness music to the quiet shoreline.

GETTING THERE
From Packwood, drive northeast on US 12 for approximately 26 miles to Forest Road 488, signed for the Sand Ridge trailhead. Turn left (north) and find the trailhead at the west end of the parking area.

ON THE TRAIL
The trail starts off by using Sand Ridge Trail No. 1104, which follows a dirt road for a short distance before narrowing into an actual trail. In no time, you'll realize why it's called "Sand" Ridge, as fine dust puffs with each step. When Mount St. Helens made an "ash" of herself on May 18, 1980, the top blew this direction and many of the trails, even to this day, are still covered with remnants of the volcanic dustup. On top of that, horses clip-clop along this trail, often hammering their hooves into the fine soil, causing even more loose dirt. While it's messy, this route is a great workout for the calves and will make you laugh about whose boots are dirtier. Besides, the trail does lead to a splendidly scenic place, so deal with the dust and get into your climbing zen.

At 0.7 mile and several switchbacks from the trailhead, pass an easy-to-miss junction with Little Buck Trail No. 1147, which shows up on the right (north). Continue on the Sand Ridge Trail, climbing steeply now to gain more than 1000 feet in less than 2 miles. Dead standing trees have shed a lot of branches through here, making the place look like a trailside stick-figure graveyard and providing fine habitat for Townsend's chipmunks to play hide-and-seek.

At around 4500 feet, approximately 2 miles from the trailhead, the path levels off a little and provides some relief from the climb. Kinnikinnick covers the ground on the sunny hillsides, and views of unnamed peaks open up through the ponderosa pines. In 2.8 miles from the trailhead, switch trails at a junction with Shellrock Lake Trail No. 1142, which heads straight (west). Continue climbing, more gently now on the Shellrock Lake Trail, which takes you through a thicker forest landscape as it traverses the wooded shoulder of Spiral Butte (Hike 27).

In just over 2 miles from where you hopped on the Shellrock Lake Trail, it levels out and passes a giant talus field to the left (southwest) and a large swampy pond to the right (northeast). This habitat attracts birds such

On a calm day, Shellrock Lake's shoreline reflection makes it hard to tell which way is up.

as wood ducks and mergansers, so keep your eyes on the water and walk quietly for the best viewing odds. The trail crosses through a small coniferous grove before it pops you out at your destination, the scenic shoreline of Shellrock Lake, 5 miles from where you started. To the north, the very tippy-top of Tumac Mountain (Hike 21) comes into view, showing its exposed summit that once held a lookout tower. Around the lakeshore, campsites beg you to stop and picnic. When lunch has gone down the hatch, trace your steps back the way you came.

29 Indian Creek

RATING/ DIFFICULTY	LOOP	ELEV GAIN/ HIGH POINT	SEASON
***/4	10 miles	1870 feet/ 4745 feet	late July– Oct

Map: Green Trails White Pass No. 303; **Contact:** Okanogan-Wenatchee National Forest,

Naches Ranger District; **Notes:** NW Forest Pass required. Free wilderness use permit at trailhead. Trail open to horses. A mudslide in late 2013 closed Indian Creek Trail. It is expected to reopen in 2014, but please check with the ranger station before setting out; **GPS:** N 46 39.046, W 121 16.767

The imagination runs wild near Indian Creek, and you can almost picture a time when Native tribes hunted and fished in this valley. These days, the solitude is plentiful and the odds are good that you'll have the whole place to yourself, save for a few elk and a blue grouse or two. This hike wanders through transitional forest before dropping you into a small, interesting canyon and leading back out the other side, allowing for a full loop.

GETTING THERE

From Packwood, drive northeast on US 12 for approximately 26 miles to Forest Road

Interesting rock and soil formations near Indian Creek beg for a closer look.

488, signed for the Sand Ridge trailhead. Turn left (north) and find the trailhead at the west end of the parking area.

ON THE TRAIL

Sure, this trail doesn't sport big views, old-growth forests, or subalpine meadows. But the Indian Creek canyon is an interesting natural feature worth exploring, and the woods nearby offer a pleasant, shady walk. The trail starts off on Sand Ridge Trail No. 1104, a defunct road that quickly turns into a narrow path. Soon you learn why it's called "Sand" Ridge. Between Mount St. Helens ash deposits and horse traffic, it's like walking on a beach, with fine dust up to an inch thick in late summer.

The trail switches back and gains 280 feet of elevation before an easy-to-miss junction with Little Buck Trail No. 1147 to the right (northeast) at 0.7 mile (left leads to Hike 27, Spiral Butte). There's an obvious big stump near the trail's start, another marker to help you find the trail. Take the Little Buck Trail and begin your descent to the crossing of Indian Creek in the valley below. Pick your way across the many fingers of Indian Creek by crossing makeshift log bridges and rock

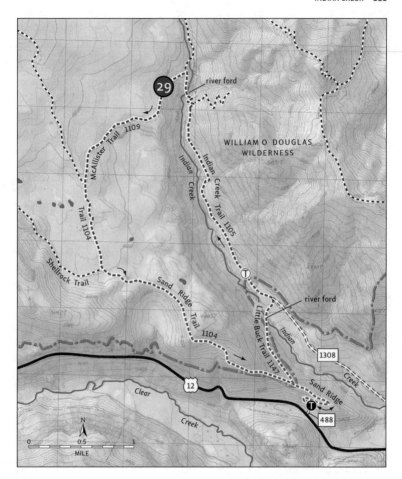

hopping. Or, if it's warm, you may choose to wade and feel a splash of cool water on your feet. Once across, arrive at a road and another trailhead, just 1.5 miles beyond where you started. This trailhead, off of FR 1308, is an alternative for those who want to make a shorter day of it, doing an out-and-back trip to visit the canyon.

Beyond the trailhead sign is Indian Creek Trail No. 1105, which turns northwest and continues the loop. The ponderosa pines in this valley remind you that you are just on the eastern side of the Cascade Crest and walking through a transition zone, or as I like to call it, a landscape that just can't make up its mind. The rocky cliffs of Bootjack Rock appear to the northeast through the trees, a towering fortress on the shoulder of Russell Ridge. Enter the William O. Douglas Wilderness before crossing a seasonal rocky creek. The tall hillsides of Indian Creek canyon begin to play peekaboo to the trail's left, causing you to wonder what's up ahead.

At 3.8 miles from the US 12 trailhead, arrive at a well-used campsite and an unsigned side trail going uphill to the right (east). This is marked Trail No. 1105B on various maps but is not worth your time, as it peters out shortly after it begins. My theory is that someone set out to find better views and the masses followed them up the hill to nowhere, each hiker dumbfounded about where the trail was supposed to lead. Alternatively, somewhere in the hills is an abandoned mine that Mother Nature took back long ago and is impossible to find—could this have been the trail to it?

Save your energy and continue on the Indian Creek Trail, which descends into a small canyon with high walls, a great place for exploring! The rock and sand sediment in the layers stand testament to water flow and erosion over the years. Indian Creek has taken the liberty of washing away the bridge that used to cross the creek here, but with a little balance, and some rock hopping, you can usually get across with dry shoes. Once across, you are technically on McAllister Trail No. 1109, which you'll stay on until you reach the Sand Ridge Trail again. For now, climb up and out of the valley, switching back through the steepness

In 0.3 mile from the canyon, arrive at a junction with Indian Creek Trail No. 1105, which heads right (north), and McAllister Trail No. 1109, which heads left (southwest) and is a continuation of the loop. Turn left and follow the McAllister Trail through the woods, climbing gently and gradually. Keep an eye out for the elk that call these open forests home, because if one of these huge beasts shows up around a trail bend unexpectedly, trust me, it will scare the bejeezus out of you.

At 2 miles past the canyon (6.1 miles from where you started), arrive at yet another trail junction, this time with Sand Ridge Trail No. 1104. This is the same trail you started on and will lead you all the way back to your vehicle. Turn left (south) and continue the final leg of your loop. In a forested 1.2 miles from the Sand Ridge junction, find yourself meeting up with Shellrock Trail No. 1142. Turn left (east) and continue on Sand Ridge another 2.7 dusty miles back to the trailhead.

Opposite: The remains of fire tower lookouts (such as this one at Smith Point) pepper the peaks in the Gifford Pinchot National Forest.

In March of 1861, William Packwood and eight other men, including five Nisqually tribal members, made their way across Skate Creek and down toward the Cowlitz River valley in search of a wagon route across the Cascades. Today the town of Packwood proudly stands in the area they discovered. Located 10 miles outside of Mount Rainier National Park and a mere hour and a half from both Mount Adams and Mount St. Helens, this area abounds with recreation possibilities. Because of the rather isolated location, many of the trails here are not used often and are in need of repair and bootprints. I did my best to select a few of the top locations that receive visitors, to provide places worthy of your effort to get here. I hope you enjoy these hikes as much as I did! After your trip, you may want to swing by Cliff Droppers Restaurant in Packwood for one of their famous burgers and homemade milkshakes—they taste amazing after a full day of cranking up mountains!

yourself with a front-row seat to Mount Rainier from the site of a former fire lookout, complete with subalpine scenery out of a movie. But getting here is more than half the battle! Right when you feel your quads screaming, the trail starts mocking you by climbing up a ridiculously steep grade. Stick with it, though, because the views are amazing, and in late summer you can eat your weight in huckleberries as you go.

GETTING THERE

From Packwood, turn north onto Skate Creek Road (Forest Road 52) near the Shell gas station. Drive 0.7 mile and turn right on Cannon Road. The pavement ends in 4.3 miles. Proceed another 0.8 mile on the rutted dirt road (unsigned FR 5290) and then turn left at a three-way intersection. Continue 2 miles and then turn right at a sign marked "Tatoosh Trail No. 161." Reach the parking area in 1.2 miles.

ON THE TRAIL

From the get-go, you might think this trail is easy, perhaps even gentle and forgiving as it wanders through a typical Northwest forest of Oregon grape, vanilla leaf, and mossy understory. Tatoosh Trail No. 161 is not wide, but starts out well-used and inviting. Cross a small seasonal creek before passing the Tatoosh Wilderness boundary, 0.2 mile from the trailhead. The next 0.5 mile is kind and gentle, gaining less than 250 feet before you hit the first of many switchbacks on the northern flank of Butter Peak. So the climbing begins!

At 1.3 miles from the trailhead, and after nearly 950 feet of elevation gain, cross Hinkle Tinkle Creek while laughing at the name and find a peculiar log shelter just beyond the crossing. Perhaps you'll find

30 Tatoosh Peak

RATING/ DIFFICULTY	ROUNDTRIP	ELEV GAIN/ HIGH POINT	SEASON
*****/5	11.4 miles	4600 feet/ 6310 feet	Aug–Oct

Map: Green Trails Packwood No. 302; **Contact:** Gifford Pinchot National Forest, Cowlitz Valley Ranger District; **Notes:** Free wilderness use permit at trailhead. Trail open to horses; **GPS:** N 46 40.013, W 121 38.294

This is perhaps one of the most beautiful hikes in our state, and one of the hardest. If you're willing to pump out a long, hard day, you'll find

Subalpine grandeur is abundant near Tatoosh Peak.

Rip van Winkle at Hinkle Tinkle, because someone has been using this shelter for a party-till-you-pass-out camp and has "forgotten" a few things. Between the partygoers and the harsh weather, the Hinkle Tinkle Shelter is in need of some love. Wish it your best, and then give your quads a serious pep talk because this trail does not mess around—you're about to begin one of the most grueling climbs of your life. Just take it a step at a time and eventually you'll get there.

In 1 mile and 1375 feet of elevation gain from Hinkle Tinkle Creek, the trail gives you some reprieve and pops you out on an open hillside near the base of Butter Peak. No official trail goes to the rocky summit, but a strong hiker/climber might want to trek cross-country for a summit bid before continuing. Just know that doing so is risky,

as the top requires a scramble on loose stone and is not for the inexperienced.

Most folks will want to continue on the trail, which thankfully slows its climbing pace and begins to reward you with views. Behind you are the snowcapped peaks of Goat Rocks, which stick their heads up high enough for a peek. The trail travels through more forest, in and out of meadows filled with corn lily, arnica, and other wildflowers. Eventually the trail opens up completely in subalpine meadows and meanders just below a large rocky band of cliffs. Paradise awaits!

Look for mountain goats on these cliffs, though they often see you before you see them and wander out of sight. Keep your eye out for bears too, which enjoy these meadows and the delicious huckleberries that grow

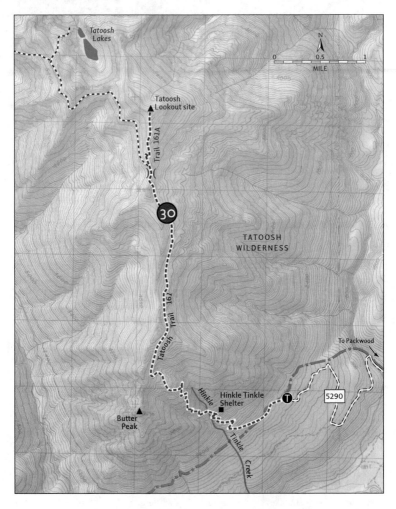

here. If you brought your flower guide, this is a great place to pull it out and see how many you can identify. Views from here get better with each step, and Mount Adams behind you shows her snowy top. Ahead of you is Tatoosh Ridge and your goal for the day.

At around 5720 feet and roughly 4.8 miles from the trailhead, the trail crosses a saddle and drops down the other side, really piquing your curiosity about how in the world you get to the top of the ridge. In approximately 200 feet, the question is answered when you arrive at a spur trail signed "Trail 161A Tatoosh Peak" heading in the correct direction. Follow this trail north, with Mount Rainier now coming into view and teasing you about the view you'll get from the top.

Climb 550 feet in 0.7 mile to arrive at the Tatoosh summit and find views in all directions that you'll never forget! Unnamed peaks of the Tatoosh Range are in the foreground, while Mount Rainier hogs the show from high above. The area where you're standing once held an L4-style fire tower, with its iconic wraparound deck, which stood guard over these hillsides from the 1930s to the mid-1960s before it was torn down. Today, concrete pillars and a bench-mark reading "Tatoosh L.O." are the only remnants left. Take as much time as possible to fill up your soul's cookie jar before heading back down, which thankfully won't feel nearly as grueling as going up.

31 High Rock Lookout

RATING/ DIFFICULTY	ROUNDTRIP	ELEV GAIN/ HIGH POINT	SEASON
*****/3	3.2 miles	1400 feet / 5665 feet	late July– Oct

Map: Green Trails Randle No. 301; **Contact:** Gifford Pinchot National Forest, Cowlitz Valley Ranger District; **Notes:** Rough road to trailhead, high-clearance vehicle recommended. Trail open to horses; **GPS:** N 46 39.986, W 121 53.487

When your spirits need a lift or you simply want to spend some time with front-row views of Mount Rainier, climb to the High Rock Lookout. The lookout tower itself is a historical relic from years gone by, when rangers were stationed here to keep an eye out for devastating storms. Around you, marmots crash out on the rocky drop-offs, peaks are in every direction, and peacefulness abides on one of Washington's grandest peaks. Seriously, get yourself here!

GETTING THERE
From Packwood, turn north onto Skate Creek Road (Forest Road 52) near the Shell gas station. In approximately 18 miles, turn left on FR 84. Travel on FR 84 for 6.7 miles, staying right at the Y (now on FR 8440). Continue another 4.6 miles to the trailhead on the right (north) side of the road.

ON THE TRAIL
You'll know this place is special even before you set foot on the trail. The trailhead is not in a dark valley, but high up on an open saddle between Allen Mountain and High Rock, with views of surrounding hillsides. The trail starts off fairly open and gently climbs, with beargrass near your feet and Cascade blueberries conveniently near your fingers. Just when the climb gets steeper and you want a break, a nicely constructed trail-side bench, the first of two you'll encounter, arrives at about 0.7 mile.

The path wanders around exposed rock ledges, with views of Mount Rainier and Mount Adams, before it enters the forest again and pops in and out of the pine and spruce. Mount St. Helens comes into view to the south, showing off its missing top. The trail switches back now, next to a steep ledge with a memorial marker to Johnnie T. Peters, one of the gentlemen who helped build this lookout along with ten others. The trail now climbs up on the side of the ridge before it traverses toward the lookout and delivers you to the rocky top.

The name says it all! The "High Rock" perch near Mount Rainier holds one of the last fire lookouts in the area.

The views are jaw-dropping in every direction, and the rock under your feet is warm and welcoming in summer months. On a clear day, four volcanoes—Mount Rainier, Mount Adams, Mount Hood, and Mount St. Helens—are all visible, as are smaller peaks in every direction. Use caution with footing when visiting the fire tower, as it's perched upon a peak that boasts sheer drop-offs of 1000 feet on three sides.

The lookout tower itself is a gem, and one of the few remaining towers of the sixty-two that used to stand tall in this region. The construction of this proud little tower took place in 1929, with mule trains delivering each piece of the four-sided, gabled-roof L4 structure. It was assembled and secured in thirty-one days by drilling steel pillars deep into the rock and fastening four strong guide wires to hold it firmly in place, a feat in itself! In 1980, when Mount St. Helens blew her top, the power of the ash and steam thoroughly rocked the building. Thankfully, it was still boarded up for the winter and partially snowed in, which prevented too much damage.

Today, the tower still gets plenty of visitors who enjoy this walk back in time, the views, and the solitude surrounding these peaks. While it's no longer staffed (modern times have given way to expensive modern equipment for watching fires), let your imagination run wild with visions of storms surrounding these mountains and fire spotters sitting on

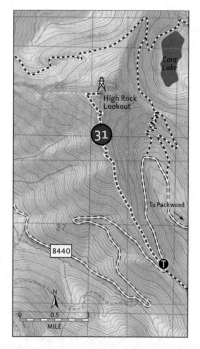

open to horses, mountain bikes, and motor-cycles. ATVs prohibited; **GPS:** N 46 33.768, W 121 42.577

At one point, a fire lookout stood tall and proud watching over the Big Bottom Valley to the north and keeping a close eye on South Point to the east. The tower has long since been removed, but the views that it once enjoyed are still here, along with a quiet retreat, a well-used trail, and a good workout to get the heart pumping. This trail is open to motorcycles, but don't let that stop you—they're usually scarce and the trail is only occasionally rutted.

GETTING THERE

From Packwood, follow US 12 approximately 4 miles south to Forest Road 20. Turn left (south) and drive approximately 0.5 mile to the trailhead on the right-hand side of the road.

ON THE TRAIL

The trail starts off in lowland shrubs and before you can say the words "Dry Creek," you're standing on its banks. Thankfully, a large log serves as a makeshift bridge and makes for a safe crossing, if you take it slowly. Seasonally, the creek dries up and becomes its namesake, but early spring and summer snowmelt can make this creek swollen and formidable.

Once you've crossed the creek, a couple of unnamed trails head off to the right. Stay left on both occasions and head up switchbacks through cool forest. As you climb, Dry Creek rages on far below you and seems to echo across the hillsides. The switchbacks give way to a straighter trail and at almost 2 miles, Mount Rainier can be seen through the trees to the trail's right (west).

special lightning stools, or "hot seats," with insulation near the stools' feet designed to protect the sitters as they looked for strikes. Enjoy the nostalgia and views and force yourself to head back home at some point.

32 Dry Creek Trail and Smith Point Lookout Site

RATING/ DIFFICULTY	ROUNDTRIP	ELEV GAIN/ HIGH POINT	SEASON
**/4	7 miles	2965 feet/ 3790 feet	late May– Oct

Map: Green Trails Packwood No. 302; **Contact:** Gifford Pinchot National Forest, Cowlitz Valley Ranger District; **Notes:** Trail

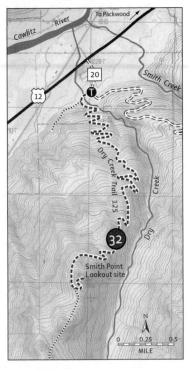

There is no mistaking the Dry Creek Trail thanks to this large sign placed by the Forest Service.

In 1 mile past these views, the landscape opens up to a beargrass hillside dotted with lupine. Elk abound in this area, so keep a close eye and nose out for the sights and smells of the large creatures. A couple of primitive trails continue south, but the former lookout site is found by staying on the main trail, which turns to the left (northeast) and continues climbing to the top where the tower once stood.

The posts of the lookout remain, as well as a very large quantity of broken glass in almost every direction, thanks to the destruction when the tower was removed. To the northwest, Mount Rainier can be seen through the healthy evergreens, which are growing high almost to spite the view. To the northeast, the Big Bottom Valley of the Cowlitz River and the town of Packwood are visible. Behind you, to the south, is the rocky peak of Smith Point. Enjoy your lunch from the top, and then head back down on the same path that brought you here.

Opposite: Clouds bring drama to a sunny day on the high ridges of the Yakima Skyline Trail.

yakima area

When the rainy, dreary days hit the western slopes of the Cascades, the eastern side is often a much better option. The semiarid climate of Yakima and the surrounding hills makes for a variety of hiking landscapes, from the near-desert sagebrush lands to the ponderosa pine forests of the transitional zones, all of them providing a smattering of options for the explorer.

33 Umtanum Creek Canyon

RATING/ DIFFICULTY	LOOP	ELEV GAIN/ HIGH POINT	SEASON
***/1	6 miles	795 feet/ 1685 feet	Mar–Nov

Map: WDFW trail map; **Contact:** Washington Department of Fish and Wildlife, Wenas Wildlife Area; **Notes:** $5 Bureau of Land Management parking fee May 15–Sept 15.

Federal passes such as Interagency Pass, Senior Pass, Military Pass, and Volunteer Pass accepted, the Discover Pass and NW Forest Pass are not. Trail closes 3.25 miles into the canyon Feb 1–July 15 to protect wildlife. Watch for rattlesnakes in summer; **GPS:** N 46 51.337, W 120 29.004

Umtanum Creek Canyon is a great place to visit, especially in the springtime when the canyon wildflowers are in bloom or in the fall when the desert displays a wide spectrum of earth tones. Kids and adults alike will enjoy exploring the canyon's nearly flat trail and challenging themselves to find wildlife, like the bighorn sheep, Rocky Mountain elk, coyote, and deer that live on these hillsides. You may even be lucky enough to see a beaver, or at least evidence of them in the form of a dam on the creek as it heads up the canyon.

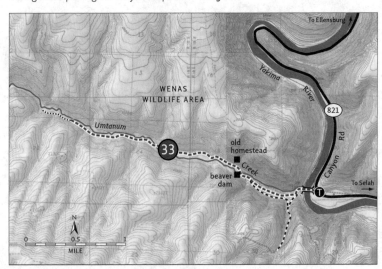

Hikers stop to admire the Yakima River on the suspension bridge near Umtanum Creek Canyon.

GETTING THERE

From Ellensburg, drive south on State Route 821 (Canyon Road) into the Yakima Canyon. In about 8 miles, find the trailhead and parking area on the road's right (west), near milepost 16. Parking is on Bureau of Land Management land, while the trail is on Department of Fish and Wildlife land.

ON THE TRAIL

The trail starts off by crossing a wide, sturdy suspension bridge over the swift Yakima River, putting you safely on the other side. A sign saying "trail" with an arrow points out the path, which guides you to an underpass located beneath a set of railroad tracks. Once through, the trail wanders a bit before splitting into two trails at an unsigned junction. Stay straight and continue northwest, following the creek.

Wildflowers and shrubs here begin showing off their seasonal colors, so watch for serviceberry, Oregon grape, golden current, arrowleaf balsamroot, lupine, and bluebells. As you walk, stop occasionally and scan the

hillsides for mammals. The bighorn sheep in these canyons blend in so well that a pair of binoculars and someone with a good eye for spotting wildlife are nice to have along. Cottonwood and aspen trees along the creek are a perfect place for birds such as lazuli buntings, yellow-breasted chat, falcons, and eagles to nest and rest, so don't forget to look between the branches.

Just shy of 1 mile from the trailhead, cross the creek on makeshift log bridges or by rock hopping. Immediately afterward, follow the creekbed 50 yards upstream (left) to find a beaver dam fit for an architect's portfolio. These little tail slappers have been busy chewing, dragging, and constructing this peaceful creek pond, which holds small fish!

Back on the trail, turn right near the creek (northeast), and see if you can find the remains of an old homestead. The buildings are gone, but the concrete foundations for the root cellar and front entrance still sit in meadows, now almost completely taken back by nature. One such piece of concrete is dated November 25, 1933, which would have been five days short of Thanksgiving that year and just in time to plant several apple trees, which still produce abundantly in the area, despite not being pruned.

If you visit in fall, grab an apple or two and savor the tartness of fresh off-the-tree fruit. The trail follows the creek, now running to the south, through steep basaltic cliffs and several groves of aspen trees before it crosses the water again about 1 mile past the homestead. Rock hop your way across and find the trail on the other side, continuing up the canyon.

In roughly 3 miles from the trailhead, the trail narrows and crosses a boulder field, becoming increasingly less obvious. This makes a fine turnaround spot and allows time for a leisurely stroll back to the trailhead, eyes peeled for the flora and fauna unique to this special place.

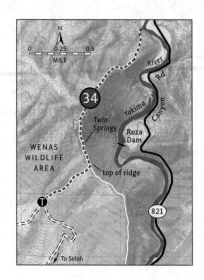

34 Yakima Skyline Trail

RATING/ DIFFICULTY	ROUNDTRIP	ELEV GAIN/ HIGH POINT	SEASON
***/3	6–7 miles	1800 feet/ 3000 feet	Mar–Nov

Map: WDFW trail map; **Contact:** Washington Department of Fish and Wildlife, Wenas Wildlife Area; **Notes:** Discover Pass or WDFW Vehicle Access Pass required. Extremely rough road to trailhead, high-clearance vehicle required. Trail open to horses and mountain bikes. Watch for rattlesnakes in summer; **GPS:** N 46 44.130, W 120 29.650

When the doldrums of the rainy season set in on the western side of the mountains, hop over to the Yakima Skyline Trail for a shot of sunshine and fantastic sights. The Skyline Trail meanders along the top of a ridgeline, exhibiting views of the Yakima Valley to the south and the Yakima Canyon to the north. Whether you go for a couple of miles or spend the day exploring, this desert ridge has much to offer.

GETTING THERE

From Ellensburg, take I-82 east to Selah and take exit 26. Off the exit, go right and travel a short 0.2 mile before turning left on Harrison Road. Drive 1.9 miles and turn right on North Wenas Road. Drive 2.8 miles and look for a rural fire station on your right. Turn right on Gibson Street and follow it for a short 0.1 mile, and then take another right on Buffalo Road. Travel 0.6 mile to where the pavement ends and the road curves right. Look to your left and find a parking area with an elk fence. If your vehicle is high-clearance, open the gate (be sure to close it behind you) and proceed a very rough 1.7 miles to the road's end and last parking area. If your vehicle is not high-clearance, park near the elk fence and

The Yakima Skyline Trail is a fine place for you (and your furry friend) to enjoy views of the desert landscapes.

walk the road, adding 3.4 miles roundtrip to your hike. If I haven't said it enough, believe me when I say, this road is ROUGH!

ON THE TRAIL

The trail starts off to the northeast of the parking area, on what appears to have been a road. Quickly the road turns to a single-track trail and the hike up the canyon begins. Climb past seasonal flowers such as sage, lupine, and balsam, while meadowlarks sing from the surrounding hills. Keep an eye out for rattlesnakes, especially in the lower areas, in all seasons but winter. Before long, a trickling spring provides some green in the desert, and a trough holding water covered with algae appears to the east.

Continue climbing up the canyon until you're standing on the top of the ridge at 1.1 miles and views of the Yakima Canyon open up in front of you like a big screen. Turn around to see, on a clear day, the snow-covered Cascades, including Mount Rainier and Mount Adams. Bitterroot plants at your

feet remind you that you are in an arid climate with delicate soils and a fragile eco-system. From here your options are to travel either right (southeast) or left (northwest).

To the southeast, you could choose an optional side trip up a small rise for better views and enjoy your lunch from a higher perch, or simply wander the ridgeline, gently gaining and losing elevation until the path begins to head down toward a different trailhead after the last peak.

To the northwest, wander up and down the ridgeline, gaining better views of Roza Dam and the Yakima Canyon as you hike. Drop down the ridge to a crossing of Twin Springs at 1.4 miles, a small oasis, and then back up slightly before you continue on a fairly level path that begins to curve east. Watch for poison ivy near the springs and use caution not to brush up against it, especially if you're wearing shorts, or you'll have a miserable day you'll never forget.

The trail crosses a fence line and then gently wanders around the hillside, teasing you to continue to see what's around the next bend. Eventually, the trail begins a descent and heads all the way down toward the Umtanum Recreation Area at the bottom of the canyon. Roam to your heart's content, and then head back the way you came to your waiting vehicle.

35 Umtanum Creek Falls

RATING/ DIFFICULTY	ROUNDTRIP	ELEV GAIN/ HIGH POINT	SEASON
**/2	2 miles	235 feet/ 2530 feet	Mar–Nov

Map: WDFW trail map; **Contact:** Washington Department of Fish and Wildlife, Wenas Wildlife Area; **Notes:** Discover Pass or WDFW Vehicle Access Pass required. Primitive dirt road to trailhead. Watch for rattlesnakes in summer, icy conditions near the falls in late fall and winter; **GPS:** N 46 53.959, W 120 38.576

Before you even set foot on the trail you are immersed in history, as the road to the trailhead is actually part of an old stagecoach route across the mountains. Be grateful you don't have wooden wheels! Once on the trail, follow Umtanum Creek to a lovely and somewhat unexpected waterfall coming off of basalt cliffs above. The grade is gentle, but the steep and somewhat precarious descent to the falls below can be tricky for those who aren't surefooted.

GETTING THERE

From I-90 eastbound near Ellensburg, take exit 109/Canyon Road. At the stop sign after the off-ramp, go right. Travel 0.8 mile, then turn left onto Umptanum Road (this is the spelling on the street sign, as opposed to other names in the area spelled "Umtanum"). Follow Umptanum Road into the hills until it turns to gravel in roughly 5.2 miles. Continue on the gravel road for 4.6 miles to

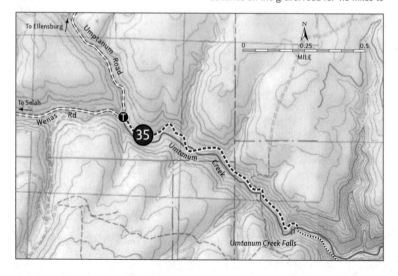

Water cascades into a thin basalt basin at Umtanum Creek Falls.

find the parking area for Umtanum Creek Falls, just off a hairpin turn.

ON THE TRAIL

The trail starts off in a transition zone filled with ponderosa pines and cottonwood trees growing happily in the arid landscape. Look for woodpeckers, including the hairy and Lewis varieties, rooting around for bugs deep in the tree bark. Also keep your eyes and ears open for elk that wander the hilltops above and bugle loudly, looking for mates in the fall.

In 0.2 mile from the trailhead, cross a small three-plank-wide bridge over the creek. The desert hills above are barren and a stark contrast to the green grasses and seasonal spring wildflowers of this little valley, for where there is water, there is life! At 0.6 mile from the trailhead, an unsigned trail junction tries to figure out which way is easiest to cross the creek. Going right is the best bet for keeping your shoes dry and keeps you solidly on the main path.

From here the trail continues through open meadows dotted with ponderosas before it climbs a small hill and shows off a beaver dam in the creek below you. Beavers are the largest living rodent in North America, and their handiwork of creating small ponds is an ecological benefit for other species, such as migratory birds who use the quiet water for resting and raccoons, weasels, and herons who stalk minnows near the water's edge. The trail skirts a hillside for a short distance before it crosses the creek, playing hopscotch for one last time.

At 0.8 mile from the trailhead, enter a talus field that steeply switches back down to the falls. Watch your footing and use caution in this area, as the soil is loose and it's easy to get caught up in where you're going instead of where your feet are planted. Umtanum Creek Falls is located in a stone punch bowl with high basalt pillars making up the edges. The contrast of the cascading water against the gray-orange stone dotted with green plants makes for some beautiful photo opportunities. A campsite across the creek is a fine turnaround spot or place to spread out a picnic.

Explorers looking to continue their journey may want to wander up the canyon until the trail peters out. When you're done, trace your steps back to the trailhead and cross the falls off of your bucket list.

36 Black Canyon

RATING/ DIFFICULTY	ROUNDTRIP	ELEV GAIN/ HIGH POINT	SEASON
**/2	7 miles	1475 feet/ 3905 feet	Mar–Nov

Map: WDFW trail map ; **Contact:** Washington Department of Fish and Wildlife, Oak Creek Wildlife Area; **Notes:** Discover Pass or WDFW Vehicle Access Pass required. Rough road to trailhead, high-clearance vehicle required. First 1.5 miles of trail open to horses, beyond that open to mountain bikes, motorcycles, and ATVs. Watch for rattlesnakes in summer; **GPS:** N 46 51.025, W 120 42.085

If you're a bird nerd like me, you'll go crazy over this canyon. I've said it before and I'll say it again: where there is water, there is life! Wildlife, including mule deer, coyotes, and the feathered ones, depend on this canyon to survive, and they raise young in the tall protected groves of quaking aspen and cottonwood. The roadbed-turned-trail also leads hikers to an old log homestead set among the deciduous trees and an opportunity to let the imagination run wild about days of yesteryear.

GETTING THERE
From I-90 eastbound near Ellensburg, take exit 109/Canyon Road. At the stop sign after the off-ramp, go right. Travel 0.8 mile, then turn left on to Umtanum Road (this is the spelling on the street sign, as opposed to other names in the area spelled "Umtanum"). Follow Umtanum Road into the hills until it turns to gravel in roughly 5.2 miles. Continue on the gravel road for 13 miles when it turns back to pavement (and changes its name to Wenas Road). Proceed another 4 miles and look for a dirt road to the left (north). Turn down the rough dirt road (high-clearance vehicle required) and drive 0.5 mile until you reach a wildlife gate. Open the gate, drive through, and then close it behind you. In 0.4 mile from the gate, stay straight at a three-way dirt road junction, and continue another 0.4 mile to find parking for approximately four vehicles at the road's end.

ON THE TRAIL
Walk around the berm and head up the canyon on the old roadbed, climbing moderately on the rocky trail. To the left, the creek trickle gives life to the nearby bitterbrush, willow, tall Oregon grape, sage, and currant

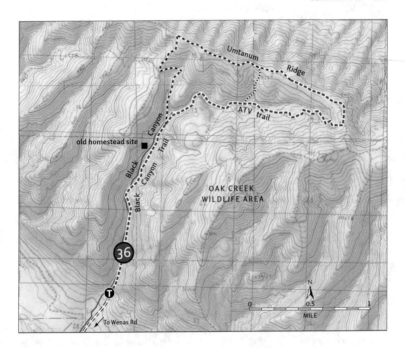

shrubs. In 0.2 mile, pass an old and decrepit snow fence and continue your climb deeper and deeper under the steep canyon walls. The dramatic basalt formations high in the hills make great nesting and hunting spots for birds of prey, such as northern harriers, golden eagles, and American kestrels, so stop and get out the binoculars if you brought them. Canyon wrens' descending musical whistles provide a distinctive soundtrack as you roam the valley floor.

In 1 mile, the climbing grade becomes gentler and the creek gives life to a large grove of mixed cottonwood and quaking aspen trees, adding a splash of green foliage and white bark to the neutral tan colors of the canyon. This grove provides even more habitat for feathered friends, especially owls, whose fledglings hide among the budding leaves in the spring. Look for long-eared, great horned, and northern saw-whet owls quietly observing you as you walk alongside their perches.

In 1.2 miles, arrive at a grassy meadow and the remains of an old log homestead tucked in the trees and worthy of exploration. The cabin, now a mass of weathered wood, causes you to stop and think about what life must have been like for the prairie folks who homesteaded here—a challenging but peaceful life for certain!

In 1.5 miles, the canyon trail meets up with an ATV road, which often is free of motorized traffic, allowing you to hike in quiet and leading you up to Umtanum Ridge. Turn right and walk the road through a transition

An old homestead makes a hiker's imagination run wild near Black Canyon.

zone of ponderosa and white pine, keeping an eye out for elk, a common visitor to this area. In spring, wildflowers such as grass widow pop up among the fallen needles in the understory, adding color and interest to the landscape.

In 3.4 miles from the trailhead, go left at a small road junction, which puts you on the top of Umtanum Ridge. Oh, the views! The snowcapped, majestic summits of Mount Stewart and peaks in the Alpine Lakes Wilderness are visible, along with the town of Ellensburg and the Kittitas Valley in the distance. This is a great place for lunch or just to sit and take in the views. Look for sagebrush violets, sagebrush buttercups, and yarrow in early spring.

Head back the way you came, or look for a faint trail leading cross-country near a

fence post just before the ridge trail starts to climb again. Follow the faint trail or simply go cross-country down into the drainage and connect back to the road you followed on the way in. From there, trace your steps back to the trailhead.

37 Waterworks Canyon

RATING/ DIFFICULTY	ROUNDTRIP	ELEV GAIN/ HIGH POINT	SEASON
***/2	3.6 miles	1235 feet/ 2685 feet	Mar–Nov

Maps: Green Trails Manastash Lake No. 273, Tieton No. 305; **Contact:** Washington Department of Fish and Wildlife, Oak Creek Wildlife Area; **Notes:** Discover Pass or WDFW Vehicle Access Pass required. Trail open to horses. Watch for rattlesnakes in summer; **GPS:** N 46 44.922, W 120 47.876

 A beautiful canyon filled with colorful wildflowers, a trickling creek, wildlife-viewing opportunities, and plenty of sunshine awaits. The moderate climb will keep your heart and lungs occupied while the interesting rock formations high up the canyon walls will give your eyes plenty of entertainment. Waterworks Canyon is a true desert gem!

GETTING THERE
From Ellensburg, drive southeast on I-82 and take exit 31A near Yakima. Follow the signs toward "US 12-West/Naches." Drive US 12 for approximately 17 miles, through the town of Naches to a junction with State Route 410. Stay straight on SR 410. Drive 0.6 mile and turn right just past a small bridge, where you'll find the trailhead and parking for roughly five cars.

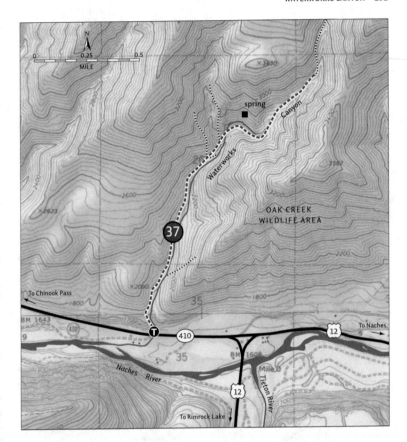

ON THE TRAIL

Begin by walking through the game fence, closing the gate tightly behind you. Just on the other side, the desert walk begins, the trail meandering up into the canyon, staying very close to the trickling creek to the trail's right. In springtime, the large yellow flower clumps of Carey's balsamroot populate these sparse hillsides, bringing life and color to the subdued desert tones. The trail crisscrosses the gently flowing creek a couple of times, keeping you smack-dab on the canyon's floor.

Where there is water, there is life! Above you, stone basalt pillars with caves, tunnels, and large pockets are interesting for the eyes to explore and for spotting nesting birds, such as red-tailed hawks, prairie falcons, golden eagles, and other species. Faint game trails made by elk, bighorn sheep, and deer cover the canyon walls above, while closer to the trail, smaller birds such as canyon wrens,

Usually sunny, Waterworks Canyon is a great place to enjoy the desert landscape.

lazuli buntings, and vesper sparrows flit from tree to tree, attracting mates and hunting for food.

In 0.3 mile, the trail splits and a faint trail goes right, but the main trail goes left. From here, the trail wanders through a couple of grassy meadows dotted with lupine and waterleaf as it climbs deeper and deeper into the canyon's fold. Trees along the path, such as cottonwood, Garry oak, hawthorn, willow, and others provide leafy green beauty to the creeks shoreline.

At 1 mile, a four-way intersection shows up, with faint trails going to either side of the main path. Continue forward on the middle one, heading up the valley toward a beautiful grove of aspen and cottonwood trees. Duck into the trees and arrive at another junction, one direction climbing up and one heading down toward the creek. Head toward the water and keep your shoes dry by balancing across a hodgepodge of small downed logs, thanks to some thoughtful hiker who took the time to place them here! Once on the other side, the hill gets steep for a few hundred yards before getting back to a moderate grade.

At 1.5 miles, stop and listen! You are very close to a natural desert spring that pops out of the ground from deep within the earth, providing water to the creek and sustaining a multitude of creatures that depend on it for existence. Just 0.3 mile beyond the spring, the trail crosses under a gently slopping, grassy bench that makes a fantastic place to perch for lunch and a great turnaround spot. Bust out your cheese and crackers, or continue strolling up the canyon to your heart's content.

38 Tieton Nature Trail

RATING/ DIFFICULTY	ROUNDTRIP	ELEV GAIN/ HIGH POINT	SEASON
***/1	3.6 miles	220 feet/ 1820 feet	Mar–Nov

Map: Green Trails Tieton No. 305; **Contact:** Washington Department of Fish and Wildlife, Oak Creek Wildlife Area; **Notes:** Discover Pass or WDFW Vehicle Access Pass required. Trail open to mountain bikes. Watch for rattlesnakes in summer; **GPS:** N 46 43.173, W 120 49.887

Kids and adults will love this hike with its abundant nature, fairly level trail, and swinging suspension bridge for channeling your inner Indiana Jones. High above you golden eagles and osprey soar, while Lewis's woodpeckers peck away at ponderosa pines near the trail looking for insects. A keen eye may pick out

Rocky Mountain elk or bighorn sheep that roam the hills above, camouflaged by the landscape.

GETTING THERE
From Ellensburg, drive southeast on I-82 and take exit 31A near Yakima. Follow the signs toward "US 12-West/Naches." Drive US 12 for approximately 17 miles, through the town of Naches to a junction with State Route 410. Turn left (south) and continue on US 12 for 3.4 miles to the parking area near a Quonset hut on the left (south) side of the highway.

ON THE TRAIL
From the parking area, walk through the defunct gate toward the river and turn right (west) through a meadow area to find the official trailhead, just before the suspension bridge. Walk up the steps and feel the swaying bridge beneath your feet as you cross above the mighty Tieton River. What makes

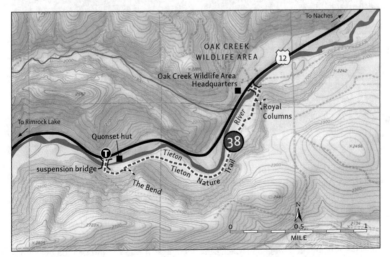

A gentle grade makes the Tieton Nature Trail a good pick for hikers of all ages and abilities.

this bridge extra exciting is the fact that the railings are simply thin metal wires, which teases you into thinking the crossing is much riskier than it actually is. If you brought the pooch, you'll have to lift him up to the bridge and entice him across—the bridge span has small metal holes cut throughout, which can

feel uncomfortable on soft paws. Thankfully, the crossing isn't very long and in no time you're on the other side, ready to wander the southern riverbank.

Happily on the other side, turn left (east) and follow the well-used trail on a gentle grade as it wanders through the ponderosa pines. Keep your eyes open for birds, especially in the springtime when a wide variety of species arrives in flocks in the Tieton area and excites birders. Bullock's orioles, western tanagers, canyon wrens, and others are just a sample of what you may see. If the weather is warm, the slithering ones may show up occasionally near the trail's edge. Using trekking poles is recommended and usually makes a snake scram before it poses any threat. Snakes are part of the diet of the golden eagles and osprey that nest in this area, so the limbless reptiles are hardwired to make themselves scarce at any sign of predators, including humans.

In 0.3 mile beyond the suspension bridge, encounter an unsigned trail fork. Continue straight (left). The right fork leads to "The Bend" rock-climbing area, which is closed seasonally to protect nesting golden eagles, a treat for the eyes. If you brought your binoculars, stop and scan the cliffs for the stick-and-moss edges of the giant nests these birds create, which are so large that a human could almost lay down inside one and take a nap! In late spring and early summer, you may even get a chance see the fledglings, which stay close to the nest even after they've taken their first flight.

The trail traverses a hillside before dropping into the meadows, which are seasonally filled with arrowroot balsam and lupine as well as flowering shrubs and white oak trees. In 0.5 mile from the trailhead, the way slightly descends again, this time swinging you closer to the river. In the summer of 2002, a 2000-acre fire swept through this area, wiping out many of the trees and plants. The recovery is astounding, and today new seedlings thrive in the nutrient-rich soils and decaying organic matter.

In about 1 mile from the trailhead, pass a concrete foundation for an old steam plant that helped create the irrigation canals in the area, now a relic from the past. Shortly afterward, the trail becomes narrower and a game fence provides a boundary to the trail's right. A few plant identification signs in the area help you learn the various species of shrubs that grow in this arid climate.

The trail finishes by guiding you along an old roadbed to a trail junction where the sign points the way to the "Royal Columns" rock-climbing area, heading off to the trail's right (southeast). Ahead of you is a wire game fence gate with a mini pedestrian door. To check out the footbridge that crosses the Tieton at the trail's end, go through the spring-loaded door or unlatch the gate (relatching it behind you) and walk through. When you've had your fill, head back the way you came.

39 Buck Lake

RATING/ DIFFICULTY	ROUNDTRIP	ELEV GAIN/ HIGH POINT	SEASON
**/2	3 miles	410 feet/ 4750 feet	late May– Oct

Map: Green Trails Old Scab Mountain No. 272; **Contact:** Okanogan-Wenatchee National Forest, Naches Ranger District; **Notes:** Free wilderness use permit at trailhead. Trail open to horses; **GPS:** N 46 48.875, W 121 09.055

The trail to Buck Lake can lead far into the backcountry by synching up with many different trails. But Buck Lake itself is accessible by a short, fairly easy approach and makes a great trip for those who want a shorter day hike or an enjoyable outing with kids. While the lake is murky and not a great place for swimming, bird life flourishes near the water's edge and your odds of seeing elk or mountain goat are good, as they use these trails more than we do!

GETTING THERE

From Ellensburg, drive southeast on I-82 and take exit 31A near Yakima. Follow the signs toward "US 12-West/Naches." Drive approximately 17 miles, through the town of Naches to a junction with State Route 410. Stay right on SR 410 and drive 7.8 miles. Look for the Wood Shed Restaurant on your left and turn left on Nile Road just before it. Proceed 1.3 miles to Bethel Ridge Road, and turn left. Follow the long, windy single-lane paved road for 7.5 miles until the pavement turns to gravel. Stay straight on Forest Road 1502 past McDaniel Lake. After the lake, go 2.9 miles to a fork and turn right. Drive 0.3 mile to the road's end at the trailhead.

ON THE TRAIL

To call this a lake is a bit of a stretch; it's more like a swamp or puddle. So why go? What's to see? During a recent visit I counted forty different varieties of birds, including orioles, jays, warblers, flycatchers, and even the rare peregrine falcon. Additionally, from my log perch I watched a bull elk wander down to the water for a dinner of aquatic grasses pulled from the lake bottom. Wildlife thrives near this trailside lake, and those who sit patiently and watch will be fully rewarded.

The trail starts to the left of the trailhead sign. Fill out your wilderness use permit before you hit the trail. Then find yourself walking in forest with pine needles cushioning your footfalls. Note that the prints on the trail are not of the human variety as much as they are goat, elk, and deer. If children are present, this is a fun place to investigate what print belongs to what animal.

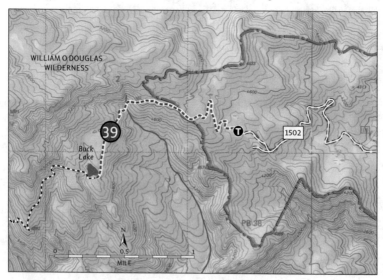

Although the water can be murky, wildlife abounds at Buck Lake.

Climb gradually before reaching a boundary sign, transitioning you to the William O. Douglas Wilderness, just under 0.5 mile from the trailhead. Blowdowns are common in early season, but the open forest allows for fairly easy navigation around them. Descend to a small seasonal spring and wetland before continuing onward and arriving at a landslide. The trail over the loose soil is fine for humans but would be tricky for stock. Cross the slide using caution and good footing.

The trail slightly descends to another seasonal creek before it levels off. In approximately 1.3 miles from the trailhead, note a faint trail leading off to the left (south), to a decent campsite with a mountain view. Shortly after the campsite, the lake appears to the trail's right (north). Enjoy the lake and the creatures that call this place home before turning back the way you came.

40 Edgar Rock

RATING/ DIFFICULTY	ROUNDTRIP	ELEV GAIN/ HIGH POINT	SEASON
***/3	2.2 miles	1470 feet/ 3700 feet	late May– Oct

Map: Green Trails Old Scab Mountain No. 272; **Contact:** Okanogan-Wenatchee National Forest, Naches Ranger District; **Notes:** Trail open to horses; **GPS:** N 46 55.180, W 121 03.358

When driving State Route 410, it's hard to miss the giant monolith on the south side of the road. Edgar Rock was once used as a fire lookout site, but little remains of the structure. Instead, the rocky top is now a fine place to reflect and enjoy views of surrounding peaks and the town of Cliffdell below. In the late 1850s a man named John Edgar, a scout and guide for military expeditions over the mountain passes, was in the area of Edgar Rock when he came upon a group of hostile Native Americans looking for the troops he was scouting for. Legend has it he heroically communicated with the Natives and defused the situation in time for the troops to retreat before casualties resulted. Sadly, he was killed a year later during one of the many battles of that time.

GETTING THERE

From Ellensburg, drive southeast on I-82 and take exit 31A near Yakima. Follow the signs toward "US 12-West/Naches." Drive north approximately 17 miles, through the town of Naches to a junction with State Route 410. Stay right on SR 410, drive 17.9 miles, and turn left onto Old River Road (signed "Old River Road, Lost Creek Village, FR 1704"). Follow the road until it comes to a T and turn left on the dirt road. Drive 0.6 mile to a hairpin turn, and look for the badly overgrown trail sign just before the creek. Park on the shoulders of the road and head up!

ON THE TRAIL

The trail starts out along the edge of Lost Creek and then turns right and heads uphill. Stay right at an unsigned trail junction and start gradually climbing through ponderosa pines. Look to your left during the months of May and June for a small patch of the rare

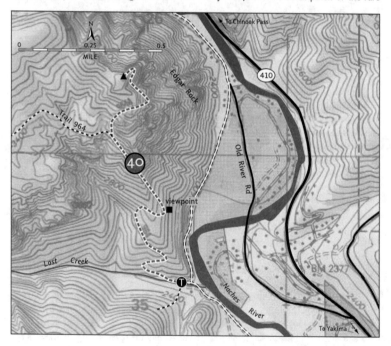

mountain lady's slipper orchid. Get a good look and take plenty of pictures, being careful not to disturb the soil, as the plants are extremely vulnerable to disruption. Members of the orchid family, they are perennial but only live about five years and require perfect soil balance, light, and temperature. This patch is such a treasure to this trail!

The trail switches back several times, giving you a good workout before it breaks out into a rock garden up above. A viewpoint at about 0.5 mile gives you a preview of what's to come and a sneak peak of the valley below. Pass a boulder stacked on a boulder bordered by a tree. How have these three rested so perfectly together all these years?

Before long, at about 1 mile, arrive at an intersection with the poorly marked Trail No. 964, which heads left. The sign simply says "trail," leading you to guess which direction leads to Edgar Rock. You want Trail No. 964A, the short spur to the right that leads to the top. Little evidence of the fire tower remains save for the metal bolts and the fantastic view it possessed. Soak it all in, and then head on back down.

The delicate white flowers of mountain lady's slipper are a rare and wonderful discovery near Edgar Rock.

Boulder Cave is a place of wonder, deep darkness, and interesting geology. Kids and adults alike will love standing inside and pondering what lives in the depths surrounded by the chilly walls.

41 Boulder Cave

RATING/ DIFFICULTY	ROUNDTRIP	ELEV GAIN/ HIGH POINT	SEASON
***/1	1.4 miles	235 feet/ 2670 feet	late May– Sept

Map: Green Trails Old Scab Mountain No. 272; **Contact:** Okanogan-Wenatchee National Forest, Naches Ranger District; **Notes:** NW Forest Pass required. Trail closed Oct 1–late May (opening day varies) to protect bat habitat. Flashlight or headlamp recommended; **GPS:** N 46 57.638, W 121 05.136

GETTING THERE

From Ellensburg, drive southeast on I-82 and take exit 31A near Yakima. Follow the signs toward "US 12-West/Naches." Drive approximately 17 miles, through the town of Naches to a junction with State Route 410. Stay right on SR 410 and drive to the town of Cliffdell. Just after the town, look for a sign saying "Old River Rd/Boulder Cave Recreation Area" and turn left. Cross the one-lane bridge and turn right at the T. Follow the road to its end at the Boulder Cave Recreation Area.

ON THE TRAIL

Locate the very popular trailhead near the parking area and begin walking up the pathway toward the cave. Dogwood, lupine, and ponderosa pines guide you up the paved

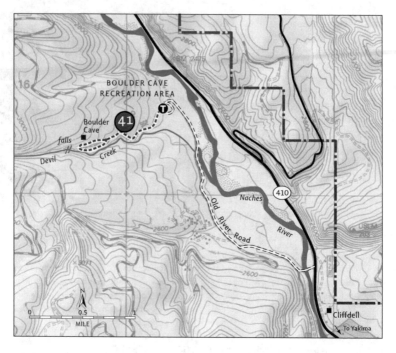

trail to a wooden platform overlooking Devil Creek canyon, the culprit responsible for the cave. Years ago, the creek cut through the hard basalt in this area, encountering soft soil and sand. When it did, it undercut the overlaying basalt and caused it to collapse into the canyon, giving birth to Boulder Cave.

Continue onward and start a short descent toward the cave, reaching it at 0.6 mile. Be glad you brought a very bright headlamp, because the cave is dark. It's also drippy in places and chilly, even in summer. If you're afraid of the dark and things that go bump in it, you're in luck! Before too long there is a light at the end of the tunnel where the trail delivers you to daylight again. Once you're through, a well-constructed plank boardwalk awaits your footsteps and guides you back up the hill, with great views of the cave from the other side.

Important: This cave is home to the very rare and sensitive Townsend's big-eared bat. These creatures are in rapid decline and have been listed by the Department of Fish and Wildlife as a species of special concern. The colony that calls Boulder Cave home depends on its darkness and quiet for hibernation, resting, mating, and raising young. For this reason the cave is only open during the summertime, when most of the activity has commenced. When visiting the cave, walk softly and if you must talk, whisper, to avoid disturbing resting bats. While dogs are permitted, it's best to leave them behind for

Two hikers enjoy exploring the trail near Boulder Cave.

this visit. Additionally, a fungus called white-nose syndrome has been killing bats by the millions nationwide and is quickly spreading across the country. Prevent it from arriving in Washington State by decontaminating all clothing, shoes, cameras, flashlights, et cetera that you might have brought into other caves, by laundering them or wiping them down with a bleach solution.

42 Cowiche Canyon

RATING/ DIFFICULTY	ROUNDTRIP	ELEV GAIN/ HIGH POINT	SEASON
***/2	5.8 miles	440 feet/ 1480 feet	Mar–Nov

Map: Conservancy trail map; **Contact:** Cowiche Canyon Conservancy; **Notes:** Trail open to horses and mountain bikes. Watch for rattlesnakes in summer; **GPS:** N 46 38.310, W 120 35.537

There are a handful of places near towns that feel so remote you can lose yourself in solitude. Cowiche Canyon, 6 miles northwest from downtown Yakima, is just such a place! With the tall canyon walls, gentle flowing creeks, well-maintained trails, and seasonal wildflowers, this place is a treasure for both those who care to stroll and those who wish to crank out a swift trail run. The fairly level path allows "elevationally challenged" hikers to enjoy a leisurely walk without much exertion. Spring and fall are the best times for this hike; summer may be uncomfortably warm.

GETTING THERE

From Ellensburg, head east on I-82 to Yakima and take exit 33B. Turn right and travel on Yakima Avenue for 1.6 miles, and then turn right on Summitview Avenue and follow it for approximately 9 miles. Look for a large wooden house on the right and turn right

Nearly anytime of year is a good time to visit Cowiche Canyon, but when spring foliage peaks, it is especially charming.

on the street immediately following, Weikel Road. In 0.5 mile, turn right at an old white building/barn and find the parking area ahead. Follow the signs past the homes and properties to the Cowiche Canyon trailhead.

ON THE TRAIL

From the parking area, head east toward the canyon on a pathway lined with private homesteads. In roughly 50 yards, reach the official trailhead and walk around the gate to begin your adventure. The relatively level trail follows an old railroad grade through

the canyon, but most of the evidence of the railway has been removed. Instead, enjoy the wide, beautiful trail beneath your feet, where several people could walk side by side. The Cowiche Canyon Conservancy, or CCC, has done a fine job of following their nonprofit mission of conserving open space, scenic vistas, and riparian corridors with this natural area.

Seasonally, plants around your feet and on canyon walls are tagged with names, so that you can learn as you walk. In April, May, and early June, the blossoms of red

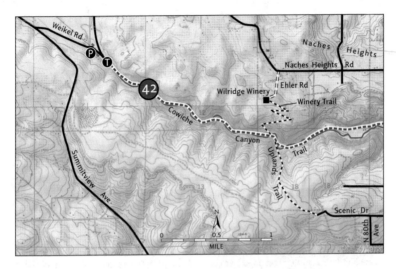

osier dogwood, wood rose, and purple sage lightly scent the air, while above you basalt and andesite rock dominate the skyline. As you walk through the riparian zone, life is everywhere. Birds such as western tanagers, Bullock's orioles, and cliff swallows are often seen building seasonal nests, amphibians can be found swimming near water's edge, and reptiles cruise around rocks hunting for food.

Farther down the trail, walk around a couple of large boulders, marvel at their size, and be glad you weren't here when they came tumbling down. At 1.9 miles, arrive at the Winery Trail (to your left) and the Uplands Trail (to your right). Make a mental note to come back and do them both (see Hike 43), or check them out now if time allows.

Just after the Uplands Trail, the main trail curves right and is marked with a sign that says "Bypass to Bridge 11." Head through a narrow riparian area for about 0.1 mile before popping back out onto wider trail.

Farther along, a couple of residences are visible from the trail, but these nice folks don't mind your visit, provided everyone is respectful. Tip your hat to the private land-owners' permission and donated easements that make this natural area and trail possible.

Cross a private road and continue onward, arriving at the canyon's west trailhead 2.9 miles from where you started. Use the portable toilet here if necessary, and then enjoy the return trip back to your vehicle.

43 Uplands Trail to Winery Trail (Cowiche Canyon)

RATING/ DIFFICULTY	ROUNDTRIP	ELEV GAIN/ HIGH POINT	SEASON
***/3	3.6 miles	790 feet/ 1804 feet	Mar–Nov

Map: Conservancy trail map; **Contact:** Cowiche Canyon Conservancy; **Notes:** Watch for rattlesnakes in summer. For tasting-room hours, visit Wilridge Winery website; **GPS:** N 46 36.671, W 120 37.522

 If you're looking for an enjoyable spring or fall hike, look no further than the Uplands and Winery Trails of Cowiche Canyon. As a bonus, the trail ends with a stroll through the romantic vineyards of Wilridge Winery and an optional stop at their tasting room. Plenty of great views surround these hillsides, and Cowiche Canyon is an exceptional area to enjoy recreation for users of all abilities. Hike here in spring or fall if possible, to avoid the hot summer weather and the rattlesnakes that become more active during warm spells. With the green Cowiche Creek flowing nearby and the high cliffs watching from above, it's easy to forget how close you are to civilization.

GETTING THERE

From Ellensburg, head east on I-82 to Yakima and take exit 33B. Turn right on Yakima Avenue and follow it for 1.6 miles. Turn right on Summitview Avenue and follow it for approximately 4.3 miles. Turn right on North 74th Avenue, and then turn left on Englewood Avenue. Drive to North 80th Avenue and go right. Then turn left on Scenic Drive and find the trailhead on the right.

ON THE TRAIL

The valley engulfs you in beauty from all sides. Head slightly uphill from the trailhead and climb a little before arriving at an interesting interpretive sign describing desert flora. Stay right and follow the well-used paths here. Several side trails connect in this area, so when in doubt, look for the gravel

The Uplands and Winery trails deliver you to a vineyard where rows of varietal grapes thrive in the warm climate.

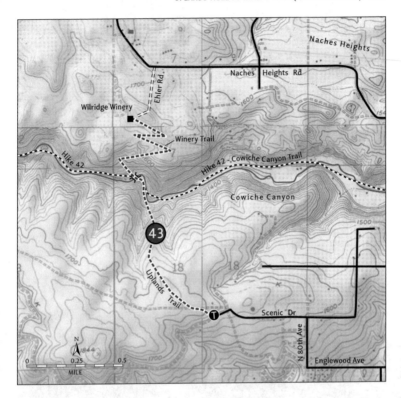

pathways and brown plastic posts that direct you to the main trail.

Head down toward the canyon and enjoy the open views of the neighboring sun-kissed hills and vineyards. In 1 mile, arrive in the bottom of the canyon. If you have time to explore, make a side trip either left or right on the main Cowiche Canyon Trail (Hike 42). If not, turn left and cross a sturdy bridge over the flowing Cowiche Creek.

This oasis in the desert is home to many birds, both resident and migratory, so keep a close eye and ear out as you walk. Just after the bridge, arrive at the Winery Trail junction to your right. The trail climbs steeply out of the canyon, with basalt rocks on either side providing a sight for the eyes as the heart gets pumping.

Near the top of the ridge, the trail eases a bit and gently meanders between two hillsides, delivering you to the vineyard. California quails are common here, running around with their silly little head plumes and providing a soundtrack with their calls that sound like *Chi-ca-go, Chi-ca-go*. Perhaps they are lost.

Follow the dirt road to the left past rows of wine grapes and then turn right, toward the tasting room. Be sure to check the tasting room hours if you intend to stop and sip. Once you've enjoyed the vineyard, head back the way you came.

44 Snow Mountain Ranch and Cowiche Mountain

RATING/ DIFFICULTY	LOOP	ELEV GAIN/ HIGH POINT	SEASON
***/3	6.1 miles	1080 feet/ 2980 feet	Mar–Nov

Map: Conservancy trail map; **Contact:** Cowiche Canyon Conservancy; **Notes:** Trail open to horses. Watch for rattlesnakes in summer; **GPS:** N 46 39.570, W 120 45.394

Acquired in 2005, and now a sanctuary for those looking to enjoy desert hiking, this 1800-acre parcel of land outside of Yakima is managed by the Cowich Canyon Conservancy (CCC). Many trails grace this property, but the finest of all is this enjoyable trek up the open slopes of Cowiche Mountain, with its seasonal wildflowers and grand views. Years ago former Supreme Court justice William O. Douglas enjoyed visiting the Snow Mountain Ranch here, then owned by friends, before starting his Cascades adventures. Today, the land is a great place to enjoy the outdoors as well as a critical place for salmon recovery efforts in Cowiche Creek.

Trails on the recently acquired lands of Snow Mountain Ranch beg for your footprints.

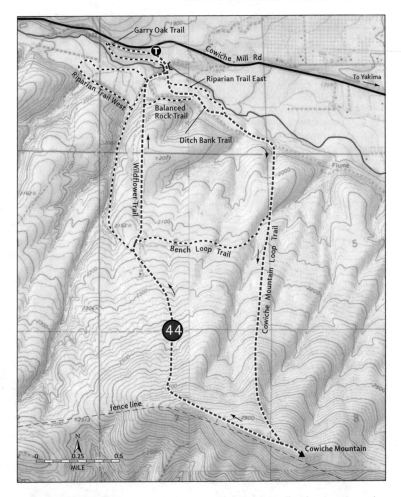

GETTING THERE

From Ellensburg, head east on I-82 to Yakima and take exit 33B. Turn right and travel for 1.6 miles on Yakima Avenue. Turn right on Summitview Avenue and follow it for a hair more than 11 miles. Turn left on Cowiche Mill Road and proceed 2.5 miles to the trailhead parking, located to the left.

ON THE TRAIL

Leave the parking area via a wooden walk-around and pass Garry Oak Trail. Make a note to come back and check out this trail full of Garry oak trees, if time permits. For now, continue on toward a defunct irrigation system and cross over a concrete bridge to the official trailhead sign. Evidence of farming is not far in the past, and the meadows in the area are being restored with natural vegetation. There are many trails here and the CCC does a decent job signing each one to help keep you from getting lost. The recent acquisition of this land means that many trails aren't well established and need your bootprints to help out!

The Cowiche Mountain Loop may be hiked from either east or west and may be combined with several trails. For the most direct approach, follow the Ditch Bank Trail left (east) approximately 0.25 mile before arriving at the junction with the Cowiche Mountain Loop Trail. Turn right (south) and follow the meandering path around sagebrush and ruins of old fences. Cairns, sticks with flags, and wooden posts mark the trail and keep reassuring you that you are on the correct path.

As you climb, the views of the Yakima Valley open up to green vineyards and orchards, while Mount Adams and Mount Rainier look on from afar. Bitterroot, lupine, and balsam show off their colors in spring near the summit in an explosion of wildflowers that at times almost engulfs the trail. At 2.8 miles,

arrive at the top at a dead-end fence line and a gate that marks the Department of Fish and Wildlife property boundary.

To complete the loop, you'll eventually head right (west), but the true summit is to the left (east). Follow the trail left to a makeshift stacked rock and stick monument and settle down to lunch with a view. Once you've treated your eyes to the Yakima Valley below, backtrack and continue following the trail past the dead-end gate, this time heading west to complete the loop. Rest assured you are on the correct trail, despite the trail markings being substantially fewer than on the eastern side of the loop. A few cairns show up to guide you as you head back down.

Bits and pieces of the farming life remain, such as bathtub troughs, which remind you it hasn't been long since this land was purchased. Several trail junctions pop up, including the Wildflower Trail and the Bench Loop Trail. The Wildflower Trail and the Cowiche Mountain Loop end in nearly the same place and both are good options; the world is your oyster, but the Wildflower is a bit more direct. Enjoy the songs of the birds, including a nest of great horned owls, who call this place home, as you arrive back at the trailhead where you started.

Opposite: A barred owl watches with wary eyes near Wobbly Lake.

The Cispus River drainage is one of the most remote areas in Washington State, accessible mostly by dirt roads. Sitting in the middle of the Gifford Pinchot National Forest, the drainage's green mossy trees and high jagged peaks create a fantastic venue for recreation. This area is multiuse and open to almost every kind of trail user possible, including horses, mountain bikes, and motorcycles. With the melting pot of various users and the long drive to get here, you might be quick to write off the area as not worthy of your time. But then you would miss out on some incredibly scenic views that are served with a side of solitude, because even though many of these trails are open to a variety of users, they get very little traffic. I encourage everyone to take a day, pick a trail, and explore some of Washington's hidden gems.

45 Sunrise Peak

RATING/ DIFFICULTY	ROUNDTRIP	ELEV GAIN/ HIGH POINT	SEASON
****/4	3.2 miles	1430 feet/ 5892 feet	late July– Oct

Maps: Green Trails McCoy Peak No. 333, Blue Lake No. 334; **Contact:** Gifford Pinchot National Forest, Cowlitz Valley Ranger District; **Notes:** Rough road to trailhead, high-clearance vehicle recommended. Trail open to horses, mountain bikes, and motorcycles, except hiker-only Sunrise Peak Trail No. 261A; **GPS:** N 46 20.121, W 121 44.601

Sunrise Peak is a prominent rocky fortress, fit for a lookout tower. Not shockingly, one stood here until the 1960s, guarding the ridges beyond. Summer wildflowers on the flanks of the peak put on one of the best shows in the area, and huckleberries in late season ripen up for a delectable feast in the sunny open meadows. During the week, you'll be lucky to see another body, and if you do, it will probably be covered in fur. If you haven't gone to Sunrise Peak, it's worth the trip. Put it on your bucket list—you won't be disappointed!

GETTING THERE
From Randle, turn south onto State Route 131. After approximately 0.9 mile, bear left at a junction onto Forest Road 23 and continue for 17.4 miles. Bear right at a fork (staying on FR 23) and drive another 4.5 miles. Turn right (west) onto FR 2324 (signed "Sunrise Peak") and continue for 5.3 miles. Turn left (east) to find the trailhead a short distance beyond, up a steep and narrow spur road.

ON THE TRAIL
The trail starts off by climbing through the trees on what feels like a small toboggan run, from wheels that have created a rounded trench in the trail. Thankfully, the climb is fairly short, only 0.5 mile to a ridgeline and then the trail's shape levels out, becoming more manageable. To the southeast, Mount Adams shows off its larger-than-life ice-cream-cone top, while the subalpine meadows of Jumbo Peak (Hike 46) to the south beckon you to continue walking for a better view. Views, wildflowers, wild strawberries, and huckleberries start on this ridgeline and don't stop until you are almost to the summit.

Follow the trail as it traverses the ridgeline northwest, climbing slightly before arriving at a junction with Sunrise Trail Spur No. 262A and a wooden sign that's seen better days. Turn right at the sign and head northwest. In late July through early August,

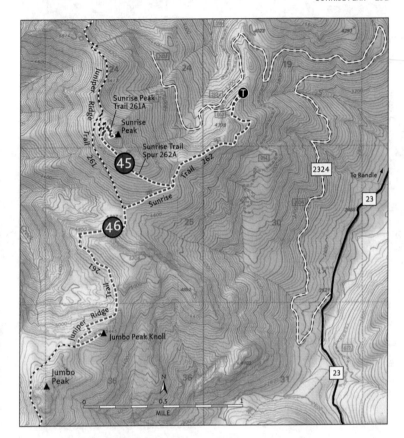

this area has an incredible meadow display filled with mariposa lily, magenta paintbrush, beargrass, lupine, tiger lily, arnica, Sitka valerian, and other wildflowers conveniently placed before a backdrop of Mount Adams. It might take you half the day to get up the trail because you'll be stopping so often for snapshots.

Thank the flowers for their welcome distraction, because this trail is steep, gaining 740 feet in a short 0.6 mile before it arrives at a junction with Sunrise Peak Trail No. 261A. Go right at this junction, climbing past a sign saying "Hikers Only Beyond This Point," a good reminder for those on wheels. As you climb toward the lookout, Mount Rainier comes into view directly to the north. A loose rocky tread shows up under your feet as the wildflowers battle it out with juniper on the steep hillside.

Near the top, at around 1.6 miles, how convenient that someone has forgotten

The lookout tower is gone but the handrail remains near the top of Sunrise Peak.

to remove the handrail that once led to the lookout—because this puppy is steep! Watch your footing carefully and use extra caution as you approach the summit. A few twisted metal bars serve as reminders of the history here, while a great flat spot provides a welcome place to spread out lunch. When you've had enough of the spectacular views in all directions, trace your steps back to the trailhead.

46 Jumbo Peak Knoll

RATING/DIFFICULTY	ROUNDTRIP	ELEV GAIN/HIGH POINT	SEASON
****/3	5.2 miles	1345 feet/5400 feet	late July–Oct

Maps: Green Trails McCoy Peak No. 333, Blue Lake No. 334; **Contact:** Gifford Pinchot National Forest, Cowlitz Valley Ranger District; **Notes:** Rough road to trailhead; high

clearance vehicle recommended. Trail open to horses, mountain bikes, and motorcycles; **GPS:** N 46 20.121, W 121 44.601

Sure, motorcycles are permitted here, but whatever you do, don't let that stop you from visiting this gorgeous place, which is filled with subalpine meadows and some of the most beautiful vistas in the state. So remote is this area that the odds of seeing another person, let alone one on wheels, is unlikely—even more unlikely if you visit on a weekday. Instead, hike in quiet solitude among rainbows of seasonal wildflowers, rocky mountain fortresses, and wide-open views. There is much to explore near Jumbo Peak!

GETTING THERE
From Randle, turn south onto State Route 131. After approximately 0.9 mile, bear left at a junction onto Forest Road 23 and continue

Near Jumbo Peak Knoll, green shrubbery guides the trail.

for 17.4 miles. Bear right at a fork (staying on FR 23) and drive another 4.5 miles. Turn right (west) onto FR 2324 (signed "Sunrise Peak") and continue for 5.3 miles. Turn left (east) to find the trailhead a short distance beyond, up a steep and narrow spur road.

ON THE TRAIL

The trail starts off on Sunrise Peak Trail No. 262 (Hike 45), which leaves from the parking area and ducks into the forest. Motorized traffic has made this trail rounded and trenched, so use caution as you walk to avoid twisting or rolling your ankles. The good news is that this area is remote and challenging for motorcycles, so the odds of

seeing them are slim. It is also very beautiful and well worth your time, so don't let some rubber tires discourage you!

Follow the trail under Douglas firs to a ridgeline only 0.5 mile from the trailhead. At this point, there is less motorized trail damage and your ankles get a break from the unpleasant trail surface. The views begin and so does the subalpine feeling of this spectacular area. To the southeast, Mount Adams steals the skyline, while the meadows of Jumbo and Sunrise peaks ahead beg you to continue, enticing you with a magnetic draw.

Traverse the ridgeline and the shoulder of Sunrise Peak before arriving at a junction with Sunrise Trail Spur No. 262A and Sunrise Peak Trail No. 261A. If time and gumption permit, hit this (Hike 45) on the way back. For now, continue straight ahead, and in a short distance find yourself at an intersection with Juniper Ridge Trail No. 261, just 1.1 miles from the trailhead. Turn left (south) and descend roughly 90 feet on a very dusty, leave-your-boot-print-as-you-go trail before climbing again.

Juniper Ridge is a popular place for motorcycles, and the trail surface proves it; dust and tire ruts are the new tread as you move forward. Climb 200 feet and enter a subalpine wonderland, with seasonal wildflowers at your feet, hummingbirds buzzing around your ears, and views that go on and on. Behind you, Mount Rainier towers over the skyline, while to the south you can see the trail as it crosses under Jumbo Peak. To your right (west), a rocky unnamed peak protrudes toward the skyline, a favorite spot for mountain goats who call this area home. Huckleberries in late summer are sweet and juicy on these hillsides, as they receive plenty of sunshine in the open fields.

At 2.5 miles from the trailhead, arrive at a small saddle and look to your left (northeast) for a very steep short trail. A keen eye will catch a sign on an adjacent tree saying "Hikers Only Beyond This Point," and soon you'll know why. No one in their right mind would take anything but agile feet up this short spur, as it's nearly straight up and contains loose soil and pebbles. It's a slip and slide, but a fun one, and it provides a good opportunity to laugh at yourself and others in your hiking party as your knees knock and your feet boogie uncontrollably.

Arrive at the top and your destination 2.6 miles from the trailhead, where you'll find rocky ledges and wildflowers of nearly every Northwest variety set against the eye-popping backdrop of Mount Adams. This is the kind of area you'll dream about when winter sets in and you need a mental lift. Jumbo Peak is beyond on the main trail, but the summit requires a scramble and has no official trail. Explore to your heart's desire, and then head back the way you arrived.

47 Dark Meadow

RATING/ DIFFICULTY	ROUNDTRIP	ELEV GAIN/ HIGH POINT	SEASON
***/3	8.4 miles	2300 feet/ 4400 feet	late July– Oct

Maps: Green Trails Blue Lake No. 334, McCoy Peak No. 333; **Contact:** Gifford Pinchot National Forest, Cowlitz Valley Ranger District; **Notes:** Trail open to horses, mountain bikes, and motorcycles; **GPS:** N 46 18.695, W 121 43.879

While the name Dark Meadow might conjure up images of moss-covered trees lurking in haunting fog, that couldn't be any less accurate for what you'll find here. The sunlit meadows in this open area give way to views of a vast landscape, where elk munch on greens and seasonal wildflowers bloom in the foreground of subalpine peaks. It makes sense, then, that the area was named not for an eerie vibe but rather after homesteader John Dark, who built a cabin in the meadow in the late 1800s as he prospected for gold nearby. The trails in this area are multiuse, but don't let that discourage you. There is much to enjoy and your odds of seeing motorcycles especially are slim. All things considered, the trails are in good shape, with only a few ruts and reinforcement with grass pavers for erosion protection.

The area's light and airy feeling is a stark contrast to the name "Dark Meadows."

GETTING THERE

From Randle, turn south onto State Route 131. After approximately 0.9 mile, bear left at a junction onto Forest Road 23. In approximately 18.5 miles, arrive at a junction with FR 21 and bear right (south) on FR 23. Find the trailhead in another 5 miles (23.5 miles from Randle) on the road's right (west).

ON THE TRAIL

From the trailhead, the path immediately crosses East Canyon Creek, which can be high and swift in early season. Thankfully, a giant old tree came to rest across the creek to the trail's south, and someone was kind enough to cut steps into the log on the approach and descent. Once across, find the trail again by walking up the creekbank to the north.

Back on the trail, ascend through brushy vegetation and keep an eye out for several trailside patches of stinging nettles, which can cause temporary skin irritation and make you wish you'd brought along your itch-be-gone cream. After getting through the nettle patches, the trail dives into a forest harvested many years ago and begins a gentle climb to the soundtrack of Dark Creek flowing to the trail's north. The smaller trees give way to a few old-growth monsters, giving tree huggers the perfect opportunity to throw their arms around one and get some photos. Through the trees to the north are steep cliff faces reaching well over 500 feet high, worth a look and possibly a camera snap, if vegetation permits.

In 1.3 miles arrive at a crossing of the wide Dark Creek, which is wadable even when it's running high. A small log also spans the creek downstream and makes for a fine crossing without having to unlace boots. From here, the climb gets steeper and heads up a few

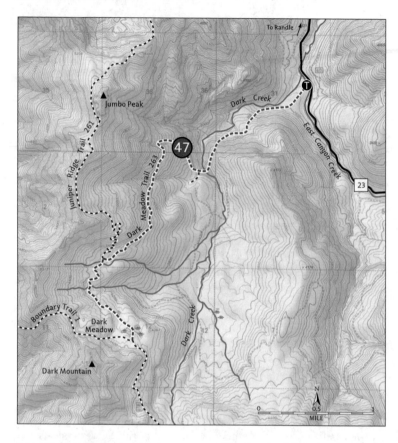

tight switchbacks before straightening out a bit and continuing to gain most of the trail's elevation. Who thought a meadow hike would require so much effort! The reward is worth it, so take plenty of breaks and enjoy the cool forest shade.

Several small tributaries dance across the path as you head uphill, requiring a jump or a step on a stone to keep the feet dry. At 3470 feet and about 1.9 miles, Dark Meadow Trail No. 263 meets up with an unsigned

trail heading downhill to the left. Stay right and continue the climb, diving in and out of sunlight and trees, eventually meeting up with the Juniper Ridge Trail at around 4300 feet at 3.2 miles. To the north is the summit of Jumbo Peak, a hike for the way back or for another day.

For now, head toward Dark Meadow by turning left (south) and meandering along a gentle grade for 1 mile, enjoying Mother Nature's landscaping as meadows guide you and afford great views of surrounding peaks. Mount Adams hugs the southern skyline, playing peekaboo through the tall trees. If you walk quietly, you may even be treated to a showing of elk or deer who frequent these meadows. The trail eventually meets up with the Boundary Trail, which can take you in a number of directions. Hike to your heart's content and head back the way you came when you are done exploring.

48 Blue Lake

RATING/ DIFFICULTY	ROUNDTRIP	ELEV GAIN/ HIGH POINT	SEASON
****/4	5.5 miles	2935 feet/ 4110 feet	late June–Oct

Map: Green Trails Blue Lake No. 334; **Contact:** Gifford Pinchot National Forest, Cowlitz Valley Ranger District; **Notes:** Rough road to trailhead, high-clearance vehicle recommended. Trails in vicinity are open to horses, mountain bikes, motorcycles, and ATVs, except hiker-only Blue Lake Hiker Trail No. 274; **GPS:** N 46 24.626, W 121 44.011

Blue Lake itself is a multiuse, beautiful forested lake tucked deep in the woods. But perhaps Blue Lake isn't the only reason you go! The hiker-only trail to the lake is a vision in green and a fascination in many ways. Running parallel to Blue Lake Creek, the trail shakes hands with high basalt canyon walls, formed by volcanic eruptions beneath a glacier. When the basalt flow cooled quickly from the melting glacier, it created long strands of rock, some of which looks like spaghetti. Small caves are also tucked in the cliff walls, piquing your curiosity about what might be living there. The raging creek drops to small seasonal waterfalls and keeps you company nearly the whole hike.

GETTING THERE

From Randle, turn south onto State Route 131. After approximately 0.9 mile, bear left at a junction onto Forest Road 23. Drive approximately 16 miles to a spur road signed for Blue Lake Hiker Trail No. 274. Turn left on the spur road and stay straight at the road's fork. Continue 1.2 miles to the trailhead. **Note:** This trailhead is not often visited and

The conifers around its shoreline can make Blue Lake look green.

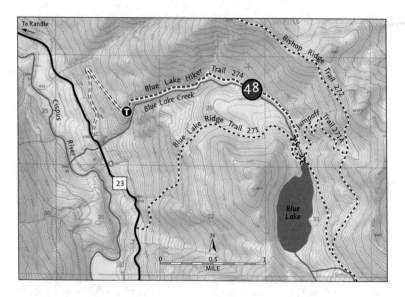

the road is somewhat neglected. Grass has grown in over tire treads and the road is very narrow and quite rough in places. Rest assured that you are on the correct spur road and that a large turnaround area exists near the trailhead to get you pointed back down.

ON THE TRAIL

The trail starts out with salal at your feet before it starts climbing, and I mean climbing! What separates this trail from others in the area is the creative trail building that makes these crazy steep slopes useable. Someone was genius enough to build rock stairs up areas that would normally challenge gravity—and still might. Use extra caution on this puppy! Because of the drop-offs and steep cliffs, it might be best to leave the little ones with a sitter for this hike. Keep your feet underneath you as you continue

climbing up and around a narrow cliff with just enough room for walking.

Before long, at about 0.7 mile, descend a bit to Blue Lake Creek and admire the fantastic high basalt cliff walls, which are better than some of the sculptures in art galleries. The trail climbs again, switching back uphill and crossing a couple of seasonal creeks with trickling waterfalls. If you visit in June, keep your eyes open for the rare calypso orchids, which are easy to miss—they peacefully grow near the seasonal creek crossings tucked in the dark soil.

Finally the trail gives the heart and the quads a break with a much gentler grade and walks along the creek, which is tamer now above the canyon. Cross the creek on a sturdy log bridge and find yourself in dark forest before arriving at the trail junction for the multiuse Blue Lake Ridge Trail No. 271, 2.5 miles from the trailhead.

Cross the trail and continue straight on the other side.

The dark forest continues before you bust out at another bridge and find yourself on the other side—at the lake! At the southern end of the lake is Blue Lake Ridge, which makes for a fine backdrop in photos. Immediately to your west and almost impossible to see from your perch is a cinder cone from the extinct Blue Lake Volcano. This lake was likely formed when lava flows from that volcano dammed a stream and created this deep, large body of water. Return the way you came or make a loop by using one of the many multiuse trails in the area.

49 Wobbly Lake

RATING/ DIFFICULTY	ROUNDTRIP	ELEV GAIN/ HIGH POINT	SEASON
**/2	2.8 miles	590 feet/ 3400 feet	June–Oct

Map: Green Trails Blue Lake No. 334; **Contact:** Gifford Pinchot National Forest, Cowlitz Valley Ranger District; **Notes:** Rough road to trailhead. Trail open to horses, mountain bikes, and motorcycles; **GPS:** N 46 26.367, W 121 36.278

The name Wobbly Lake paints a funny mental picture of a basin of blue gelatin instead of water. But you won't find gelatin or water that's too wobbly; instead, a peaceful lake tucked into a valley awaits your arrival. The name "Wobbly" was given to this lake and the creek to the lake's south for the firefighters who dug the fire lines here in 1918. Back in the day, the fire crew belonged to the Industrial Workers of the World union, who were referred to as Wobblies. Long gone are Wobblies and the fires that burned hot back then. Nature has long since repaired the burn zones, and life has sprung back to the lake and surrounding hillsides. Because it's considered easy, this multiuse trail gets a fair amount of motorized traffic; however, it's still a scenic place to visit.

GETTING THERE

From Randle, turn south onto State Route 131. After approximately 0.9 mile, bear left at

The author consults her map along the shoreline of Wobbly Lake.

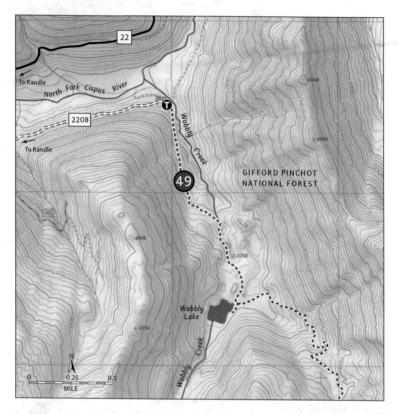

a junction onto Forest Road 23. In approximately 10 miles, turn left (north) on FR 22. The roadway turns to gravel in another 5.6 miles. Stay straight and continue for another 2.6 miles until you reach FR 2208 (signed for Wobbly Lake Trail No. 273). Go straight and reach the trailhead in just under 3 miles.

ON THE TRAIL

The trail is wide and enjoyable for all forms of travel, including feet. The decent cruising surface is light on ruts and divots, making this path enjoyable walking and not too tough on the ankles. Be grateful for the wide trail, as it helps prevent spider-web-across-the-eyeball syndrome, which is an epidemic in these parts come summer. The trail climbs through sparse forest for a bit, crossing a few small creeks trickling down hillsides. Keep your senses sharp! Evidence that elk and deer use these trails as much as (or more than) humans is everywhere in the form of prints and droppings.

The trail climbs out of the forest and begins to level off, showing off views of the neighboring ridge near Elk Peak. Keep your eyes peeled for barred owls that roost in the trees here, giving you the feeling that someone is watching you. Although they are nocturnal hunters, they sit very still during daylight hours, their large yellow eyes and swiveling heads keeping a lookout from their perches. A lakelet on the trail's east comes into view in early season, sporting a turquoise color and looking delightfully like a blue topaz gem.

Before long, at about 1.3 miles, a campsite appears on the trail's west—the first sign you are close! Next up, Wobbly Lake. Arrive at the lake's northern tip and look out across the water to the backdrop of an unnamed peak looming above. The lake you are enjoying was formed when a landmass slid off the peak to the lake's east, damming a creek. If you choose to dip your feet in the water, or jump in for a swim, be sure to look around for misplaced fishing lures or line, since this place is popular with the hook-and-bullet crowd. The lake makes a perfect place to turn around and head back, or, if you've still got some pep, the trail continues onward, climbing out of the valley and eventually meeting up with spur road FR 060.

50 Camp Creek Falls

RATING/ DIFFICULTY	ROUNDTRIP	ELEV GAIN/ HIGH POINT	SEASON
****/1	0.5 mile	100 feet/ 1420 feet	Mar–Nov

Map: Green Trails McCoy Peak No. 333; **Contact:** Gifford Pinchot National Forest, Cowlitz Valley Ranger District; **GPS:** N 46 26.904, W 121 49.986

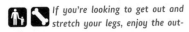 If you're looking to get out and stretch your legs, enjoy the out-

An easy goal for small kids or those with physical challenges is the forested vision of Camp Creek Falls.

doors, and/or show off the Northwest to visitors, this is your hike! A very short trail goes through green forest understory to a spectacular 30-foot waterfall. The accessibility of this short trail to such a beautiful place makes this a great hike for kids and grandparents alike.

GETTING THERE
From Randle, turn south onto State Route 131. After approximately 0.9 mile, bear left at a junction onto Forest Road 23. Drive approximately 8.5 miles to a pullout on the right side of the road, directly across from the sign for Camp Creek Falls.

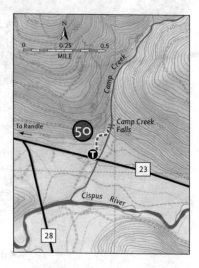

ON THE TRAIL

The trail starts off cruising through Oregon grape, salal, and vanilla leaf under a canopy of deciduous and evergreen trees. In fall, the big-leaf and vine maples show off spectacular color, while the evergreens provide shade and steady forest green year-round. Pacific tree frogs thrive here and come in colors from brown to green, changing colors as the landscape dictates. They are the only frog that truly says *ribbit*! Keep an eye and an ear out for them as you wander.

The trail meanders along the forest floor for a short distance before a gentle climb begins. Ferns of various varieties show up on the hillside, including maidenhair, western sword, deer fern, and oak. The sound of water is a constant companion throughout the hike and gets slightly louder as you climb, but the hillside blocks the true volume.

Turn the corner after the short climb and be blown away at the sound and the sights! Before you is Camp Creek Falls, a gorgeous

30-foot waterfall dropping from the rocks high above. The sound and the power of the rushing water are enough to stop you in your tracks. The narrow trail continues down toward the falls and stops at a small turnaround spot where you may want to grab your jacket if you're catching some spray. The trail here is narrow and steep, so use caution if the little ones are along. When your camera is tired, head on back.

51 Curtain and Angel Falls

RATING/ DIFFICULTY	LOOP	ELEV GAIN/ HIGH POINT	SEASON
***/3	3.75 miles	1240 feet/ 2095 feet	Mar–Oct

Map: Green Trails McCoy Peak No. 333; **Contact:** Gifford Pinchot National Forest, Cowlitz Valley Ranger District; **GPS:** N 46 26.317, W 121 51.101

Have you ever seen the backside of a waterfall? This is your chance! Believe it or not, the trail goes directly under one of the waterfalls here, which drops from an overhanging cliff above, allowing you the opportunity to duck behind its white curtain. In late snow years, this early season hike is a great way to get out on the trail for a deep forest day of fun, waterfalls, and even some bonus cave exploration on this lowland hiking adventure.

GETTING THERE

From Randle, turn south onto State Route 131. After approximately 0.9 mile, bear left at a junction onto Forest Road 23. In approximately 8 miles, turn right (south) on FR 28 (Cispus Road) and follow the signs toward the Cispus Learning Center. After 1.4

Walk around the backside of a waterfall as the trail sneaks behind Curtain Falls.

miles, turn right onto FR 76 and continue to the learning center on your right. Parking is near the Elderberry Lodge to the left, just after entering the campus. The learning center is kind enough to let visitors park on their property, so please be courteous by packing out trash and showing respect for their generosity.

ON THE TRAIL

From the learning center, cross over FR 76 and find Covel Creek Trail No. 228, just across from the center's entrance. The wide

trail welcomes you with the usual forest suspects, such as vanilla leaf, vine maple, and Oregon grape. Moss here will remind you how much rain this area gets!

Almost immediately, arrive at a junction with the Braille Trail. This fantastic loop was developed for the vision impaired and provides rope along the entire route for guidance and direction. Make the loop if you desire, or simply continue onward. Head right (southwest) along the Braille Trail before the Covel Creek Trail continues by turning right again and crossing over Covel

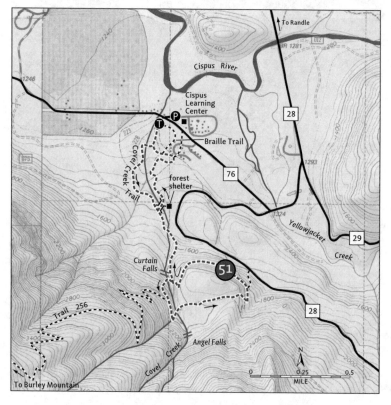

Creek, only 0.2 mile from the trailhead. The bridge here has washed out but, thankfully, the creek doesn't get too swollen, and with a little balancing act over rocks and downed logs, you can make it across without wet shoes. **Note:** If you don't want to attempt the crossing, follow the Braille Trail to the Forest Trail, turn right, and follow it to the forest shelter, where you can cross on a log bridge.

Once across the creek, continue on the trail for 0.4 mile, arriving at a bridge that crosses the creek and takes you to a forest shelter. This is your return route, and you'll cross this bridge on the way back, but for now, continue heading up the west side of Covel Creek and note the sign high in the tree above pointing you to Angel Falls. The trail begins climbing and guides you across the creek on a log footbridge higher up, before a series of trail stairs begin. As you climb, the creek gets louder and a series of small cascading waterfalls accompany you. This is just an appetizer for the main course up ahead!

Before long, Curtain Falls, also known as Covel Creek Falls, is visible through the trees and the trail makes a T. The waterfall beckons, so head right (west) and stand in awe of the falling white curtain of water as you make your way down the trail, just 1 mile from the trailhead. The trail does, in fact, go directly behind the waterfall—what a treat! This rare trail feature allows you to experience walking behind the waterfall and looking out from behind the veil of roaring water. Use the handrail and watch your footing, as the mist can make the path slippery.

As you begin to climb the adjacent hillside, be sure to look behind you and snap a few more pictures. Climb several large switchbacks and reach a junction at 1.4 miles with Burley Mountain Trail No. 256. At this point, head left for the return loop and

a little bit of downhill mixed with flat trail to give the heart and quads a break. Drop into a small valley and at 1.7 miles arrive at the foot of the large and cascading Angel Falls, the second waterfall on this hike.

Cross the riparian areas of seasonal foliage such as western corydalis and devil's club, before a flat section has you cruising along at a good clip. In 0.4 mile from Angel Falls, a trail junction appears with some confusing and outdated signage that will cause to you scratch your head in wonder. Disregard the confusing signs and head left (northwest) to walk the baseline of some high cliffs sporting mystery caves—some that pique your imagination as you look inside.

This might be a good time to remind you that Sasquatch sightings are common in this area—spooky! After high-fiving Bigfoot, you'll be back at the T near Curtain Falls. Head back the way you came until you reach the bridge that leads to the forest shelter. Cross the creek, explore the forest shelter, and head back down to the Braille Trail, which will lead you back to the trailhead and your waiting vehicle.

52 Tongue Mountain

RATING/ DIFFICULTY	ROUNDTRIP	ELEV GAIN/ HIGH POINT	SEASON
*****/3	3.1 miles	1070 feet/ 4678 feet	May–Oct

Map: Green Trails McCoy Peak No. 333; **Contact:** Gifford Pinchot National Forest, Cowlitz Valley Ranger District; **Notes:** Rough road to trailhead. Trail open to horses, mountain bikes, and motorcycles, except hiker-only Tongue Mountain Lookout Trail No. 294A; **GPS:** N 46 23.811, W 121 45.926

Excellent views of Mount Rainier and Mount Adams await on Tongue Mountain.

Tongue Mountain waits for you. Seriously, get here—you'll love it! Conveniently, if you're starting from Seattle the drive isn't too far, either. There is almost no better place on a clear day for views in every direction. Sitting on the top will make you feel glad to be alive and will give your soul a lift as you look down on the Cispus River valley below and out to the in-your-face views of Mount Rainier, Mount Adams, and Mount St. Helens. Not to mention that the hike up is fairly short and direct, so even those who are unable to do longer hikes can still get views that most people work hours to find.

GETTING THERE

From Randle, turn south onto State Route 131. After approximately 0.9 mile, bear left at a junction onto Forest Road 23. In approximately 8 miles, turn right (south) on FR 28 (Cispus Road) and follow it for 0.9 mile. The main road here heads right, but you want the gravel road that goes straight ahead (FR 29). Follow FR 29 for 3.7 miles to FR 2904 and

turn left. Drive 4 miles to the trailhead on the left, directly across from the Juniper Peak trailhead (Hike 53).

ON THE TRAIL

The way starts off on the multiuse Tongue Mountain Trail No. 294. You'll feel like you're walking on waves, rolling up and down over the bumps and divots created by the motorbikes that cruise around occasionally. The trail that turns off to Tongue Mountain summit is strictly hiker, though, so bear with this first part and realize that soon you'll be on more hiker-friendly terrain. Dense foliage near your feet consists of the usual Northwest forest greens, such as bunchberry, vanilla leaf, and Oregon grape, as you climb higher and higher. Through the trees the surrounding hillsides fade in and out as dense forest limits views.

After 1 mile, reach a trail junction with some wooden posts helping folks remember that this trail is for feet only. Turn right and follow Tongue Mountain Lookout Trail No. 294A, huffing and puffing harder now as

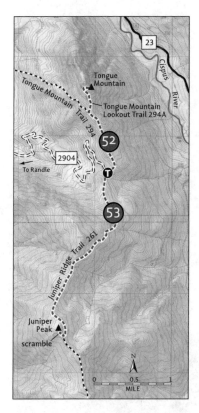

Tongue Mountain, an area once used by the Taidnapam Indians for goat hunting. The true summit is to your left, but the views are actually better by continuing up the trail to the right. Use care and caution with footing, and hold tight to kids and dogs; there is a 3000-foot drop!

When you arrive at the table of the false summit, you'll be rewarded with a fantastic flat top to sit, snooze, or spread out a picnic, the edges naturally landscaped with purple spreading phlox. Park yourself and take it all in. From 1934 to 1948, a lookout tower stood here protecting the forested mountains around you. It has long since been removed and not a trace of its existence can be found. To the north, Mount Rainier is so giant it almost seems like a hologram. To the southeast, Mount Adams shows off her snowy west face, and to the south, Mount St. Helens displays her missing summit, having blown her top in 1980. If that's not enough to make your head spin, below you is the winding Cispus River valley and the Dark Divide area, and to the west are more peaks such as Burley Mountain and Tower Rock. There is so much to enjoy, you'll want to take a lot of pictures, both mental and physical. When you've soaked it all in, head back down the way you came.

the trail climb really begins. Thankfully, before long the trail breaks out above the tree-line with views of Mount St. Helens and Juniper Peak to the south—a reward for your efforts! Giant rock faces appear above you, foreshadowing coming attractions. Several switchbacks keep you on your game as the climb continues next to seasonal berries and wildflowers such as paintbrush and lupine.

Before long, at about 1.4 miles, arrive at the saddle of the peak, your first glimpse of views. What a place! You are standing on the rocky shoulders of the summit of

53 Juniper Peak

RATING/ DIFFICULTY	ROUNDTRIP	ELEV GAIN/ HIGH POINT	SEASON
****/3	5.8 miles	1885 feet/ 5610 feet	mid-July– Oct

Map: Green Trails McCoy Peak No. 333; **Contact:** Gifford Pinchot National Forest, Cowlitz Valley Ranger District; **Notes:** Rough road to trailhead. Trail open to hikers, horses, mountain bikes, and motorcycles; **GPS:** N 46 23.802, W 121 45.927

 *You might not expect to find gorgeous subalpine meadows and amazing views on a trail that starts off by switching back and forth on a rutted trail in deep forest. But the Juniper Ridge Trail is full of wonderful surprises. The top is magnificent, boasting wide-open views of Mount Rainier, Mount Adams, Mount Hood, and Mount St. Helens, as well as local peaks such as Sunrise Peak, Jumbo Peak, and Tongue Mountain. Put this one on your list for sure!*

GETTING THERE

From Randle, turn south onto State Route 131. After approximately 0.9 mile, bear left at a junction onto Forest Road 23. In approximately 8 miles, turn right (south) on FR 28 and follow it for 0.9 mile. The main road heads right, but you want the gravel road that goes straight ahead (FR 29). Follow FR 29 for 3.7 miles to FR 2904 and turn left. Drive 4 miles to the trailhead on the right, directly across from the Tongue Mountain trailhead (Hike 52).

ON THE TRAIL

The trail starts off by climbing in second-growth forest under an umbrella of green. Where light hits the forest floor, bushes such as huckleberry and twinflower thrive in the acidic soil. Motorcycles have rutted the trail, causing a V shape in places, so take your time and watch your ankles.

In roughly 2 miles, the forest gives way to open hillsides, subalpine landscapes, and views of Mount Adams to the southeast. Wild-flower shows here are some of the grandest around and worthy of the time it will take you to photograph them all! Unfortunately, mosquitoes are drawn to these meadows too and can have you dancing

Three hikers meander along the ridge near Juniper Peak.

with bug spray just when the flowers are at their peak.

A stone hill to the trail's right (west) begs you to climb it. Explore it if you wish, but there is more ahead, so save some energy! Traverse under the broad shoulders of Juniper Peak before arriving at a saddle on the ridgeline at 2.5 miles. Ahead of you in the distance is Sunrise Peak, standing tall with its rocky summit. Beyond is the appropriately named behemoth Jumbo Peak surrounded by green meadows. Juniper Peak is just behind you to the north, beckoning you to pick a path up its steep shoulders.

There is no official trail to the top of Juniper, but it's easily climbed by putting one foot in front of the other, choosing your steps carefully so that they land on soil or stone. The top is a fantastic place for a picnic, with views in literally every single direction. When your PB&J is down the hatch, head back to the trailhead, or explore the ridgeline to your heart's content.

54 Layser Cave

RATING/ DIFFICULTY	ROUNDTRIP	ELEV GAIN/ HIGH POINT	SEASON
**/1	0.4 mile	190 feet/ 2370 feet	Apr–Nov

Map: Green Trails McCoy Peak No. 333; **Contact:** Gifford Pinchot National Forest, Cowlitz Valley Ranger District; **Notes:** NW Forest Pass; **GPS:** N 46 27.680, W 121 51.608

If you happen to be in the area checking out other hikes, or are in the market for a good hike for young kids, don't miss Layser Cave, a short interpretive hike that will get the imagination running wild about what life must have been like long ago for Native Americans. As a bonus, the trail pops out at a nice vista of Mount Adams, Tongue Mountain, Tower Rock, Burley Mountain, and other local peaks.

GETTING THERE

From Randle, turn south onto State Route 131. After approximately 0.9 mile, bear left at a junction onto Forest Road 23. In 7 miles, turn left (northeast) onto FR 083. Continue another 1.7 miles to a hairpin turn and the easily missed trailhead located on the road's right. Parking is on the road's left.

ON THE TRAIL

Just imagine bushwhacking and exploring around an area of cliff band and stumbling upon an ancient cave of great archeological value! This is exactly what happened in 1982 to Tim Layser, a Gifford Pinchot National Forest employee, when he was on patrol in the area. When scientists went back to explore Layser's discovery, they were astonished by the cave's contents. Inside were stone tools used by Native Americans seven thousand

Layser Cave is a must-see for those who are interested in history.

years prior, as well as animal bones and debris, all buried in soil layers. The mystery of the cave's uses began to unravel in a clear historical picture. The bones indicated that at least 108 deer were brought to the cave to be butchered and preserved. The meat was then dried over several small fires near the cave's entrance. Stone tools were made inside the shelter, and excavated beads nearby indicated that the Native people had some trade connections with coastal tribes.

Today, a main trail ends in a short loop that stops off at a viewpoint for enjoying Mount Adams and surrounding peaks before it wanders over to the cool, 32-foot-long cave. A flashlight is good to have for examining the walls, floors, and ceilings, but if you left it at home, light trickling in from the entrance will still allow you to make out the shape of the cave. Enjoy this trip back in time and then finish the loop by connecting back to the main trail.

Opposite: A tapestry of fall colors makes up the foreground on the top of Green Mountain.

fr 23/takhlakh lake area

A mariposa lily opens up to the light near Hamilton Buttes.

Off of Forest Road 23, near Babyshoe Pass, in a very remote area of Washington State, sits the beautiful Takhlakh Lake. In spite of this area's isolation, or perhaps because of it, the lake and car-camping area are popular with those looking to get away from it all and to explore the trails near Mount Adams and the surrounding peaks. The lake itself has a couple of trails worth your time and a fine beach for a refreshing splash on a warm day. Or you could always just find a place to sit and enjoy the perfect image of Mount Adams reflected in the lake on a calm day.

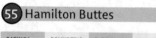

55 Hamilton Buttes

RATING/ DIFFICULTY	ROUNDTRIP	ELEV GAIN/ HIGH POINT	SEASON
****/2	1.8 miles	680 feet/ 5772 feet	mid-July– Oct

Map: Green Trails Blue Lake No. 334; **Contact:** Gifford Pinchot National Forest, Cowlitz Valley Ranger District; **Notes:** Rough road to trailhead, high-clearance and four-wheel drive required. Trail open to horses, mountain bikes, and motorcycles; **GPS:** N 46 23.532, W 121 36.980

Let me be perfectly honest. The road to this place is extremely rough, and by rough I mean that it's fit only for high-clearance vehicles burly enough to drive up what feels like a riverbed gone bad. If you have one of those, or can sweet-talk a friend who has one into going, you'll very much enjoy this short climb to a fantastic rocky summit, perched high above the Cispus River valley with great Mount Adams views. Road notwithstanding, this short and fairly easy hike is perfect for newbie hikers, kids, or those otherwise unable to reach mountain views like this under their own steam. Sadly, motorized users are permitted to cruise up this pristine peak, but they generally approach from a different trail and they can't go as far as feet on the exposed summit.

GETTING THERE
From Randle, drive State Route 131 south for approximately 0.9 mile and bear left at a junction onto Forest Road 23. Continue 10.3 miles and then turn left onto FR 22. After another 5.7 miles, turn right on FR 78 then, in 7.2 miles, reach a fairly large junction at which you turn left onto FR 7807. Travel 1.7 miles on FR 7807, then, just past the crest of a hill, turn right onto an unsigned road. Continue straight for 0.4 mile to park in a pullout near the road sign, as the road past here is not fit for most vehicles.

ON THE TRAIL
From where you parked, walk up the very rough road a short distance until the road magically starts turning into a trail and is marked by two signs. The first sign is a plastic post with worn-off numbers, noting the permitted trail users, which is everything but quads (ATVs). The next sign, located

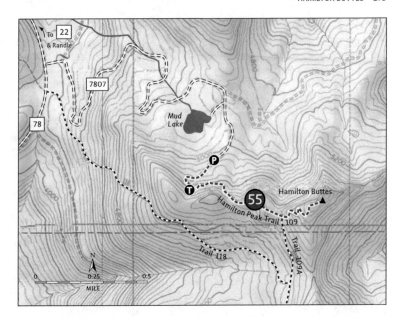

0.4 mile beyond where you parked, is on a tree to the trail's right (we'll call this the trailhead), stating that you are, in fact, on Hamilton Peak Trail No. 109. The dusty loose soil is an indicator that motorized traffic has been through here, but don't despair—it's still worth the trek!

The trail zigzags up the hillside, getting more and more open until you break out into open meadows under a stone shelf. Seasonal wildflowers put on a show, with varieties such as mariposa lily, paintbrush, columbine, Sitka valerian, lupine, aster, tiger lily, and the list goes on! Below you, the brown murky water of Mud Lake is visible, the only thing clear about it being how it got its name.

In a short 0.8 mile from the parking area, the trail makes one last steep push to deliver you to the summit of Hamilton Buttes. Two

peaks make up the summit, and a trail goes from one to the next. Those who aren't sure-footed will be content to sit among the stone of the first peak and enjoy the view, which is nearly identical to the one from its neighbor. To the southeast is Mount Adams in all her glory, while to the north in the distance is Mount Rainier and the craggy peaks of the Goat Rocks. From your perch, keep an eye out for bears wandering around in the open meadows below, eating huckleberries on the sunny hillsides attempting to get their fill before winter.

In the late 1920s a lookout tower was constructed on this mountain, but it was abandoned by the 1960s. Like so many lookouts of that time period, the tower was of L4 construction—the iconic windowed structures with wraparound decks and thick shutters—but this one in particular hung over the edge of the cliff, with views directly down the north side. Little remains of the lookout today but the striking landscapes over which it reigned. Enjoy the views to your heart's content before heading back.

56 Green Mountain

RATING/ DIFFICULTY	ROUNDTRIP	ELEV GAIN/ HIGH POINT	SEASON
**/3	5.6 miles	1235 feet/ 5100 feet	mid-July– Oct

Map: Green Trails Blue Lake No. 334; **Contact:** Gifford Pinchot National Forest, Cowlitz Valley Ranger District; **Notes:** Rough road to trailhead, high-clearance vehicle recommend. Trail open to horses, mountain bikes, and motorcycles; **GPS:** N 46 19.732, W 121 34.474

From the top of Green Mountain, Mount Adams bursts through the skyline to the southeast, just a hop, skip, and a jump away. In the distance, the summits of Mount St. Helens and Mount Rainier beg for recognition. This trail is gentle enough to be enjoyed by those unable to climb more difficult routes, but it's challenging in its own way. The dust created by motorized traffic can be cough-worthy at times, so plan your visit after a showery weather pattern for a more enjoyable hike.

GETTING THERE

From Randle, drive State Route 131 south for approximately 0.9 mile and bear left at a junction onto Forest Road 23. Continue 17.5 miles and then bear left onto FR 21. After another 4.5 miles, turn right at a road signed for Horseshoe Lake. Bear left in 0.5 mile at

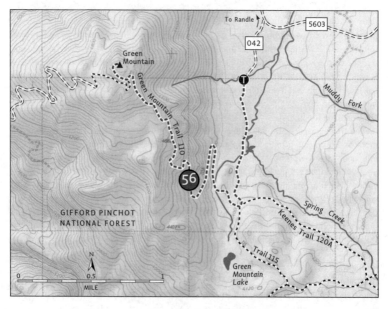

the road fork onto FR 56. Drive 2.5 miles, then turn right onto unsigned FR 5603. Continue for 3 miles, then turn right onto FR 042, a small spur road signed "Spring Creek Tr No. 115." Park when you've had enough of the trees pin-striping your vehicle and walk to the trailhead at the road's end, or continue on the very brushy narrow road to a small parking area where the road dead-ends.

ON THE TRAIL

Begin on Spring Creek Trail No. 115, which is marked by a couple of signs, both in need of some TLC. Head south on the mostly level trail and pass through a tall-grass meadow with peekaboo views of Mount Adams, foreshadowing the views to come. Duck back into the forest, continuing on level grade before arriving at a junction with Keenes Trail No. 120A, just 0.7 mile from the trailhead. The sign here is somewhat confusing, pointing in various directions and maybe causing you to pull out your map.

Stay on Spring Creek Trail No. 115 southbound, which is the main path you've been following, and in just 75 feet arrive at the junction with Green Mountain Trail No. 110, heading west. Follow Trail No. 110 as it crosses some small creeks on sturdy bridges before it begins to climb. Thank the wheels for these bridges, since they were built and are maintained by the folks who enjoy zipping around these mountains in helmets and padding.

From here, the trail switches back, gradually climbing under lichen-covered Douglas firs before crossing several open hillsides. Views of the Goat Rocks to the northeast make you stop to look, a good excuse to catch your breath. These open hillsides are favored among red-tailed hawks, who hunt rodents from trees above, so be sure to scan

A lenticular cloud signifying changing weather forms over Mount Adams as seen from Green Mountain.

the trees and skyline. The trail pops back into the woods and jogs left (southwest) for a short distance before heading back right (west).

In 1.9 miles from the turn-off onto Green Mountain Trail No. 110, arrive at a junction with a short spur leading to the summit. Stay straight at the sign and proceed to climb the final 0.2 mile to your final destination, the top of Green Mountain. Play "name that peak," with your map out for a cheat sheet, as you turn in circles looking at everything from Hamilton Buttes to Council Bluff and beyond. When you've enjoyed the vista, trace your steps back to the trailhead.

57 Takhlakh Lake and Takh Takh Meadow

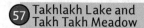

RATING/ DIFFICULTY	LOOP	ELEV GAIN/ HIGH POINT	SEASON
**/2	2.3 miles	410 feet/ 4620 feet	July–Oct

Map: Green Trails Blue Lake No. 334; **Contact:** Gifford Pinchot National Forest, Cowlitz Valley Ranger District; **Notes:** Rough road to trailhead; **GPS:** N 46 16.803, W 121 35.901

Those who have never been to Takhlakh Lake all have the same response when they arrive: "WOW!" This gorgeous lake, teeming with rainbow trout, sits nestled in evergreens with a jaw-dropping reflection of Mount Adams. While it offers good fishing, it also has a spacious camp-ground and a relatively short figure-eight loop trail that explores the Takh Takh lava field. Somewhat deceptively, this trail is not about the meadow, but rather the interesting lava in the area. Make a weekend of it!

GETTING THERE

From Randle, drive State Route 131 south for approximately 0.9 mile and bear left at a junction onto Forest Road 23. At 32 miles, turn left on FR 2329 toward Takhlakh Lake. In 0.8 mile, stay right at a fork, staying on FR 2329. In another 0.7 mile, bear right again, locating the lake and the day-use parking area on the left, 0.1 mile farther.

ON THE TRAIL

Mosquitoes enjoy this lake as much as people do, so hose yourself with bug spray before you romp to save yourself bites and aggravation. Once the repellent suit of armor

Takhlakh Lake kicks off the start of the Takh Takh Meadow Hike.

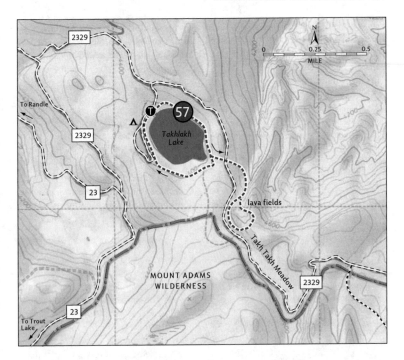

is donned, you'll be ready to start off. The trail starts to the north (left) of the day-use area and winds around the lake on a wide path through seasonal huckleberry bushes.

In about 0.5 mile, arrive at a junction with Meadow Trail No. 136. Turn left (east) and follow the signs on the trees pointing you toward Takh Takh Meadow. Another sign just afterward announces the junction with FR 2329. Continue forward on the Meadow Trail and cross over the road, finding the trail again on the other side in cool forest. Large lava rocks show through the trees to the trail's north, an indication of what's to come.

At 0.8 mile, arrive at a fork at the toe of the lava field, with the way going north and south. Neither direction is better than the

other, as they both bring you back to this very spot, so flip a coin. Heading south, the trail winds around past the giant lava rocks, with birds flitting around in dead ghost trees overhead. The trail flirts with the shoulder of FR 2329 before it continues the loop.

As a side note: Those looking to get a better view of Takh Takh Meadow may want to take a short detour here and walk the road 0.4 mile roundtrip (out and back), as the trail mainly stays with the lava field. "Takhlakh," or "Takh Takh," is a Taidnapam/Yakama word meaning "small prairie," so perhaps the meadow, with its rich wildflowers, inspired the name long ago.

Back on the trail, the loop continues swinging around the lava rocks and begins a small climb to put you on top of the field, with in-and-out views of Mount Adams and Mount Rainier. The basalt lava field you are exploring poured down from Mount Adams more than three thousand years ago and serves as an ancient reminder of volcanic power. Dead standing trees provide insects for Clark's nutcrackers, gray jays, northern flickers, and pileated woodpeckers.

Watch your step as you crest the final loop of lava and pay attention when following the trail, as the stone makes it easy to wander off the main path. Before you know it, you're back where you started less than 0.5 mile before. Wander back through the forest the way you came, crossing back over the road and backtracking to Takhlakh Loop Trail No. 134, also known as "the trail around the lake." From here, turn left (west) and follow the lakeshore, meandering on a wide, flat trail back to the day-use area.

58 Council Bluff

RATING/ DIFFICULTY	ROUNDTRIP	ELEV GAIN/ HIGH POINT	SEASON
****/3	3.2 miles	890 feet/ 5180 feet	mid-July– Oct

Map: Green Trails Blue Lake No. 334; **Contact:** Gifford Pinchot National Forest, Cowlitz Valley Ranger District; **Notes:** Rough road to trailhead. Boundary Trail No. 1 is open to horses, mountain bikes, and motorcycles. Council Bluff Trail No. 117 is hiker-only. **GPS:** N 46 15.779, W 121 37.976

Getting to Council Bluff is not nearly as exciting as the destination itself. A defunct Forest Service road leads the way to the short spur trail that puts you on the top. The summit views are vast and well

worth the yawns to get there. Years ago, a fire tower stood here, watching over Council Lake below and the Mount Adams Wilderness not far in the distance. Today, the fire tower is gone, leaving behind a perfectly flat place to enjoy a picnic with a bird's-eye view.

GETTING THERE
From Randle, turn south onto State Route 131. After approximately 0.9 mile, bear left at a junction onto Forest Road 23 and continue another 32.6 miles. Turn right (west) toward Council Lake on FR 2334 and drive 1.2 miles. Turn right (north) and follow the road to the campground. Park near the gated road.

ON THE TRAIL
Begin by walking up the defunct Forest Service road, which passes a couple of designated campsites near the campground. In a short distance, find the official trailhead for Trail No. 1, otherwise known as the Boundary Trail. The road-turned-trail turns north and continues climbing on the wide swath bordered by a forest of Douglas firs.

In roughly 1 mile, just before the road-trail turns left (west), a short trail to the right (east) breaks the monotony with a view down to Council Lake below and out to Mount Adams on the skyline. After enjoying the view, hop back on the defunct road and follow it left (west), where soon it begins to level out.

In 1.3 miles from the the parking area, look to the right (north) and locate a very well-used trail that shoots off into the forest near a barrier for motorized users. Although it's not well marked, this is Council Bluff Trail No. 117. From here, switchback on open hillsides among huckleberries and juniper shrubs, watching the views get better and better.

Mount Adams keeps a close eye on Council Lake as viewed from Council Bluff.

In 1.6 miles from where you started, plant your feet firmly on the top of Council Bluff. To the southeast is one of the best views of Mount Adams around, complete with the aqua-colored Council Lake in the foreground. To the north is Mount Rainier, shining high in the sky, along with the jagged ridge of the Goat Rocks just slightly to the

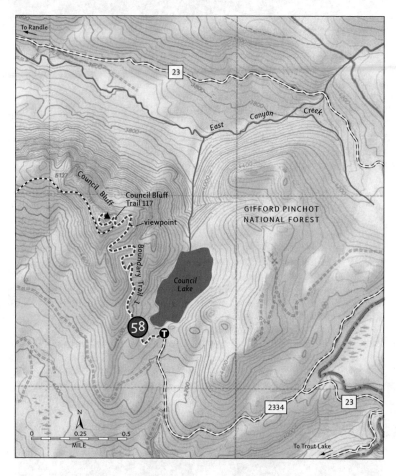

northeast. The lookout tower that stood here was a classic L4 construction, complete with wraparound deck; it graced this peak from the 1930s to 1967, when it was destroyed. Today, no evidence remains except a great spot to sit, commune with nature, and enjoy the views. When you've seen enough, head back the way you came. Or continue along the defunct road, a.k.a. the Boundary Trail, for as long as you wish before heading back.

Opposite: Lakes, creeks, and waterways abound in Indian Heaven Wilderness.

indian heaven wilderness

Inside the Gifford Pinchot National Forest are more than 20,000 protected acres of wilderness, with more than 175 small lakes and countless meadows. The area, called Indian Heaven Wilderness, has long been culturally important to Native Americans as grounds for hunting, fishing, and berry picking. Today, a number of trail systems give visitors countless opportunities for exploration of this area's scenic splendor. In early summer, mosquitoes can suck you dry, so wear plenty of bug spray or opt to visit after August for better odds beating the biters.

59 Lake Wapiki

RATING/ DIFFICULTY	ROUNDTRIP	ELEV GAIN/ HIGH POINT	SEASON
***/3	7 miles	1600 feet/ 5260 feet	late July– Oct

Map: Green Trails Indian Heaven No. 365S; **Contact:** Gifford Pinchot National Forest, Mount Adams Ranger District; **Notes:** Free wilderness use permit at trailhead. Trail open to horses; **GPS:** N 46 01.721, W 121 41.156

Above Lake Wapiki sits Lemei Rock, the highest point in the Indian Heaven Wilderness and the last remnant of an ancient volcano. Lake Wapiki now fills up what was its crater. Thinking of this geology helps you get a visual picture of what this area may have looked like millions of years ago. Today, the lake is one of the most remote and beautiful lakes in the Indian Heaven Wilderness and gives you a true sense of solitude and quiet. Filled with small brook trout and dotted with numerous campsites, this place is perfect for the day or for a weekend getaway.

GETTING THERE
From the town of Trout Lake, head west on State Route 141. Although the highway sign says "north," the road actually goes west. After 5.4 miles, you enter the Gifford Pinchot National Forest, and the highway becomes Forest Road 24. At 7.5 miles beyond Trout Lake turn right to continue on FR 24 for

Lake Wapiki is one of the most remote and serene lakes in the Indian Heaven Wilderness.

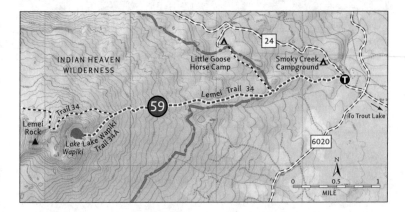

another 4.9 miles. Find a small parking area on your right and the Lemei trailhead (Trail No. 34) on your left.

ON THE TRAIL

Begin hiking through sparse trees and huckleberry-meets-beargrass understory, using care to watch for Pacific tree frogs. One nearly met its demise by holding perfectly still, likely scared senseless, as I stepped forward in this area.

The trail gains little elevation and in 1 mile meets up with a trail that leads toward Little Goose Horse Camp. Proceed straight at this junction and continue roaming through the forest, passing a wilderness boundary sign. The trail begins climbing now, gaining elevation gradually. Give a look back down the trail and see if you can spy Mount Adams popping up occasionally. It hides well among the timber, and only a keen eye on a clear day will find it.

In 2.1 miles and 1060 feet of gain beyond the Little Goose Horse Camp trail junction, arrive at another junction, with Lake Wapiki Trail No. 34A leading to the left (southwest). Follow Trail No. 34A for 0.4 mile as it tra-

verses a forested hillside and delivers you to the serene shores of Lake Wapiki. Jeffrey's shooting star and buttercup adorn the meadows, which turn to swamps in early season snowmelt. Follow the footpath around the lake, or just relax by the shoreline and soak it all in.

60 East Crater and Bear and Elk Lakes

RATING/ DIFFICULTY	LOOP	ELEV GAIN/ HIGH POINT	SEASON
***/3	10.3 miles	1535 feet/ 5015 feet	mid-July– Oct

Map: Green Trails Indian Heaven No. 365S; **Contact:** Gifford Pinchot National Forest, Mount Adams Ranger District; **Notes:** Free wilderness use permit at trailhead. High-clearance vehicle required. Trail open to horses; **GPS:** N 45 58.879, W 121 45.477

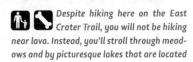 *Despite hiking here on the East Crater Trail, you will not be hiking near lava. Instead, you'll stroll through meadows and by picturesque lakes that are located*

The crystal-clear waters of Elk Lake beg you to stop for a look.

in the shadow of East Crater, an old shield volcano. While the land's contours make the volcano difficult to see, plenty of other natural beauty keeps your camera shutter clicking! Elk and deer frequent the scenic meadows filled with seasonal wildflowers, while gray jays squawk amongst the trees near Elk Lake, the perfect side trip for a picnic. Just make sure your vehicle has high clearance as the road to the trailhead is a doozie.

GETTING THERE

From the town of Trout Lake, head west on State Route 141. Although the highway sign says "north," the road actually goes west. After 5.4 miles, you enter the Gifford Pinchot National Forest, and the highway becomes Forest Road 24. At 7.9 miles from Trout Lake, near Petersons Prairie, go straight to get onto FR 60. In 1.7 miles, veer slightly right, toward Goose Lake/Carson to remain on FR 60, and continue another 1.7 miles before turning right onto FR 6030 toward Forlorn Lakes/East Crater. Continue 4.2 miles on FR 6030, (which becomes FR 6035) to reach the East Crater trailhead on the road's left (west).

ON THE TRAIL

East Crater Trail No. 48 begins under the forest canopy, with huckleberries and forest shrubs such as rosy spirea near your feet as you start to gently ascend. In just under 0.5 mile, the trail crosses into the Indian Heaven Wilderness and continues gradually gaining elevation, crossing seasonal creeks and wetlands on stable bridges as the forest begins to feel more open.

In just under 1.5 miles from the trailhead, the path levels out a bit and shallow ponds show up trailside, first on the left and then to the right—an ideal nursery for the biting battalions. Be generous with bug-be-gone spray if you are getting nailed, because the little hemoglobin hunters are horrible in this area during early summer. Evidence of logging many, many years ago still shows itself in the occasional cut stumps, which have become perfect planters for huckleberry seedlings.

Cross an intermittent stream and find yourself walking near meadows to the trail's right, with the shoulder of East Crater on your left. Besides bugs, these wet meadows also attract wildflowers such as Jeffrey's shooting star, marsh marigold, and bog gentian, so

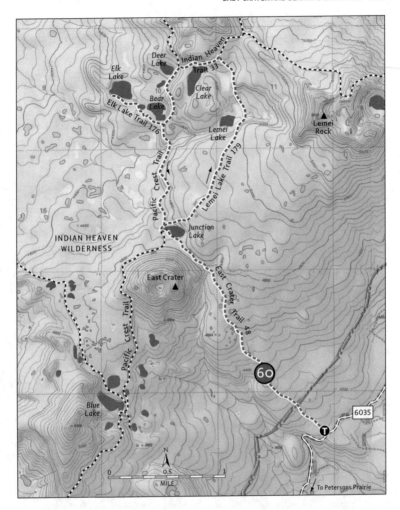

keep your flower guide handy, or take a few pictures so you can ID them later.

In 2.6 miles from the trailhead, the appropriately named Junction Lake shows up through the trees on the trail's right, the biggest "pond" yet. Just afterward, arrive at a

junction with the Pacific Crest Trail. Go right (north) and follow the PCT a short distance to the west corner of Junction Lake, where our loop officially begins. Turn right here onto Lemei Lake Trail No. 179, a muddy mess just after snowmelt, but nothing that waterproof hiking boots can't handle! Hey, some people pay good money for mud treatments at the spa.

Go north past the edges of Junction Lake before ducking back into the woods for a brief period, climbing gently to arrive at some gorgeous grassy-green meadows. Keep your eyes peeled for deer and elk, which graze in this area and have left almost as many (if not more) footprints along the trail as humans have. Also visible in the distance is Lemei Rock, the highest point in the Indian Heaven Wilderness at 5925 feet.

The trail then descends into the Lemei Lake basin, where the meadows continue and press up against the Lemei Lake shoreline, 4.2 miles from the trailhead. A couple of decent campsites at the south end of the lake are good places for a packs-off break. Leave Lemei Lake and cross a couple of small streams by rock hopping before popping back into the trees for a gradual climb of 165 feet to the next trail junction. Watch your step through the creek areas, as froggies go a hoppin' in many places—and getting frog goo off a shoe is not an easy thing to do!

In 4.8 miles from the trailhead, arrive at a junction with Trail No. 33 and turn left (west) to round the top part of the loop. Pass the rather large Clear Lake before descending and meeting up with the PCT in just over 0.5 mile from the junction. Turn left (south) on the PCT, passing several unnamed shallow lakes and tarns. In 0.6 mile from catching the PCT, arrive at a junction with Trail No. 176 going to Bear and Elk Lakes—well worth the 0.8-mile roundtrip detour. These two lakes are among the most stunning forested lakes in the Indian Heaven Wilderness and don't see many visitors. You'll likely have the whole place to yourself.

Back on the PCT, continue southbound in wooded terrain, crossing several little creeks and descending back to the junction with East Crater Trail No. 48, completing the loop 7.7 miles since the trailhead. Turn left (east) on the East Crater Trail, and trace your steps back to your waiting vehicle. Afterward, immediately drive back to Trout Lake to indulge in a huckleberry smoothie from the restaurant near the gas station. Seriously, it will change your life.

61 Indian Race Track

RATING/ DIFFICULTY	ROUNDTRIP	ELEV GAIN/ HIGH POINT	SEASON
***/3	6.8 miles	1615 feet/ 4965 feet	mid-July– Oct

Map: Green Trails Indian Heaven No. 365S; **Contact:** Gifford Pinchot National Forest, Mount Adams Ranger District; **Notes:** Free wilderness use permit at trailhead. Trail open to horses; **GPS:** N 45 58.062, W 121 50.794

Years ago, during the fall berry harvest, thousands of people from Native American tribes would gather in this area, which was part of a cross-Cascades trade route. One large meadow in particular was used for horse racing and competitions in horsemanship, speed, and agility. The soft, level meadow provided the perfect place for the horses to avoid injury while powerfully sprinting to the finish line. Today, this meadow is known as the Indian Race Track, and while Mother Nature has mostly reclaimed the actual track area, divots and channels in the meadow from the hooves are still visible to a keen eye. The trail ends with a trip to the historical Red Mountain

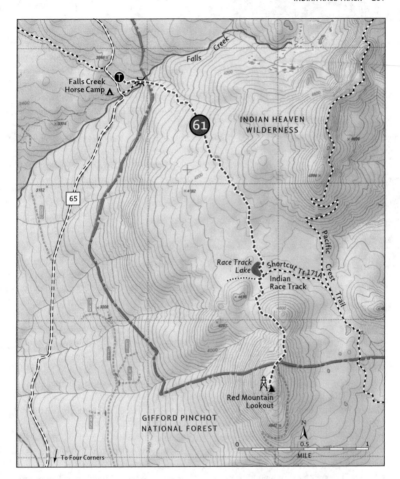

Lookout, giving you a bird's-eye view of much of the Indian Heaven Wilderness.

GETTING THERE

From the town of Trout Lake, head west on State Route 141. Although the highway sign says "north," the road actually goes west. After 5.4 miles, you enter the Gifford Pinchot National Forest, and the highway becomes Forest Road 24. At 7.9 miles from Trout Lake, near Petersons Prairie, go straight to get onto FR 60. In 1.7 miles, veer slightly right, toward Goose Lake/Carson to remain on FR 60, and continue another 10.2 miles before coming to a four-way intersection, known as Four Corners. Turn right here onto the unsigned

From the historic Red Mountain Lookout you get a fantastic view of the Indian Heaven Wilderness.

FR 65 and drive for 1.9 miles to a Y where the pavement ends. Veer right at the Y and travel another 3.2 miles to the Indian Race Track trailhead, just beyond Falls Creek Horse Camp, to the road's right (east).

ON THE TRAIL

The gentle climb begins in a sparse conifer forest dotted with beargrass and soon crosses Falls Creek on a sturdy log bridge surrounded by riparian plants such as thimbleberry. In 0.2 mile from the trailhead, a horseman's spur trail, coming in from the Falls Creek Horse Camp, joins your trail. In 0.1 mile beyond the trail junction, enter the Indian Heaven Wilderness at the boundary sign. The green lichen makes the trees look hairy and in need of a good barber to trim their beards.

The climbing becomes moderate as you make your way through the forest, which begins to open up a bit more in about 1 mile from the trailhead. Huckleberries thrive in the acidic soil, but only those few bushes that receive sunlight through the trees produce fruit. In 1.7 miles from the trailhead, the grade begins to flatten out, giving you a reprieve. The trees become sparser and the meadow-like landscape begins, with grasses and wet marshes popping up here and there.

At 2 miles, shallow Race Track Lake appears on the trail's right (west), covered in yellow pond lilies—like so many of the so-called lakes in the Indian Heaven Wilderness, it's more of a pond. The trail makes its way around the lake's perimeter before delivering you to the meadow known as the Indian Race Track. Today, it's hard to tell what was created by pockets of standing water versus hooves, but it's fun to let your imagination run a little wild as you attempt to figure it all out.

From here, your map and the signage might make you a bit confused. The trail essentially peters out before it seems to dead-end at Shortcut Trail No. 171A, which heads left and hooks up with the Pacific Crest Trail to the east. When you arrive at the well-used Shortcut Trail, go right (west) and follow it about 0.1 mile; then look left (south) for the continuation of Trail No. 171, which leads to Red Mountain. It's not well marked, so you have to follow what looks to be a beaten boot path through meadow before the defined trail in the trees makes you say "Ah-ha!" Pat yourself on the back with your trekking pole for successfully navigating, and then continue on Trail No. 171, watching your step to avoid the Pacific tree frogs that are hopping happily among the lakes and meadows and doing us all a favor by eating mosquitoes!

The trail from the race track to Red Mountain climbs moderately until it gets near the top, where the loose sandy soil can mean one step forward, one step back. Taking your time with your steps can help avoid the feeling that you are on skis. Luckily, the views open up and distract your slipping feet and burning lungs with sneak previews of coming attractions, looking down into Indian Heaven below.

At 3.1 miles from the trailhead, notice that you are leaving the wilderness. Unfortunately, Red Mountain is just outside of the boundary. There's a gated access road, which you'll cross just 0.3 mile farther. Thankfully, the only way the public can visit the peak is by muscle power, so don't expect much company or traffic. Before long, the trail connects with the road and the lookout tower can be seen up ahead. Follow the road around to its back side, and then follow the trail up to the ladder of the old beauty, which has some interesting history.

This tower was Washington State's very first fire lookout, built in the early 1900s by hauling split cedar siding and roofing over 20 miles of rugged terrain with horse and wagon. During World War II, the tower was used as a guard station and was converted to a US Army Aircraft Warning Service post in an effort to secure a mainland defense system. Full-time guards were stationed in the tower for up to a year at a time, through harsh winters of deep snow, icy windows, and little entertainment to keep them from getting cabin fever. It was unquestionably difficult and miserable work. Also during that time the small garage just below the tower was built to accommodate supplies and firewood, as well as for use as sleeping quarters for whomever was fortunate enough to be off duty and resting. The original tower

was replaced in 1959 to accommodate wear and tear. Sadly, in December of 2006 a fierce windstorm nearly shook the lookout off the map. In the summers of 2007 and 2008, a group of volunteers donated labor and expertise to reconstruct the structure, using salvaged authentic materials. Thanks to the Forest Service and these volunteers, today the Red Mountain Lookout lives on! Enjoy the views of Mount Adams, Mount St. Helens, and Indian Heaven from the decking of this engaging building before heading back the way you arrived.

62 Thomas, Blue, and Tombstone Lakes

RATING/ DIFFICULTY	ROUNDTRIP	ELEV GAIN/ HIGH POINT	SEASON
****/4	7 miles	1015 feet/ 4150 feet	mid-July– Oct

Map: Green Trails Indian Heaven No. 365S; **Contact:** Gifford Pinchot National Forest, Mount Adams Ranger District; **Notes:** NW Forest Pass required. Free wilderness use permit at trailhead. Trail open to horses; **GPS:** N 46 00.344, W 121 50.347

The Indian Heaven Wilderness is the land of many lakes, and perhaps no trail showcases the variety better than the Thomas Lake Trail. Not far from the trailhead, Thomas Lake teems with small brook trout and has several shoreline camp spots for picnicking or making a weekend of it. From Thomas, the trail gains elevation gently and leads past more lakes that peek out from the trees. Meadows populated with deer and elk are up next before you arrive at your destination, Blue Lake, the largest and most visited of all the lakes in the Indian Heaven Wilderness.

GETTING THERE

From the town of Trout Lake, head west on State Route 141. Although the highway sign says "north," the road actually goes west. After 5.4 miles, you enter the Gifford Pinchot National Forest, and the highway becomes Forest Road 24. At 7.9 miles from Trout Lake,

Meadows, such as this one near Blue Lake, guide you from lake to lake in Indian Heaven.

near Petersons Prairie, go straight to get onto FR 60. In 1.7 miles, veer slightly right, toward Goose Lake/Carson to remain on FR 60, and continue another 10.2 miles before coming to a four-way intersection, known as Four Corners. Turn right here onto the unsigned FR 65 and drive for 1.9 miles to a Y where the pavement ends. Veer right at the Y and travel another 6.7 miles to find the Thomas Lake trailhead on the right (east).

ON THE TRAIL

As in all areas of the Indian Heaven Wilderness, the mosquitoes can be atrocious in July and August. Once you've tangled with bug spray, grab your wilderness permit at the trailhead and head east, passing seasonal thin-leaf huckleberry bushes and wandering through an old clear-cut.

Before long, leave the clear-cut, pass the wilderness boundary, and begin a gentle forested climb, gaining 210 feet through larger hemlocks and firs before Dee and Heather lakes show up to the north. Thomas Lake follows at 0.7 mile from the trailhead.

Just past Thomas Lake the trail splits. Straight ahead takes you down a small spur trail to Eunice Lake, while right (southeast) takes you onward toward Blue Lake. Head right and gain a bit of elevation before leveling out in some broad and grassy meadows. If you're quiet, you might find yourself observing some of the meadows' inhabitants, including deer, elk, or even the occasional black bear. The trade-off for the mosquitoes are the beautiful blooming marsh-variety wildflowers, such as marsh marigold and Jeffrey's shooting star, which grow with reckless abandon in the moist soil.

Ahead of you through the trees is East Crater Peak, giving you some elevation in this flat and open country. The very small Naha

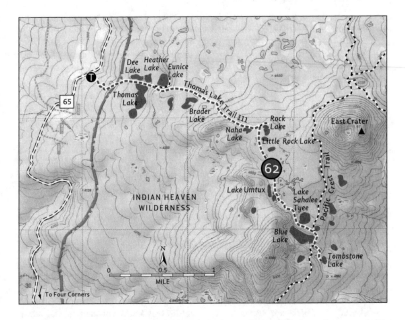

Lake appears to the trail's south, looking more like a pond but giving the meadows some dimension. In wet weather this section of trail can be very, very muddy and difficult to negotiate, with large puddles. Waterproof boots come in handy as you focus on staying on the path and doing your best to protect fragile vegetation.

In 2 miles from the trailhead, the trail confusingly seems to dead-end at Rock Lake and Little Rock Lake. The two lakes look like delicate, clear ponds surrounded by firs and protected from the wind. The trail turns sharply to the right just before you arrive at the lakes and makes its way southward across the marshy meadow's edge.

In 1 mile from the sharp turn at Rock Lake, Lake Sahalee Tyee shows up to the trail's left. This lake, larger than many along this trail, interestingly is the crater of an ancient volcano. Native Americans frequented this area, building trenches for slow-burning fires, which helped preserve their berries for long, cold winters. The lake's namesake translates loosely in Chinook Jargon (a tribal trade language) to "the chief's high, heavenly ground."

After passing Lake Sahalee Tyee, duck back into the evergreens and descend gently to Blue Lake and ample lunch-breaking opportunities near its shoreline. In 3.5 miles, the trail meets up with the Pacific Crest Trail. Curious types may want to check out Tombstone Lake, located off a short 0.5-mile spur trail to the southeast of Blue Lake. Tucked deep in the forest, Tombstone Lake was not named for a creepy burial sight, but rather a rock resembling a tombstone that sticks out of the lake. Soak it all in and return the way you came.

63 Cultus Creek and Deep Lake

RATING/ DIFFICULTY	LOOP	ELEV GAIN/ HIGH POINT	SEASON
***/3	7.3 miles	1615 feet/ 5237 feet	mid-July– Oct

Map: Green Trails Indian Heaven No. 365S; **Contact:** Gifford Pinchot National Forest, Mount Adams Ranger District; **Notes:** NW Forest Pass required. Free wilderness use permit at trailhead. Trails open to horses; **GPS:** N 46 02.885, W 121 45.334

Like nearly all of the hikes in the Indian Heaven Wilderness, this loop features a plethora of lakes, ponds, and grassy meadows. As a bonus, you'll catch a glimpse of the subalpine terrain just under the shoulders of Bird Mountain, have an opportunity to dip your toes in the clear waters of Deep Lake, and enjoy several good views of Mount Adams to the northwest, which reigns over these lands.

GETTING THERE

From the town of Trout Lake, head west on State Route 141. Although the highway sign says "north," the road actually goes west. At Trout Lake Creek Road (Forest Road 88), turn right (north) and proceed 12.3 miles to Tire Junction and turn left onto FR 8851. In 3.2 miles arrive at a three-way intersection and go straight on FR 24. After another 3.3 miles, turn left at the Y, to stay on FR 24 for another 4.1 miles. Find the trailhead for Cultus Creek Trail No. 108 near the campground.

ON THE TRAIL

Begin the loop northeast of Cultus Creek Campground at the well-marked trailhead for Cultus Creek Trail No. 108. Climb moderately through forest and wet pockets of soil containing slide alder, lupine, columbine, and the familiar sight of huckleberries. Dead standing trees here are remnants of old fires, the biggest of them in 1902, which burned hot and fast, destroying the forest but leaving nutrient-rich acidic soil in which today's huckleberries thrive. Keep your ears open for deer in this stretch, as they are common visitors.

Before long, at about 1.2 miles, the forest gives way to a rocky open hillside filled with wildflowers and views of Lemei Rock to the south and Sawtooth Mountain to the north. Wildflowers in the summertime attract rufous hummingbirds, which zip around your head chattering to protect their food sources and doing aerial acrobatic flips with a high-pitched *dood-ity-doo.* I'm fairly certain that translates to "I'm not sharing my nectar with you."

In 1.4 miles, the trail tops out at a saddle at 5237 feet, and Mount Adams's west-facing slopes are visible through a parting in the treeline. From here, the trail ducks back into the forest and arrives at a junction with the Pacific Crest Trail 1.5 miles from the trailhead. Head south (left) on the PCT, walking through airy forest dotted with meadows and ponds—scenery so familiar in Indian Heaven!

A junction with Placid Lake Trail No. 29 connects to the PCT in 0.9 mile from the last junction. Continue on the PCT, and in another 1 mile from the Placid Lake junction turn left (east) on Indian Heaven Trail Trail No. 33, which gradually climbs to pass Clear Lake. Stay on Trail No. 33, passing trail junctions for Lemei Lake Trail No. 179 and Lemei Trail No. 34.

In 1 mile from leaving the PCT, arrive at the shores of Cultus Lake. This pretty little lake has a big brother hiding in the trees,

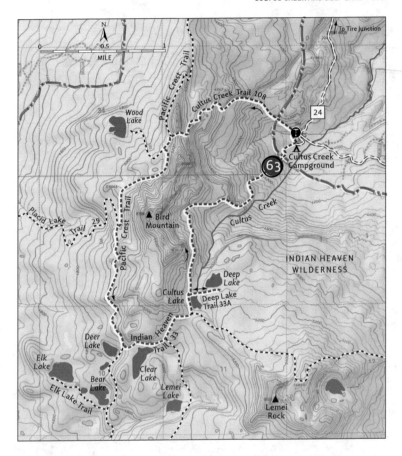

and it's one of my favorites in all of the Indian Heaven Wilderness! Just past Cultus Lake, look for a junction with Deep Lake Trail No. 33A and go right (east). Follow the trail past the north end of Cultus Lake, and then cross a creek and arrive at the shoreline of Deep Lake, just 0.2 mile beyond turning off onto Trail No. 33A and with a view of the very tippy-top of Mount Adams on a clear day. Going left (north) around the shoreline

leads to a couple of well-used camps— perfect places to sit, enjoy the sunshine, watch small brook trout catch bugs, and enjoy the afternoon.

Back on Trail No. 33, traverse the shoulder of Bird Mountain underneath stony outcroppings before traveling through grassy meadows freckled with clumps of heather. From here the trail wanders a bit before ducking back under the trees and

Mount Adams plays peakaboo near Deep Lake.

descending fairly quickly. In about 1.5 miles from leaving Trail No. 33A, you'll pop out at a viewpoint on a hairpin switchback. From here, Mount Adams, Mount Rainier, the Goat Rocks, and Sawtooth Mountain are all visible and worth stopping for a look and possibly a few pictures. From this vista it looks like a long way down to the campground to complete the loop, but shockingly, it's only about another mile. Finish the journey by descending the heavily timbered slope and crossing Cultus Creek to arrive back at the campground.

64 Placid and Chenamus Lakes

RATING/ DIFFICULTY	ROUNDTRIP	ELEV GAIN/ HIGH POINT	SEASON
**/2	3.2 miles	330 feet/ 4240 feet	mid-July– Oct

Map: Green Trails Indian Heaven No. 365S; **Contact:** Gifford Pinchot National Forest, Mount Adams Ranger District; **Notes:** Free

wilderness use permit at trailhead. Trail open to horses; **GPS:** N 46 02.918, W 121 48.552

The trail to Placid Lake is almost completely flat and a fantastic walk through the woods for young kids, those who may have physical limitations, or folks who just want to take it easy and enjoy a change of pace from steep hills. Just a short distance beyond Placid, the climbing is very gentle and easygoing to forested Chenamus Lake, whose silty-bottomed waters are a fine place to stick your feet on a warm summer's afternoon.

The remoteness of Placid Lake makes it a quiet gem.

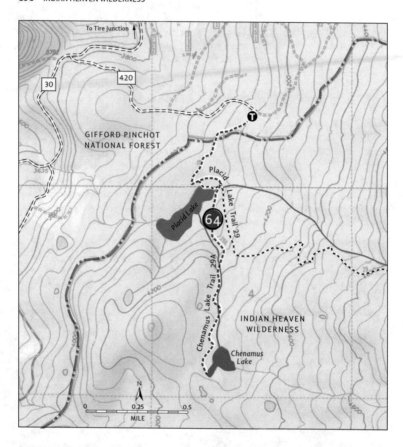

GETTING THERE

From the town of Trout Lake, head west on State Route 141. Although the highway sign says "north," the road actually goes west. At Trout Lake Creek Road (Forest Road 88), turn right (north) and proceed 12.3 miles to Tire Junction and turn left onto FR 8851. In 3.2 miles, arrive at a three-way intersection and go straight on FR24. After another 3.3 miles, bear right onto FR 30. Continue 5.4 miles, then turn left onto FR 420 (signed "Placid Lk TR No. 29"). Stay on FR 420 for 1.2 miles, ignoring any unsigned spurs you encounter, to reach parking on the left and the trailhead on the right.

ON THE TRAIL

Placid Lake Trail No. 29 begins by crossing over a seasonal creek before first opening up into a wide pathway and then narrowing. The trail wanders under the canopy of lichen-covered Douglas firs, mountain hemlocks, and silver and noble firs. Listen for northern flickers knocking and pecking stumps and dead trees to hunt insects and build nests. As you near the lake, the trail opens up to meadows, which in summer months contain wildflowers such as lupine, corn lily, and beargrass.

At 0.5 mile, the main trail curves to the left (east), but the spur trail to Placid Lake is straight ahead. If you wish to stop at Placid and have a bite to eat, take a dip, or do some fishing, head straight and park your pack or spread out your picnic on one of the many logs near the shoreline. When you're ready to check out Chenamus, travel 0.1 mile from Placid and arrive at a Y in the trail. The trail to the left is the main trail, while the one to the right is an impostor, perhaps made by accident by someone who was lost or looking for a shortcut. If you take the wrong one, you'll eventually end up on the main trail again, so don't sweat it.

Roughly 1 mile from the trailhead, arrive at a junction with Chenamus Lake Trail No. 29A. Trail No. 29, which you were following, begins heading uphill toward the Pacific Crest Trail and Bird Mountain, deeper into the Indian Heaven Wilderness. Instead, follow Trail No. 29A straight ahead under the forest canopy before crossing a small creek and entering a marshy meadow area. Look for the delicate blue flowers of common camas in midsummer, growing abundantly in the wetlands.

In 0.6 mile from the trail junction, arrive at the shallow shores of 4-acre Chenamus Lake, a typical example of a flat, forested Indian Heaven–style lake. The bootpath that follows the lake to the trail's right is actually an abandoned section of the Cascade Crest Trail. A good navigator can still follow this old trail to the PCT via Rush Creek and make a

loop, but don't attempt this if you aren't a pro with a map and compass. The old trail is no longer well defined, and everything looks the same out here and you could find yourself going in circles—fun on a merry-go-round, not in the woods. Most folks will want to turn back after enjoying Chenamus Lake and follow the path back to their waiting vehicle.

65 Squaw Butte and Skookum Meadow

RATING/ DIFFICULTY	ROUNDTRIP	ELEV GAIN/ HIGH POINT	SEASON
**/3	9.2 miles	1672 feet/ 4325 feet	late July– Oct

Map: Green Trails Lone Butte No. 365; **Contact:** Gifford Pinchot National Forest, Mount Adams Ranger District; **Notes:** High-clearance vehicle recommended. Trail open to horses and mountain bikes. Open June 15–Nov 1 only, to protect wildlife habitat; **GPS:** N 46 07.484, W 121 47.000

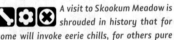 *A visit to Skookum Meadow is shrouded in history that for some will invoke eerie chills, for others pure amusement. It was here in 2000 that a supposed imprint of Bigfoot, a.k.a. Sasquatch, was located. It was also here, in these marshy meadows, that the Rainbow Family of Living Light had their annual gathering of twenty thousand people celebrating love, unity, and peace under a full moon. Whether or not you're interested in the history, there is beauty to enjoy. The area's large meadows offer a sanctuary for bear, elk, and deer to graze and raise young, while the wildflowers of beargrass, false Solomon's seal, and dwarf dogwood are a welcome seasonal sight.*

GETTING THERE

From the town of Trout Lake, head west on State Route 141. Although the highway sign says "north," the road actually goes west. At Trout Lake Creek Road (Forest Road 88), turn right (north) and proceed 12.3 miles to Tire Junction and turn left onto FR 8851. In 3.2 miles, arrive at a three-way intersection and go straight on FR 24. After another 1.1 miles, turn right onto FR 271 toward the Tillicum Campground and Squaw Butte Trail. Arrive at the campground in another 0.3 mile

and turn right. Find the trailhead 0.2 mile farther, on the left.

ON THE TRAIL

One of the most challenging things about this hike is finding the actual start of the trail. Due to defunct forest roads, the trailhead sign is deceivingly placed away from the actual trail, but a short walk gets you there with no problem. Once you've found the trailhead sign, follow the overgrown roadway either on foot or with a high-clearance

The mystery of Sasquatch shrouds the area near Skookum Meadow.

vehicle (if the way is cleared of downed logs) to the sign's right until the roadway starts to turn back left. Look on the right and find a small sign indicating the start of the Squaw Butte Trail.

The trail hugs the shoulders of Squaw Butte on an old skid-road-turned-trail through second-growth forest for 1.5 miles before starting a gentle descent toward Skookum Meadow. In 2.4 miles, the trail takes an ugly walk through a clear-cut before it ducks back into the forest. On a positive note, the stumps of the clear-cut provide good sunny places to sit for a break, while fireweed does its best to hide the scars on the land.

In just over 3 miles, arrive at the first meadow and look for elk, as this is one of their favorite spots to graze. The trail through the grassy meadow stays to the right, even though the grasses are trying to overtake the pathway. From here, meadows alternate with forest before the trail turns east and crosses Big Creek on a decrepit old bridge, in need of repair—it was originally built by the Civilian Conservation Corps in the 1930s.

After the crossing, Skookum Meadow proper can be seen to the right through the

SKOOKUM MEADOW HOME TO SASQUATCH?

"Skookum" in Chinook Jargon can be translated a few ways, including "monster" or "sasquatch," so it stands to reason that the Bigfoot Research Organization would search in Skookum Meadow for their namesake elusive creature. In September of 2000, researchers creatively set up a plate of fruit in hard-packed mud, in hopes of capturing footprints or hairs of the great beast. During the night, vocalizations were heard, and the next day the researchers eagerly gathered at the bait to see what had transpired. To their delight, they saw that their plan had worked; but instead of leaving a footprint, the beast had sat down in the mud, leaned in, and grabbed the fruit, leaving an imprint of its ankle, forearm, hip, and thigh. A mold was created and soon became known worldwide as the famous Skookum Cast. Scientists, including wildlife biologists and anthropologists who examined the cast, extracted primate hairs and determined that they could not be attributed to any known species. Others were more skeptical and calculated that the imprint was most likely an elk wallow. Either way, we're left to wonder about what mysterious beasts walk among us as we wander around these lush green meadows.

trees, and in no time you dead-end at FR 32, 4.6 miles from where you started. The road is gated, so lack of car traffic has it looking more like another meadow. Keep your senses alert for Sasquatch, who is known to throw objects such as sticks and pinecones at hikers; he also has a pungent odor. Or . . . is it your hiking partner?

On your way back, if time permits, be sure to stop and wander out to Skookum Meadow, where the Rainbow Family had their twenty-thousand-strong, multiday gathering in July 2011. In agreement with the Forest Service, and in keeping with the Rainbow belief in sustainability, participants promised to fully restore the meadow. True to their word, many members stayed for up to a month afterward, reseeding the meadow, picking up trash, and restoring the backcountry to its pre-event state. Only a few years later, it's difficult to find any evidence of such a large gathering.

Opposite: Keep your eyes and ears open for elk and deer in meadows like these near Killen Creek.

mount adams wilderness/
trout lake area

In the south Cascades lies the second-highest mountain in Washington State, an active stratovolcano surrounded by rugged wilderness. The Mount Adams Wilderness contains some 47,000+ acres, perfect for exploring and complete with unique trails, water features, and mind-blowing views. Because Mount Adams is remote, the human pressure it receives is primarily on the summit route by those longing to climb to the top, leaving the rest of the place primed for quiet exploration. The trail systems both in the wilderness area and just outside its boundaries are vast and offer a wealth of solitude for those willing to put in the time to get here. Making a weekend of it, by throwing down a base camp at one of the many nearby campgrounds, is a great way to explore this underused and abundantly nature-rich area.

Note: If you plan to hike or climb above 7000 feet between June 1 and September 30, you'll need to purchase a Cascades Volcano Pass from the Mount Adams Ranger Station in Trout Lake or the Cowlitz Valley Ranger Station in Randle.

66 Bird Creek Meadows and Hellroaring Viewpoint

RATING/ DIFFICULTY	LOOP	ELEV GAIN/ HIGH POINT	SEASON
****/3	3.3 miles	850 feet/ 6510 feet	mid-July– late Sept

Map: Green Trails Mount Adams No. 367S; **Contact:** Yakama Nation land, information from Gifford Pinchot National Forest, Mount Adams Ranger District; **Notes:** $5 five-day self-issued permit for Yakama Nation land. Access is July–Sept only. Very rough road, high-clearance and all-wheel or four-wheel-

drive vehicle recommended. Horses permitted on Round the Mountain Trail No. 9; **GPS:** N 46 09.227, W 121 25.501

There are only a few places you can get views of the east side of Mount Adams that are this beautiful and vast. The wildflower meadows that line the trail are an inspiring foreground at the picturesque viewpoint of Hellroaring Meadow's basin to the east and the giant shoulders of Mount Adams to the north. Bird Creek Meadows has some interesting management history. After the reservation treaty of 1855, the federal government and Yakama Tribe disputed the location of the tribal reservation boundary. Bird Creek Meadows and the surrounding area was long managed as part of the Mount Adams Wilderness by the US Forest Service and was thought to be public land. However, in 1966, the Indian Claims Commission determined that a portion of the boundary was incorrectly identified and included land originally intended to be part of the Yakama Indian Reservation. In 1972, under the direction of President Richard Nixon, the boundary was relocated and 21,000 acres were returned to the Yakama Tribe. Since then, Bird Creek Meadows and the surrounding areas have been managed by the sovereign nation, which allows access to their land for recreation from early July to late September, with permit fees for entry, camping, and fishing.

GETTING THERE

From the town of Trout Lake, head north at the Y at the town's gas station, on the Mount Adams Recreation Highway. After 1.2 miles, bear right toward Forest Road 80/82. Continue 3 miles and, when the pavement ends, turn right onto FR 82. (You'll enter the

HIDDEN LAKES: A SHORT WALK IN THE WOODS

If exploring a very short trail sounds like fun, or if you have kids who may not be old enough for longer outings, the trail to the largest of the Hidden Lakes may be the perfect way to get them outside for a mini hiking adventure. While not often used, the 0.2-mile (roundtrip) trail is easy to follow and descends just 100 feet to the shoreline of big Hidden Lake. Two smaller lakes lie beyond but are a bushwhack on old fisherman's trails—not recommended unless you're good with map and compass and don't mind the brush. Bring water shoes for kids to walk on the logs, wade in the water, or get in an old-fashioned water fight.

To get here follow State Route 141 west out of the town of Trout Lake. In about 8 miles, turn right on Forest Road 24. In about another 7.8 miles, look to your right (northeast) for a small easy-to-miss sign for Hidden Lakes Trail No. 106.

The remains of a makeshift raft lie on the grassy shoreline of Hidden Lakes.

Yakama Nation in 5.9 miles, where the road becomes FR 8290.) Continue straight on FR 82/8290 for a total of 10.5 miles, passing Mirror Lake roughly 0.1 mile before spotting a self-issue permit kiosk to your right. Pick up your permit, then continue straight and find the trailhead on your left, roughly 1 mile past the kiosk.

ON THE TRAIL

Once you arrive, you might be taken aback—this trailhead is in need of some serious TLC. Picnic tables have fallen over, trash cans are bulging and need emptying, and the trail signs that haven't fallen down are catawampus and weathered. But since when does disarray stop us hikers from wandering

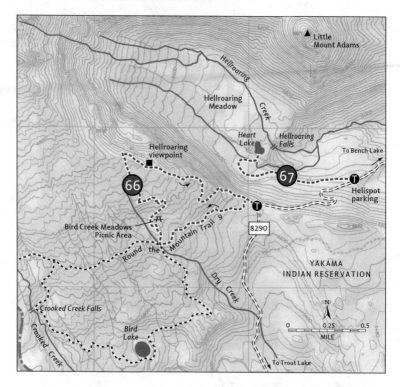

around spectacular meadows? Once you get past the eyesore of the trailhead itself, you'll find the trail, northwest of the parking lot, to be in much better shape.

Follow Round the Mountain Trail No. 9 toward Bird Creek Meadows. Pass Dry Creek Trail No. 90 to your left, 0.2 mile from the trailhead, and proceed on Trail No. 9. This is a good time to tell you that most of the maps of this area are incorrectly labeled or simply don't have good data on this area. Dry Creek Trail No. 90 is not labeled on the Green Trails map, and that's probably a good thing. This trail is so lightly used and is

in such sad shape that it's nearly impossible to navigate and not worthy of a sign. Round the Mountain Trail No. 9, however, is in great condition and provides an enjoyable walk through a conifer forest before it breaks out into a more subalpine landscape.

In 0.8 mile from the trailhead, arrive at a trail junction with a large sign welcoming you to Bird Creek Meadows Picnic Area. Turn right (north) toward the sign and continue on the trail past what must once have been a fine area to spread out lunch. Sadly, once again the picnic tables are not maintained and the water spigots around the area are

In early season, snow still lingers on the low shoulders of Mount Adams near Hellroaring viewpoint.

no longer functional. The trail, however, is maintained beautifully due to plenty of boots climbing through the meadows filled with wildflowers of nearly every Northwest variety, including mariposa lily and marsh marigold.

In 1 mile past the Bird Creek Meadows sign, arrive at the Hellroaring viewpoint, with its extensive views up to Mount Adams's east flanks. From here, the symmetrical red cinder cone of Little Mount Adams, located near the Ridge of Wonders on the mountain's southeast side, can be seen. There are more views to be found, so follow the trail as it turns a hard right (east), guiding you along the ridge high above

Hellroaring Meadow before beginning a gradual descent.

Another showy view of Mount Adams, Little Mount Adams, and Hellroaring Meadow is found just 0.6 mile from the first viewpoint and is worth pulling out the camera and snapping a few memories. Heading down, the trail is less used and at times can be hard to follow, especially where it crosses slabs of stone, so look for the cairns and follow the most obvious-looking path. In no time, the trail ducks into the evergreens and continues to descend, eventually hooking up with Trail No. 9 and making a full loop. At the junction, turn left (east) and follow Trail No. 9 back to your waiting vehicle.

67 Heart Lake

RATING/ DIFFICULTY	ROUNDTRIP	ELEV GAIN/ HIGH POINT	SEASON
****/1	2.2 miles	190 feet/ 5390 feet	mid-July– late Sept

Map: Green Trails Mount Adams No. 367S; **Contact:** Yakama Nation land, information from Gifford Pinchot National Forest, Mount Adams Ranger District; **Notes:** $5 five-day self-issued permit for Yakama Nation land. Access is July–Sept only. Very rough road, high-clearance and all-wheel or four-wheel-drive vehicle recommended; **GPS:** N 46 09.414, W 121 24.736

 *Heart Lake is clear, scenic, and somewhat unexpectedly tucked into the hillside at the base of Little Mount Adams, with plenty of places to stick your toes into the chilly waters, if you dare. While the forested shorelines prevent views of* the big Mount Adams, this trip is still worthwhile. Getting here is fun too, with plenty of flower-filled subalpine meadows to keep your eyes occupied with rainbows of colors. If that's not enough to entice you, the trail grade is very gentle, gaining less than 150 feet of elevation and making this a very easy first hike for young kids or those unable to do more rigorous hikes. The access road is atrociously rough and the lake remote, which works in your favor, since only a handful of visitors make the trek to the lake each year. The odds of having the whole place to yourself to picnic and play are very good. If you can hack the road to the trailhead, you'll join me in giving this one a thumbs up.

GETTING THERE

From the town of Trout Lake, head north at the Y at the town's gas station, on the Mount Adams Recreation Highway. After 1.2 miles, bear right toward Forest Road 80/82. Continue 3 miles and, when the pavement

Peaceful Heart Lake twinkles on a sunny summer day.

ends, turn right onto FR 82. (You'll enter the Yakama Nation in 5.9 miles, where the road becomes FR 8290.) Continue straight on FR 82/8290 for a total of 10.5 miles, passing Mirror Lake roughly 0.1 mile before spotting a self-issue permit kiosk to your right. Pick up your permit, then continue straight and pass the Bird Creek Meadows trailhead on your left. Descend on a very narrow, rough road to find the trailhead for Hellroaring Meadow Trail No. 184, on the left (north) near the helispot parking, roughly 1.9 miles past the kiosk.

ON THE TRAIL

Hellroaring Meadow Trail No. 184 to Heart Lake begins in a light forest of mixed conifers, with an understory of huckleberries. Because the trees hog most of the light, limited berries are produced in this shady spot. In about 0.5 mile, the forest becomes sparser and small meadows allow for glimpses of Mount Adams through the Douglas firs.

When the meadows are in their prime in late July to mid-August, the varieties of wildflowers here are countless, making this a good place to practice your flower identification. Unfortunately, the bugs also think this is the best time to visit, so keep that repellent handy. Bears frequent this area, so use good bear-country etiquette as you travel in and out of the wildflower fields and wander through pockets of evergreens. In midsummer, the damp meadow trail can be muddy in spots, but nothing that waterproof hiking boots can't handle.

A well-constructed stone pathway leads through one particular trouble spot, where the "yellow brick road" of stones gives your feet some reprieve from sloshing around. Cross an unnamed creek on a sturdy log before ascending a gentle hill to arrive at the edge of Heart Lake, just 1.1 miles from the trailhead. A faint trail goes around the lake, directing you to a fine flat lunch spot at the far end.

After reaching the far side of the lake, if you feel adventurous, are good at navigating, and enjoy bushwhacking, challenge yourself to locate the falls on Hellroaring Creek, found by way of a very faint trail heading to the northeast. When you're all explored-out, head back the way you came.

68 Shorthorn Trail

RATING/ DIFFICULTY	ROUNDTRIP	ELEV GAIN/ HIGH POINT	SEASON
**/3	5.6 miles	1445 feet/ 6160 feet	late July– late Sept

Map: Green Trails Mount Adams No. 367S; **Contact:** Gifford Pinchot National Forest, Mount Adams Ranger District; **Notes:** Free wilderness use permit at trailhead. Rough road to trailhead, high-clearance vehicle recommended. Trail open to horses. Forest fires of 2012 affected this area; **GPS:** N 46 07.831, W 121 30.930

This trail was heavily used in the 1800s by sheepherders who traveled this path to graze their livestock on high-country grasses during the summer months. Today, the trail is used by hikers and horsemen who enjoy the small meadows, creeks, and views of Mount Adams that still exist despite the fire damage of 2012.

GETTING THERE

From the town of Trout Lake, at the Y at the town's gas station, head north on the Mount Adams Recreation Highway. At 1.2 miles, bear right toward Forest Road 80/82, following the signs toward the South Climb. Proceed 4.3 miles on FR 80 and turn right onto FR 8040. Follow FR 8040 for 5.3 miles to a Y junction with the road to Morrison Creek Campground/Shorthorn Trail. Stay left and follow the rough road toward Morrison Creek Campground. If your vehicle is not high-clearance, find parking in several pullouts near the campground. Otherwise, you can follow the road a short distance farther to the trailhead, located to the northeast just past the campground.

ON THE TRAIL

Shorthorn Trail No. 16 begins climbing through the charred trees that stand testament to Mother Nature's decision that it was time to clean house. In early September 2012, this area burned hot, leaving blackened trees throughout most of the climb. As in most fire zones, the landscape is renewing. itself. Look for the new growth in tiny shoots of plant life at the bases of the burned giants. Overhead,

birds such as red-breasted nuthatches and hairy woodpeckers love clinging to the darkened trunks. Enter the Mount Adams Wilderness and continue climbing on a moderate grade, with pearly everlasting, Lewis's monkey flower, and arnica making their way back in the sooty soil.

In roughly 1.8 miles, the grade becomes more gradual and enters a small grassy meadow with limited views of Mount Adams through burned conifers. Continuing onward, the trail begins crossing a series of creeks and marshy areas—you'll be happy you have waterproof footwear as you mambo through the wetlands. Look for cairns that mark the main trail near the crossings, since seasonal runoff creates many faint paths in this area. Past the creeks, the trail becomes rocky and begins to feel more volcanic in nature.

At about 2.3 miles from the trailhead, arrive at a large rocky ravine that channels the lightly flowing Crofton Creek. Over the years, massive floods have swept down

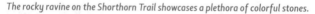

The rocky ravine on the Shorthorn Trail showcases a plethora of colorful stones.

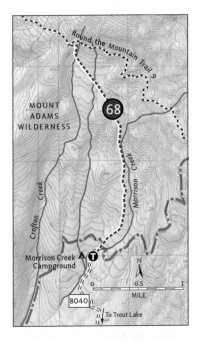

MOUNT
ADAMS
WILDERNESS

Round the Mountain Trail

68

Morrison Creek

Crofton Creek

Morrison Creek
Campground

N

0   0.5   1
MILE

8040

To Trout Lake

Trail ends at a junction with Round the Mountain Trail No. 9, where you'll catch views of Mount Adams's summit as well as Avalanche Glacier, the Pinnacle, and Pikers Peak on the mountain's southern slope. There are plenty of rocks for sitting and enjoying a break before heading back. Otherwise, explore Trail No. 9 in either direction before calling it a day.

69 Mount Adams South Climb

RATING/ DIFFICULTY	ROUNDTRIP	ELEV GAIN/ HIGH POINT	SEASON
*****/5	11.6 miles	6950 feet/ 12,276 feet	May–Oct

Map: Green Trails Mount Adams West No. 366; **Contact:** Gifford Pinchot National Forest, Mount Adams Ranger District; **Notes:** NW Forest Pass, Cascade Volcano Pass ($10–15 per person), Climbing Register Form (free) all required. Free wilderness use permit at trailhead. Trail open to horses. Forest fires of 2012 affected this area; **GPS:** N 46 08.138, W 121 29.877

For those who have longed to challenge themselves with mountaineering in the Cascades, but perhaps aren't ready for the technical aspects of Mount Rainier, the Mount Adams South Climb is the perfect little sister to get you started. The nontechnical south side of the peak puts your boots and your eyes directly on the summit of the second-highest peak in Washington State, where the views in every direction are unobstructed. A photo of you standing high on the summit is a frame-worthy shot and will go down as a proud accomplishment—this climb is difficult! With challenging elevation gain and loss, steep pitches, altitude demands, and year-round

the mountain from glaciers above, creating a deep, slightly foreboding channel that will make you want to get across quickly, even though the water is just a trickle. The sediment in the nearby rocks brandishes pink, rust, tan, gray, and orange, outlined by the deep greens of the nearby conifers—a colorful vision! The creek opens up to views south, of Mount Adams's sister volcano, Mount Hood, and then the trail climbs steeply out of the Crofton Creek ravine, staying with the rocky volcanic theme as it switches back, allowing for increasingly good views to the south. Seasonal wildflowers tucked into the gloriously colored rocks soften up this harsh environment and invite you to continue.

In 0.5 mile from the ravine, the Shorthorn

snow, this hike is best suited for those who are in optimal shape and willing to accept all the hazards that volcanoes can throw down. Before attempting this climb, you should be equipped with proper mountaineering skills and gear such as crampons and ice axes. Also, I'd be remiss not to mention that this climb is wildly popular and buzzing with folks who are excitedly promenading to the summit. While you won't have solitude, you'll likely have plenty of people to chat with as you stop to catch your breath high on the snowfields.

GETTING THERE

From the town of Trout Lake, at the Y at the town's gas station, head north on the Mount Adams Recreation Highway. At 1.2 miles, bear right toward Forest Road 80/82, following the signs toward the South Climb. Proceed 4.3 miles on FR 80 and turn right onto FR 8040. Follow FR 8040 for 5.3 miles to a Y junction with the road to Morrison Creek Campground/Shorthorn Trail, which are to the left. Turn right instead, now on FR 500, and drive roughly 3 miles to the road's end at Cold Springs Campground. Locate the trailhead for South Climb Trail No. 183 to the campground's north.

ON THE TRAIL

Before you begin your climb, swing by the ranger station in Trout Lake to secure a Cascades Volcano Pass ($10 per person weekdays, $15 weekends, $30 annual unlimited) and to fill out the Climbing Register (free). The Forest Service uses the information you provide to assist in finding overdue climbers. The ranger station also provides free human waste bags (a.k.a. blue bags), requiring everyone to pack out their duty and to strictly follow Leave No Trace ethics. Be sure to put that blue bag somewhere it won't get smashed when you glissade back down! I'm not kidding.

The author sits on the top of Mount Adams after hiking the South Climb.

CIRCUMNAVIGATING MOUNT ADAMS

Unlike Mount Rainier, Mount Adams does not have a premium backpacking trail that goes completely around its base. However, with a series of connecting trails and some off-trail hiking, it is possible for experienced navigators to make the trek. Round the Mountain Trail No. 9, Pacific Crest Trail No. 2000, and Highline Trail No. 114 connect to help backpackers loop the south, east, and north sides of the volcano, but the true challenge is a large stretch of trailless terrain on the east side, which is Yakama Nation land. In order to cross this very rough section of 7+ miles, you must be able to navigate alpine obstacles such as glaciers, volcanic stone, and swift, glaciated creeks.

Though toughness prevails, the trip is incredibly rewarding, with outstanding alpine and subalpine scenery, endless mountain views, grassy meadows dotted with wildflowers, and even the possibility of a mountain goat or two for company.

Contact the Gifford Pinchot National Forest, Mount Adams Ranger District, for the most current information. The trip is roughly 35 miles with a high point of 8310 feet, and 7000 feet of elevation gain.

This is a stiff day hike that will challenge even those who are in tip-top shape. Most climbers huff and puff up to an area called the Lunch Counter, a large rocky outcropping at about 9000 feet, and make camp on day one. On day two, they climb the rest of the way to the top and then head down and break camp. Depending on the time of the year, the trail may be rocky and difficult walking almost all the way to the Lunch Counter, or completely covered in snow! In early season you might find wildflowers down low, followed by snow patches and kicked-in steps almost all the way to the summit. Be sure to ask about conditions and challenges in the ranger station when you get your permit.

The trail leaves Cold Springs Campground and feels like any other well-traveled trail. It's dusty and forested, with limited views through the burn zone for 1.3 miles until you intersect with Round the Mountain Trail No. 9. After the junction, the South Climb Trail continues climbing, either over volcanic rock or snow, passing to the west of Crescent Glacier before the official trail peters out. The throngs of climbers before you generally have made a good path leading from the official trail's end first to the Lunch Counter at around 9000 feet and then all the way to the top, but footsteps can go everywhere, so bring your map and compass and be prepared to navigate. Also, look for snow wands, which seasonally mark the safest route. The steep climb up to the false summit from the Lunch Counter is next.

From a distance, the climb from the Lunch Counter to the summit looks fairly straightforward, if not easy, but that bad boy is tough! Not only is the pitch steeper than it looks, but the false summit, known as Pikers Peak, can be a motivation stopper if you're unaware that it's merely a stop along the way. The true summit is still 800 feet higher! Most folks stop at Pikers Peak, at 11,657 feet, to take a breather, enjoy some eye candy, and refuel their bellies. If you do so, have a windproof jacket handy. Between

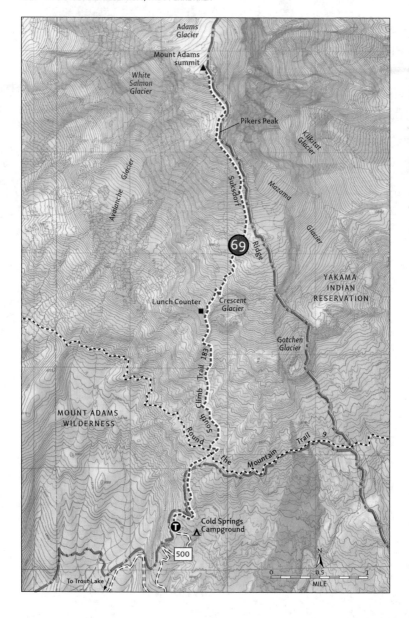

the rivers of sweat coming off you and the icy winds, you'll be a "climber-sicle" in no time. Once you've rested, leave Pikers Peak and travel across a fairly level snowfield before climbing the final wall to the real summit of Mount Adams at 12,276 feet (roughly 5.8 miles). Once on top, the unobstructed views in all directions are truly photo worthy.

If you're climbing in late summer, you may be surprised to see parts of a fire lookout peeking out from under the snow. In 1918 construction of a tower smack-dab on the summit began, taking three summers to complete. Sadly, the lookout was only used for two seasons before it was deserted (one of those "it seemed like a good idea at the time" situations). Eight years after the lookout's doors shut, a sulfur mining claim was filed by Wade Dean on the summit's plateau. The lookout tower served as the mining camp's summer base, and a sturdy trail was built, allowing horses and mules to carry equipment up here. The amount and quality of the sulfur sludge was insufficient for profitability, however, and mining was abandoned in the late 1950s.

The return trip is almost as much fun as standing on the top. Glissading, or sliding on your rear end, using an ice ax as a brake, is a fun way to shave off some time and enjoy the ride down. During most seasons, a "slide" is well established from the top of Pikers Peak and you can plop yourself in the shoot and sail. Slushy snow later in the day allows for a slower, more controlled ride, while icy conditions can be somewhat scary and cause you to pick up speed. Remove crampons before hopping into the slide, as catching them can result in leg fractures, which can really ruin a good day. As always, use good judgment to weigh snow conditions and your abilities if you choose to glissade to the bottom.

Important: As with any volcano, be prepared for climbing hazards. While this route is nontechnical and does not require ropes, it should be treated seriously. Slushy or icy snow conditions may be present on steep climbs. Carry crampons and an ice ax year-round and brush up on your self-arrest skills. Watch for signs of changing weather; snowstorms and fog make navigating difficult. Be aware of the signs of altitude sickness, and keep a close eye on climbing partners. Bring extra emergency supplies, including extra clothing, food, and water. Be physically prepared to tackle one of the state's highest peaks and know that it will be very strenuous. Just forget that I said that mules did it and you'll feel much better about yourself.

70 Snipes Mountain and Crooked Creek Falls

RATING/ DIFFICULTY	ROUNDTRIP	ELEV GAIN/ HIGH POINT	SEASON
**/4	12.8 miles	2500 feet/ 6280 feet	mid-July– late Sept

Map: Green Trails Mount Adams No. 367S; **Contact:** Gifford Pinchot National Forest, Mount Adams Ranger District; Yakama Tribe; **Notes:** Free wilderness use permit at trailhead. Rough road to trailhead. Trail crosses into Yakama Indian Reservation, but there's no self-serve pay station—have $5 on hand to pay the fee if asked. Trail open to horses. Mountain bikes permitted only from Snipes Mountain Trail No. 11 to Pineway Trail No. 71. Range area, cattle may be present mid-July–late Sept—bring plenty of water or thoroughly treat stream water. Forest fires of 2012 affected this area; **GPS:** N 46 05.581, W 121 28.801

Stop, look, and listen—there is much to be learned from fire zones, like this one on Snipes Mountain.

In 2009, the Cold Springs Fire badly burned this trail. Then in 2012, the Cascade Creek Fire came by to clean up anything that was missed, leaving black stands of ghost trees high on the hills, but there is still beauty to be found here and things to see. This trail takes hikers very close to the Aiken Lava Bed, a black field of basalt lava 4.5 miles long and 0.5 mile wide. Up higher, the trail crosses the subalpine scenery of Round the Mountain Trail No. 9 and drops to the scenic Crooked Creek Falls, which is seasonally surrounded by wildflowers. Be sure to bring plenty of water, as the exposed burn zone gets very hot in summer months.

GETTING THERE

From the town of Trout Lake, head north at the Y at the town's gas station, on the Mount Adams Recreation Highway. After 1.2 miles, bear right toward Forest Road 80/82. Continue 3 miles to the pavement's end. Stay straight, now on FR 8225, through a four-way junction, to reach the trailhead (left/north) and parking (to the right/south) in 3.8 miles. Note that although there is a "Road Closed" sign at the four-way junction, it is open as far as the trailhead and parking.

ON THE TRAIL

In the first 3 miles of Snipes Mountain Trail No. 11, you'll gain roughly 1000 feet of elevation and wander in and out of blackened trees, which allow plenty of light through for the plants to spring back to life in the nutrient-rich soil. Fireweed, scarlet gilia, pearly everlasting, aster, black elderberry, and a variety of grasses are making their reappearance after the fire devastation. To the west is the Aiken Lava Bed, complete

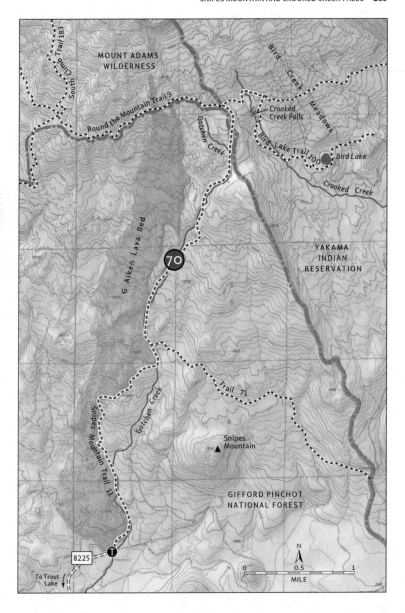

with little pikas that live among the black rocks and sound their *eeeeep* alarm when you walk by.

Due to a somewhat controversial grazing allotment, free-range cattle are permitted to graze in this area, so don't be alarmed if you spot a large lumbering beast through the trees. On a humorous note, they wear bells, and one time, when I startled a behemoth bovine, the whole herd began clanging and clambering at a full trot downhill, causing the quiet hillside to sound more like New Year's in Times Square.

In 2.8 miles, cross Gotchen Creek, which is just a trickle but is producing life on this dry hillside. Quaking aspen trees are trying to make a comeback, twinkling with wind and sunlight. Also keep an eye and ear out for Anna's hummingbirds, which come here seasonally to enjoy the sweet nectar of the fireweed.

At 0.1 mile beyond the creek, arrive at a junction with Pineway Trail No. 71 coming in from the east, with signs on trees pointing the way. Turn left (northwest) and continue on the Snipes Mountain Trail, following the sign toward Trail No. 9. As you continue climbing, you'll be able to see the width of the Aiken Lava Bed—an impressive amount of rock!

In 4.5 miles from the trailhead, arrive at a pedestrian gate with a sign noting that the gate must stay closed to help protect Gotchen Creek Meadows. As part of the grazing allotment, the fencing, gate, and signs were constructed to help preserve the fragile subalpine meadows above from wayward livestock. The Forest Service and the ranchers try their best to corral the cattle, but sadly, between snow damage and limited resources to make repairs, the cows find a way through. This is a case where the grass truly is greener on the other side of the fence, so you can't really blame the bovine! Keeping the cattle out of these meadows is a group effort, and you can help. Should you see them above the gate, the Mount Adams Ranger Station requests that you contact them within twenty-four hours so that they can ask the rancher to relocate the cattle and make fence repairs. And be sure to close the gate tightly behind you.

Hooray for the green and what a change! You've stumbled back into the world of living trees, trickling creeks, and beautiful meadows. Cross Gotchen Creek again with a hop, skip, and a jump before picking your way across a series of bountiful wildflower meadows, one right after the next. In just under 1 mile, cross the Yakama Indian Reservation boundary. The Yakama Nation requires a $5 permit but does not have a very good way to collect the fee. Unless you've been to the self-service pay station near Mirror Lake off Bird Creek Road recently, you'll have a difficult time figuring out where to deposit your bucks. The Yakama Nation suggests having a $5 bill handy, in case you're asked to pay the fee.

At 5.7 miles, the trail joins Round the Mountain Trail No. 9. Turn right (east) for the final leg of our journey to Crooked Creek Falls. The trail crosses over Crooked Creek and wanders through subalpine meadows for 0.5 mile to reach a junction with Bird Lake Trail No. 100. Leave Round the Mountain Trail and turn right (south), to descend 0.2 mile to the cascading waters of Crooked Creek Falls. The Bird Lake Trail continues, but the falls make a fine destination for the day. When you've taken enough pictures and splashed your tired feet, trace your steps back to the Snipes Mountain trailhead.

Stagman Ridge, Horseshoe Meadow, and Lookingglass Lake

71

RATING/ DIFFICULTY	ROUNDTRIP	ELEV GAIN/ HIGH POINT	SEASON
****/4	10.4 miles	2450 feet/ 6020 feet	late July– late Sept

Map: Green Trails Mount Adams No. 367S; **Contact:** Gifford Pinchot National Forest, Mount Adams Ranger District; **Notes:** Free wilderness use permit at trailhead. Rough road to trailhead. Trail open to horses. For-

est fires of 2012 affected this area; **GPS:** N 46 08.409, W 121 35.841

Subalpine meadows, eye-popping views of Mount Adams, and a showy mountain lake teeming with small trout await you! But this trip isn't for everyone because of its challenging water crossings and routefinding. In several places, swift water requires a steady walk over precarious downed logs, and you'll also need good navigation skills to find your way past creek washouts. The 2012 Cascade Creek Fire burned much of this route, and the trail tread is sooty

This picture, taken one month before the Cascade Creek Fire, shows Lookingglass Lake without today's charred trees.

dust in places. But if you're up for the adventure, you'll have fun exploring and enjoying all that this area has to offer.

GETTING THERE

From the town of Trout Lake, at the Y at the town's gas station, head north on the Mount Adams Recreation Highway. After 1.2 miles, bear left on Forest Road 23. Proceed 6.5 miles, then turn right onto FR 8030. Drive 0.4 mile and then bear left onto FR 070 (signed for Stagman Ridge Trail No. 12). Take the right fork after 3.2 miles to get onto FR 120. Continue 0.8 mile more to find the trailhead at the road's end in a big turnaround.

ON THE TRAIL

During the fires of 2012, a long finger burned down to the tip of Stagman Ridge and played hopscotch, dancing from pockets of trees to forest understory. Some of the area avoided damage, while other sections burned so hot and furiously that even nutrient-loving plants have not made a resurgence. As you walk through the charred sections on this hike, note the recovery that is taking place. Hairy woodpeckers flit from tree to tree, hunting down lunch in the dead standing trees, while new shoots from burned beargrass are tenderly starting anew.

Stagman Ridge Trail No. 12 begins on an old roadbed, affected by fire all the way from the hike's beginning to timberline. The trail narrows as it climbs the west side of Stagman Ridge, passing through pockets of thick vegetation such as thimbleberry, bracken fern, and lupine, making a comeback in the sooty soil.

In 0.7 mile, enter the Mount Adams Wilderness as the trail briefly levels out before continuing the moderate climb. Through the darkened trees, the snowy shoulders of Mount Adams begin to tease you and entice you to continue upward. In 1.9 miles, the trail starts climbing a bit more steeply and turns northwest, away from the ridgeline, before traversing the shoulder of a small knoll known as Grassy Hill. From here, the trail descends 145 feet in a short distance to cross a small trickling stream, amazingly unaffected by the fire, before climbing back to the northeast.

In 3 miles from the trailhead, cross a giant picturesque meadow with gorgeous views of Mount Adams as its backdrop, the maroon colors of darkened trees around its perimeter adding a bit of "fall" to your photos. So beautiful is this green mountain field that you might decide to stay here all day instead of pushing on to finish the loop portion! But there is more to see, including Lookingglass Lake, so enjoy the trail as it passes directly through the meadow's center before delivering you back into the trees at the other side.

In a short distance from the meadow, arrive at a sign pointing you toward the Pacific Crest Trail, hard to the left (west). This intersection can be a little confusing, because the trail appears to also be going straight ahead, crossing a creek and continuing on the other side; however, it is not noted on most maps. The trail does, in fact, go straight, and this is where you'll come out once you make the loop around through Horseshoe Meadow. The straight-ahead route is known as Graveyard Camp Trail, or the Graveyard Cutoff, and it's an unofficial, alternate way to get to Lookingglass Lake.

For now, turn left (west) and follow the final leg of Stagman Ridge Trail No. 12 as it climbs another 0.6 mile to connect with the PCT. Turn right (east) and follow the PCT for 0.5 mile before arriving at another junction, this time with Round the Mountain Trail

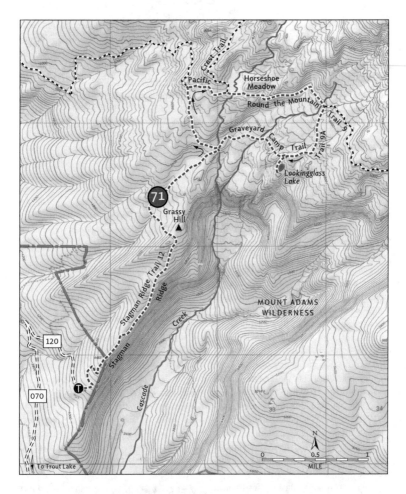

No. 9. Go right (east) and follow Trail No. 9 as it crosses just under the scenic area known as Horseshoe Meadow. These subalpine fields filled with grasses and seasonal wildflowers offer more excellent views of Mount Adams and are a great place to stop for a couple of photo souvenirs. Thankfully,

the fires only affected the trees here—the lupine seems to have no idea that a fire lapped the outskirts of the meadow.

Continue on Trail No. 9 for 1 mile before arriving at a junction with Lookingglass Lake Trail No. 9A. Turn right (south) and begin your descent toward the lake and your creek washout adventure! In 0.2 mile, come to the first creek washout and look for cairns. Each year, when the snow melts off of Mount Adams, the water comes fast and furiously down these slopes, spilling over the creekbanks and wiping out the trail. Locating the main trail at this point is challenging, as you usually have to navigate your way through the various faint trails that other folks have created. Thankfully, most of those faint trails eventually lead you to the main path, and onward you go.

A short distance later a second creek crossing awaits. Once you've navigated your way around the water feature, the trail pops into charred timber and takes you to a Y intersection, located 0.8 mile from where you left Trail No. 9. Although the intersection is not well marked, it's fairly obvious and a cairn leads the way. The trail to the left (southwest) descends to Lookingglass Lake, but the trail you've been following continues straight, or just a touch to the right. You'll want to return to this spot after your visit to Lookingglass Lake, so look around and memorize some landmarks, or hang a hat on a tree.

Then take the trail to the left (southwest) and drop a short 0.3 mile to Lookingglass Lake. From the southern shoreline on a still day, Mount Adams's reflection greets you, hence the lake's name. Just for fun, slap a mosquito or two, toss them in the water, and watch the little brook trout go crazy for a snack.

When you've had your fun, head out of the lake basin the way you came and find your way back to the Y intersection. If you put your hat on a tree, don't forget to grab it, and then head straight (west and also the right side of the Y). Follow the trail as it drops into a riparian area, which gives way to the swift Cascade Creek, with views

of Mount Adams and stones colored with shades of rust and pink.

The great adventure continues as you figure out the best way to cross the rushing water. Usually, those gone before you have fashioned makeshift crossings using rocks and/or logs, and with a little balance you'll get across with dry shoes. If you have to wade, find the flattest water possible by walking up and down the bank before making your choice. Once you're across, the trail continues and crosses a couple of smaller creeks before spitting you back out onto Stagman Ridge Trail No. 12 and concluding your loop, at 7.2 miles. Follow the Stagman Ridge Trail southwest and in no time you'll be walking through that spectacular meadow and on your way back down to your waiting vehicle at the trailhead.

72 Salt Creek

RATING/ DIFFICULTY	ROUNDTRIP	ELEV GAIN/ HIGH POINT	SEASON
*/2	6.2 miles	1040 feet/ 3710 feet	July–Oct

Map: Green Trails Mount Adams West No. 366; **Contact:** Gifford Pinchot National Forest, Mount Adams Ranger District; **Notes:** High-clearance vehicle recommended. Trail open to horses. Forest fires of 2012 affected this area; **GPS:** N 46 06.328, W 121 36.241

The Salt Creek Trail offers pleasant walking through a cool forest past beaver ponds and marshes until it comes to an end near Salt Creek. Kids will enjoy the fairly level hike, with plenty of pine cones and birds to discover as well as the possibility of seeing elk or deer grazing aquatic grasses in the marshes.

GETTING THERE

From the town of Trout Lake, at the Y at the town's gas station, head north on the Mount Adams Recreation Highway. After 1.2 miles, bear left on Forest Road 23. Proceed 7.7 miles, then turn right onto FR 8031. Drive 0.4 mile, staying right on FR 8031 at a junction with FR 070. Follow the sign for Salt Creek Trail No. 75, and turn left. Find the trailhead 0.1 mile farther on. **Note:** If your vehicle is not high-clearance, you may want to park off of FR 8031 and walk the 0.1 mile to the trailhead at the spur road's end.

ON THE TRAIL

The trail starts off on an old road-turned-trail, with a wide cruising lane and plenty of pine needles to cushion the soles of your feet. The white pines signal the transition zone between the cold volcanic climate and the warm desert of the eastern part of the state. The fires of 2012 came all the way down to Salt Creek Trail, but hit it only in pockets and mostly stayed low as a ground fire. Some trees burned, while others managed to escape the flames. Thankfully, the damage is minimal compared to some trails in the vicinity.

In about 0.75 mile, a faint old trail shoots off to the right. Stay straight and continue following the main path as it heads deeper into the forest. Elk and deer frequent this area and have made some well-used game trails, which could fool you into heading off into the brush to explore their pathways; in contrast, the main trail beckons, wide and easy to follow. The trail heads through a small riparian marsh with cottonwoods and alder before it heads back into the forest.

At 1.3 miles, enter the Mount Adams Wilderness, with a sign posted prominently on a tree to the trail's right (east). Almost

Bridges like this one prevent hikers from getting wet shoes on Salt Creek Trail.

suddenly the trees become larger and the path narrows, leaving the old roadway for a more defined trail. Beaver ponds and marshes appear through filtered trees to the trail's left (west), and in less than 0.5 mile from the wilderness boundary you come to a better view. Stop, look, and listen, for where there is water, there is life! Birds flit from tree to tree, deer and elk are often seen grazing and drinking, and beavers swim almost silently through these ponds, leaving only a small wake behind.

At 2 miles, the trail crosses a tributary of Cascade Creek over a small bridge before the actual Cascade Creek shows up trailside,

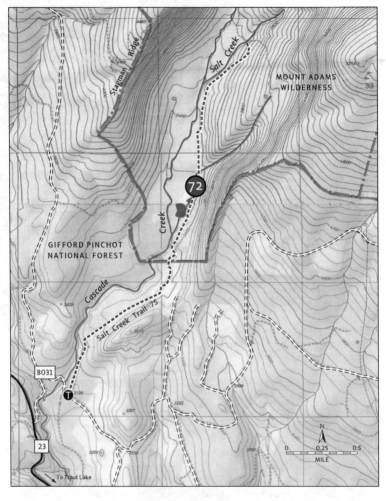

roaring in early season. Trees choked on glacial silt stand frozen dead in time, a reminder that despite this trail's being in the trees, Mount Adams is not far. As a final teaser, the trail climbs up and away from the creek for a couple hundred feet, the only real climb on the way in, before it descends about 120 feet to the end of the maintained trail, marked by a sign I found humorous: it simply says "Trail's End." Since all good things must end, head back the same way you came and check Salt Creek Trail off of your list.

73 Crofton Ridge

RATING/ DIFFICULTY	ROUNDTRIP	ELEV GAIN/ HIGH POINT	SEASON
*/2	5.2 miles	1280 feet/ 4700 feet	July–Oct

Map: Green Trails Mount Adams West No. 366; **Contact:** Gifford Pinchot National Forest, Mount Adams Ranger District; **Notes:** Trail open to horses. Forest fires of 2012 affected this area; **GPS:** N 46 07.281, W 121 33.655

The Crofton Ridge Trail runs along the shoulder of Crofton Butte near Mount Adams, in sparse forest with occasional peekaboo views and a gentle cruising grade. On a warm day, this hike offers a cool creekside reprieve, dropping to the babbling Crofton Creek before ending at Forest Road 8040. While it's not the most scenic trail in this book, especially since the fires of 2012 burned many trees here, this is a great place to stretch your legs and get some exercise if you're in the area.

GETTING THERE
From the town of Trout Lake, at the Y at the town's gas station, head north on the Mount Adams Recreation Highway. After 1.2 miles, bear left on Forest Road 23. Proceed 7.7 miles, then turn right on FR 8031. Drive 0.4 mile, staying right on FR 8031 at a junction with FR 070. Bear left at a fork in 1.5 miles and proceed onto FR 050. Find the trail on the road's left in 2.9 miles. A pullout on the road's right provides room for a couple of cars.

ON THE TRAIL
Leave the trailhead and start out with a gentle climb on dusty soil and plenty of evidence of horse usage—watch your step! Wild strawberries near your feet provide ground cover as you climb, while flowering red currant with drooping clusters of pink flowers give the eyes a worthy distraction

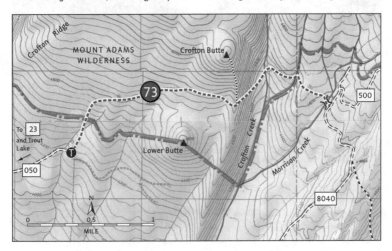

The trail invites you to follow near Crofton Ridge.

and the Anna's and rufous hummingbirds a delicious treat.

In 0.2 mile from the trailhead, enter the Mount Adams Wilderness, where swallowtail and fritillary butterflies gracefully waltz overhead, fluttering from bush to bush, and winter wrens and Oregon dark-eyed juncos carry on feeding in the darkened trees. In short order, the trail ducks into a cool, well-lit forest and ascends briefly before offering a bit of reprieve. Beargrass owns the underbrush, and what wasn't affected by the fires tries to take over the trail in places. Dead standing snags provide woodpeckers a fantastic buffet of ants and beetles high above.

At 1.7 miles from the trailhead, the trail crests a ridgeline near Crofton Butte. A faint trail heads up the ridge, while the main trail begins to drop like a rock, down toward Crofton Creek, descending 250 feet in 0.4 mile. Stop at the creek and soak your feet or splash your face in the icy snowmelt water from the volcano high above. In early season, you may have to wade the shallow waters, unless you've mastered the fine art of balancing and log rolling.

Once across the creek, the trail climbs and meanders for 1 more mile before reaching a sturdy bridge across Morrison Creek, near a flat trailside camping spot. Pop out at FR 8040, in a large parking lot with mostly odor-free pit toilets and near Morrison Creek Horse Camp, the trail's end and your turnaround spot.

74 Pacific Crest Trail to Horseshoe Meadow

RATING/ DIFFICULTY	ROUNDTRIP	ELEV GAIN/ HIGH POINT	SEASON
**/4	11 miles	1975 feet/ 5920 feet	late July– late Sept

Map: Green Trails Mount Adams No. 367S; **Contact:** Gifford Pinchot National Forest, Mount Adams Ranger District; **Notes:** NW Forest Pass required. Free wilderness use permit at trailhead. Trail open to horses. Forest fires of 2012 affected this area; **GPS:** N 46 10.238, W 121 37.588

Pacific Crest Trail through-hikers and section-hikers will tell you that the portion of trail in the shadow of the giant volcano of Mount Adams holds some of the most spectacular scenery in Washington State. The fires of 2012 altered the landscape, allowing for even more peekaboo views through the blackened trees. The day hike described here allows you to sample the heavily used PCT and climbs up to Horseshoe Meadow, a subalpine wonderland filled with seasonal wildflowers and great views.

GETTING THERE
From the town of Trout Lake, at the Y at the town's gas station, head north on the Mount Adams Recreation Highway. At 1.2 miles, bear left on Forest Road 23. Proceed 12.6 miles to FR 521, signed "PCT North Trailhead." Turn right (east) and follow the spur road 0.3 mile to its dead end at the trailhead.

ON THE TRAIL
The trail begins by gently climbing northbound under the sparse forest canopy of young mixed conifers. At your feet, beargrass and huckleberries make up the trailside foliage, while fritillary butterflies flirt with pockets of pearly everlasting. In 0.2 mile, cross a small bridge over a reliable stream, the best place for water along the route. If you think you may need some, pop out the filter and fill your bottles before the climb continues, which gets steeper as the trail quickly gains elevation.

At 1.5 miles, the trail meets up with Riley South Trail No. 64A, which is a connector trail to the Riley Trail to the north. In another 0.3 mile, the trail flattens out a bit from climbing and turns southeast for just shy of 1 mile, giving your heart and lungs a bit of

Mount Adams shows its glaciated face along the PCT toward Horseshoe Meadow.

a reprieve. Right about here, the fire zone begins, with blackened trailside trees and nutrient-loving plants trying to grow new shoots, springing back with color and life.

Just before the trail turns back to the north, a spring shows up to the trail's right—the headwaters of the White Salmon River. It's hard to believe this is the very start of a river

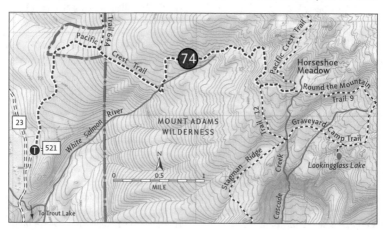

that sees hundreds of summer river rafters bounce over class 3 and 4 rapids just south of Trout Lake.

After climbing steeply for 2.4 miles beyond the spring, the trail comes to a junction with Stagman Ridge Trail No. 12 (Hike 71), coming from the south. Stay on the PCT, which heads east now for 0.4 mile to a junction with Round the Mountain Trail No. 9 on the outskirts of Horseshoe Meadow. The PCT continues north here, while the Round the Mountain Trail goes east and heads toward the large, grassy meadow. Wander and explore! Go as far as you wish before heading back on the PCT to the trailhead.

75 Riley Creek

RATING/ DIFFICULTY	ROUNDTRIP	ELEV GAIN/ HIGH POINT	SEASON
***/3	9.4 miles	2160 feet/ 5750 feet	late July– late Sept

Map: Green Trails Mount Adams No. 367S; **Contact:** Gifford Pinchot National Forest, Mount Adams Ranger District; **Notes:** Free wilderness use permit at trailhead. Trail open to horses; **GPS:** N 46 13.023, W 121 38.052

The Riley Trail leads hikers through a sample of just about everything the Mount Adams Wilderness has to offer. A deep forest climb allows the lungs to feel alive from the start, while the bigger rewards come three-quarters of the way to the end with a series of small ponds, wildflower meadows, the laughing Riley Creek, and photo-worthy views of Mount Adams. These are all great reasons to pack up a picnic and hit this trail!

GETTING THERE
From the town of Trout Lake, at the Y at the town's gas station, head north on the Mount Adams Recreation Highway. At 1.2 miles, bear left on Forest Road 23. Proceed 17.1 miles to a parking pullout on the left (west) side of FR 23.

ON THE TRAIL
The trail begins on the east side of FR 23, across the road from the parking area. Because the treeline comes down to the road and no large trailhead sign is present, the well-used path is somewhat incognito as it ducks into the Douglas firs and western red cedars, making you work to find it. To the left (north), a small but well-placed tree sign tells you that you are on Riley Trail No. 64, while a lonely wilderness permit box trailside awaits your permit request. Dwarf dogwood, twinflower, and beargrass make up the understory as the tall trees sway above.

Find yourself climbing at a moderate but occasionally steep clip in timber before entering a patch of open areas where sunlight has warmed the ground and wildflowers, such as lupine, have sprouted. In 1.2 miles, the trail becomes more level and arrives at an intersection with Riley Shortcut Trail No. 64A, which leads south to meet up with the PCT. Interestingly, this trail does not appear on many maps!

Continue on the main trail, entering the wilderness just a short distance from the junction. Just beyond, the old trail has been replaced, updated, and slightly relocated by volunteers—thank them for the more enjoyable grade, which even with a couple of switchbacks is pleasant climbing.

In 3 miles from the trailhead, small unnamed lakes and ponds introduce trail travelers to new sights, and the landscape

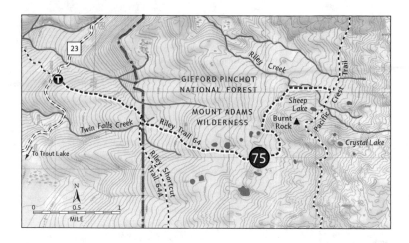

changes to a more subalpine feel. At 3.3 miles, the largest lake presents itself on the trail's left (north), a few downed logs around its shoreline serving as makeshift chairs—a great place to stop for a break or a bite, provided the mosquitoes aren't swarming.

The trail climbs a bit more before it turns north and then drops into Riley Creek Meadows, offering great Mount Adams views. The trailside posts guide you along and point out the trail in places where the blankets of purple lupine just can't help themselves from

Small tarns and lakes like this one populate the upper section of the Riley Trail.

covering up the path. Riley Creek playfully flows through the meadow and provides a reliable water source for nearby campsites. At 4.7 miles from the trailhead, arrive at the trail's end, a junction with the PCT. Explore the PCT if you wish, or head back toward the trailhead at this turnaround spot.

76 Steamboat Mountain

RATING/ DIFFICULTY	ROUNDTRIP	ELEV GAIN/ HIGH POINT	SEASON
***/3	1.4 miles	625 feet/ 5385 feet	mid-July– Oct

Map: Green Trails Mount Adams West No. 366; **Contact:** Gifford Pinchot National Forest, Mount Adams Ranger District; **GPS:** N 46 08.104, W 121 43.656

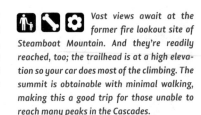 *Vast views await at the former fire lookout site of Steamboat Mountain. And they're readily reached, too; the trailhead is at a high elevation so your car does most of the climbing. The summit is obtainable with minimal walking, making this a good trip for those unable to reach many peaks in the Cascades.*

GETTING THERE

From the town of Trout Lake, head west on State Route 141. Although the highway sign says "north," the road actually goes west. At Trout Lake Creek Road (Forest Road 88), turn right (north) and proceed 12.3 miles to Tire Junction and turn left onto FR 8851. In 3.2 miles, arrive at a three-way junction with FR 8854 and FR 021. Make a hard right (hairpin turn) onto the unsigned dirt road

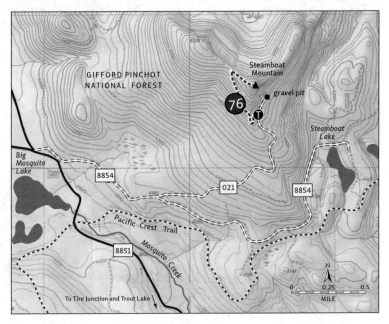

Use extra caution with footing when visiting the prow on Steamboat Mountain.

(FR 021), and in less than 1 mile stay left at the road's fork with a spur road. Continue 1.3 miles to reach the trailhead in a large quarry.

ON THE TRAIL

The trail starts out climbing in timbers, delivering you to the backside of Steamboat Mountain before heading up through thick trailside huckleberry bushes—eat up! Big Mosquito and Little Mosquito Lakes show up to the trail's west, just as the real things show up on your arms, confirming that the lakes' names are appropriate—bug repellent is your friend.

Behind you, Mount Hood shows through the trees, and in no time you gain the ridgeline at 0.4 mile and begin your final ascent toward the top. Seasonal wildflowers such as glacier lilies, paintbrush, and columbine paint a colorful picture near your boots, while Mount Rainier views tease through the conifers to north. If the kiddos came along, grab little hands as you arrive at the first rocky viewpoint, looking southeast out to Steamboat Lake, Lemei Rock, Mount Hood, and the famous Mount St. Helens.

In a couple hundred feet, reach the top of the peak and behold the sights! The footings of the old fire tower are still in place, like a ghost of history. The tower, a 20-foot treated timber structure, stood here until 1966, watching over the southern Gifford Pinchot National Forest and keeping a close eye out for smoke in inclement weather. If you are coordinated and brave, you may want to walk out to the Steamboat's prow, the rocks at the far end. Use extra caution with your footing—that's a long way down! Once you've enjoyed the spectacular views and counted all the volcanoes, head back the way you came.

77 Langfield Falls

RATING/ DIFFICULTY	ROUNDTRIP	ELEV GAIN/ HIGH POINT	SEASON
****/1	0.4 mile	100 feet/ 3565 feet	July–Oct

Map: Green Trails Mount Adams West No. 366; **Contact:** Gifford Pinchot National Forest, Mount Adams Ranger District; **GPS:** N 46 05.934, W 121 43.204

Sure it's short, sure it's remote, but this trip is definitely worth checking out. Langfield Falls is a picturesque 60-foot veil of water cascading over volcanic breccia to a small pool, with a backdrop of thick forest. This short hike is suitable for both kids and adults, as well as those unable to do longer hikes and everyone who enjoys the beauty of Northwest waterfalls.

A short hike leads to Langfield Falls and this interpretive sign.

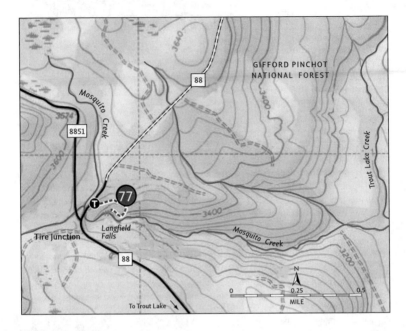

GETTING THERE

From the town of Trout Lake, head west on State Route 141 (the highway sign says "north," but the road actually goes west). At Trout Lake Creek Road (Forest Road 88), turn right (north) and proceed 12.3 miles to Tire Junction and bear right. Find the trailhead on the right in less than 0.1 mile.

ON THE TRAIL

The trail leaves the parking area and heads into cool forest, gently descending through deep evergreens. The purr of Mosquito Creek makes a great soundtrack as you anticipate the coming feature attraction. Through the conifers, the falls! The view just keeps getting better as you arrive at a sign recognizing the falls' namesake.

Mount Adams District forest ranger K. C. Langfield, who served from 1933 to 1956, had a significant impact on forest protection and preservation. The memorial plaque makes a fine vantage point from which to enjoy the falls, or you may want to continue all the way down to the creek.

Benches along the way provide sturdy seats for those who want to sit and take it all in. Kids will love the final, very short descent to the creek, which uses a makeshift rope to help with balance over the slippery soil. The falls itself varies with snowmelt and can be anywhere from 75 feet wide in early season to just a few yards by late summer. Once you've had a chance to snap a few pictures and enjoy the power of water, it's only a short climb back to the car.

PEELED CEDAR INTERPRETIVE TRAIL

Kids, senior citizens, folks with disabilities, or those wanting to stretch their legs and learn some history will enjoy this 0.3-mile walk along an interpretive loop near Trout Lake that rewards with some fascinating Native American history. The trail starts off near a picnic area overgrown from underuse. The trail, however, is in fine shape. As you walk through the large evergreens, small signs identify the tree varieties, while larger signs explain the rich forest ecosystem. The explanations are simple and short, intended to not outstrip your attention span.

The trail winds around and ends at two peeled cedar trees, also known as giving trees. The interpretive plaque explains that, long ago, Native Americans peeled sections of bark off of these two trees to use for making baskets, mats, bags, diapers, brooms, and even infant bedding. While historical peeled cedars have been found as far away as Alaska, the largest concentration of them is in the Gifford Pinchot National Forest.

After your mind has had fun wandering back in time, arrive back at the trailhead to finish off the short loop. For some added fun, you may want to combine this walk with a trip to nearby Langfield Falls (Hike 77), located a short distance away. To get

The scars of harvested bark still show on peeled cedars in the Gifford Pinchot National Forest.

here from Trout Lake, head west on State Route 141 to Trout Lake Creek Road (Forest Road 88). Find the trailhead in 12 miles, to the road's west.

78 Sleeping Beauty

RATING/ DIFFICULTY	ROUNDTRIP	ELEV GAIN/ HIGH POINT	SEASON
****/4	2.6 miles	1410 feet/ 4900 feet	May–Nov

Map: Green Trails Mount Adams West No. 366; **Contact:** Gifford Pinchot National Forest, Mount Adams Ranger District; **GPS:** N 46 05.112, W 121 39.507

From the east, this prominent peak looks like a woman sleeping on her back, hence the name Sleeping Beauty. In 1931 her nose was blasted off (ouch) to build a fire tower (her replacement nose), which stood here until the late 1960s, keeping a close watch when storms approached. She needs more rhinoplasty since the tower has been destroyed. Sadly, it must be hard for her to smell the delicious winds that blow off of the nearby Mount Adams! Today, this peak offers scenery that is anything but sleepy—you'll find some of the finest views anywhere in the south Cascades, well worth the challenging short climb to the top. Despite its remoteness, you'll probably be shocked by how many people climb this peak on any given day, their bootprints and local volunteers responsible for the wide, well-maintained trail to the summit.

GETTING THERE

From the town of Trout Lake, drive west on State Route 141 to Trout Lake Creek Road (Forest Road 88). Turn right (north) and continue 4.5 miles to FR 8810 (signed for Sleeping Beauty Trail). Turn right on FR 8810 and in 1.2 miles turn left before Trout Lake

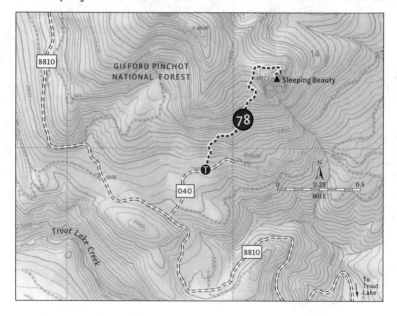

The view of Mount Adams from the top of Sleeping Beauty cannot be beat.

Campground to stay on FR 8810. Ignore the small spur road you encounter in 2.8 miles and veer right in another 2.1 miles to get onto FR 040. Stay on FR 040 for 0.4 mile to reach the trailhead on your left.

ON THE TRAIL

Climbing is the name of Sleeping Beauty's game. Mercilessly, the trail gains roughly 1400 feet in just 1.3 miles, letting up the steep grade for only a stretch of about 100 feet (an indicator you are nearing the top). Thankfully, the silver lining is that most of the climbing is done under a cool forest canopy, usually accompanied by a cross-breeze through the trees. There is no water on the trail, and the rocks on top can be very warm in summer months; take plenty of liquid to keep yourself hydrated.

At 1.1 miles, the trail arrives at the base of the cliff bands and you find yourself face-to-face with a grand view of Mount Adams, only 11 miles south of here. The trail switches back as it continues to climb up to the top of the rocky summit in an engineering marvel of walls built by the Civilian Conservation Corps in the early 1930s. The summit's crest is long but narrow and leads to a number of spots to enjoy lunch and a well-earned break. Heading right (south) takes you to the old fire lookout site, the eyebolts and fasteners still visible. Exercise caution getting there, as the trail is very narrow and crosses rocks made only for the nimble and sure-footed.

The tower was built in 1931 and boasted L4 construction with a four-sided gabled roof, a popular style at the time. The structure was removed in the late 1960s. From nearly every perch where the lookout once stood there is something to see. Mount St. Helens, Mount Hood, Mount Rainier, and Mount Adams make showy appearances, as does the Cascade Crest in its entirety through the Indian Heaven Wilderness. The significant geological history is also evident, as the ground you stand upon is andesitic magma that pushed older volcanic rocks up as it cooled. The andesite was exposed over time, and the older rocks eroded away. When your eyes and soul have feasted on the grand landscape around you, prepare your quads for the short downhill burn back to the car.

79 Killen Creek

RATING/ DIFFICULTY	ROUNDTRIP	ELEV GAIN/ HIGH POINT	SEASON
***/3	6.2 miles	1520 feet/ 6125 feet	late July– late Sept

Map: Green Trails Mount Adams No. 367S; **Contact:** Gifford Pinchot National Forest, Mount Adams Ranger District; **Notes:** Free wilderness use permit at trailhead. Cascade Volcano Pass required for exploring above 7000 feet on High Camp Trail. Trail open to horses; **GPS:** N 46 17.296, W 121 33.144

The first couple of miles of Killen Creek Trail might feel like just another trail following a stream, but the last mile offers large colorful meadows filled with wildflowers, beautiful views of Mount Adams, a playful little creek, and plenty of wildlife-viewing opportunities. Just be sure to bring your camera, so you can remember your time spent in these enchanted meadows.

GETTING THERE

From Randle, drive 0.9 mile south on State Route 131 and bear left onto Forest Road 23. Continue 30.1 miles (stay right to stay on FR 23 at the junction at 17.5 miles), then

Dusty soil surrounds your feet while Mount Adams entertains your eye on the Killen Creek Trail.

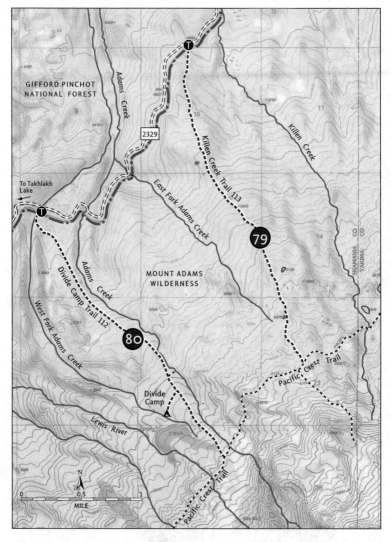

turn left at a sign pointing toward Takhlakh Lake. Proceed 0.8 mile and then turn right onto FR 2329. After another 0.7 mile, bear left at the road fork to stay on FR 2329. Continue another 4.3 miles to the Killen Creek trailhead (Trail No. 113) to the road's right (southeast).

ON THE TRAIL

Like so many trails in the Mount Adams Wilderness, Killen Creek Trail No. 113 starts out in sparse conifers, with beargrass and huckleberries lining the trail. Between Mount St. Helens ash deposits, stock traffic, and hiking boots, the trail's surface is a fine ashy dust, which poofs around your feet as you climb. Imagining you're walking on a beach in Maui helps occupy the mind! Just when you're daydreaming about ocean waves and palm trees, some erosion-preventing wooden steps bring you and your quads back to reality. Thankfully, the grade is gentle and consistent, allowing you to get into a good hiking and breathing cadence as you travel.

In just over 1.5 miles, the forest thins a bit more and there are pockets of small meadows with seasonal wildflowers where sunlight has warmed the ground. Look for lupine, aster, and mountain bistort among the various grasses. In 2.2 miles, reach the edge of a rather large meadow with even more wildflower varieties and Mount Adams looking on from above. Keep your eyes open for elk and deer, since this is one of their favorite stompin' and grazin' grounds.

In another 0.1 mile after entering the large meadow, cross a clear and reliable creek—runoff from melting mountain snow. Rock-hop your way across, or stop and get out the filter if your water bottles are getting low. A few campsites in this area provide flat places to stop for a break, grab a snack, or get out the camera to snap some flower macros.

Continue to gently climb through the meadow, with Mount Adams a prominent companion magnetically drawing you forward to explore her lower flanks. Meadows and wildflowers accompany you from here until the trail meets the Pacific Crest Trail, 3.1 miles from where you parked.

If you want to explore farther, you may want to take High Camp Trail No. 10 at this intersection and climb onto the rocky volcanic shoulders of Mount Adams. Or, if you just want to a good lunch spot, follow the PCT east (right) for 0.2 mile to a seasonal tarn. When you're done with your adventure, retrace your steps back to the trailhead.

80 Divide Camp

RATING/ DIFFICULTY	ROUNDTRIP	ELEV GAIN/ HIGH POINT	SEASON
***/3	6.8 miles	1415 feet/ 6090 feet	late July– late Sept

Map: Green Trails Mount Adams No. 367S; **Contact:** Gifford Pinchot National Forest, Mount Adams Ranger District; **Notes:** Free wilderness use permit at trailhead; **GPS:** N 46 16.146, W 121 34.722

Divide Camp Trail might conjure up images of a camp perched on a high divide, but don't let the name fool you. While there is a forested camp near a trickling spring just off this trail, the features of this hike are the volcanic creekbed cut out by the angry Adams Creek and the wildflower meadows rich in color and fragrance that line the hillsides. The subalpine foreground to the mighty Mount Adams is sure to turn your head and make you want to grab your camera.

GETTING THERE

From Randle, drive 0.9 mile south on State Route 131 and bear left onto Forest Road 23. Continue 30.1 miles (stay right to stay on FR23 at the junction at 17.5 miles), then turn left at a sign pointing toward Takhlakh Lake. Proceed 0.8 mile and then turn right

The nutrient-rich volcanic soils near Divide Camp make a healthy nursery for wildflowers.

onto FR 2329. After another 0.7 mile, bear left at the road fork to stay on FR 2329. Continue another 2 miles to the Divide Camp trailhead (Trail No. 112) to the road's right (southeast).

ON THE TRAIL

Divide Camp Trail No. 112 starts out gently ascending on an old wide roadbed for approximately 175 feet before it narrows and guides you into mixed conifers. In just over 0.5 mile, the sounds of Adams Creek flowing out of sight to the trail's left (northeast) make a fine muffled soundtrack until the creek comes loudly into view through the trees just shy of 1 mile from the trailhead. The forest guides you for the next 1 mile, getting more and more sparse as you climb and introducing trailside rock gardens along with small wildflower meadows where the sun has reached the understory.

In 1.8 miles from the trailhead, a small bootpath leaves the main trail and heads downhill to the trail's left (northeast) to the shoreline of Adams Creek. Take the detour, if you like, to reach a giant riverbed of stone that cuts across a large swath of land. It is a fascinating natural feature worth exploring.

Back on the main trail, a short distance farther, arrive at a large meadow just 2 miles from the trailhead. Seasonal wildflowers such as lupine, mountain daisy, arnica, and paintbrush mingle with grasses to give lively color to the lush fields. An odd metal pole standing to the meadow's northeast is an old snow gauge from years ago when Forest Service officials used to fly over the area and keep track of snow accumulations. The rusty relic seems grossly out of place in the summer, standing tall among the field of purple lupine.

At 2.1 miles from the trailhead, arrive at a trail junction with a wooden sign pointing you toward Divide Camp to the trail's right (southwest). The trail here has no doubt been followed by a lot of people, like us, curious to explore this camp made so famous that the very trail we are following is named for it. The camp is really nothing to write home about, just a couple of flat tent sites

near a dribbling spring. But the trail getting to it crosses a couple of pretty meadows and is worth the 0.6-mile roundtrip.

Back on the main trail, duck in and out of sparse pockets of trees intermixed with smaller meadows, staying very close to Adams Creek. If you haven't explored the wide, rocky, sand-laden riverbed enough, now is your chance! In 0.7 mile from the turnoff to Divide Camp, arrive at the trail's end, a junction with the Pacific Crest Trail. Explore the PCT if you wish, or turn back the way you came.

81 Muddy Meadows and Foggy Flat

RATING/ DIFFICULTY	ROUNDTRIP	ELEV GAIN/ HIGH POINT	SEASON
***/3	11.6 miles	1845 feet/ 5970 feet	late July– late Sept

Map: Green Trails Mount Adams No. 367S; **Contact:** Gifford Pinchot National Forest, Mount Adams Ranger District; **Notes:** Free wilderness use permit at trailhead. Rough road to trailhead, high-clearance vehicle recommended. Trail open to horses; **GPS:** N 46 18.485, W 121 32.365

Everyone loves meadows, and this trail starts out smack-dab in the middle of a scenic one. From there, the gentle climb takes you up to a level (hence the name) grassy expanse with views of Mount Adams. Foggy? Perhaps, but not when I was there! Odds are you'll be enjoying your picnic with a great view, nary a soul around, and plenty of peace and quiet, save for the clacking Clark's nutcrackers carrying on in the nearby trees.

Mount Adams peeks out of a smoky haze near Muddy Meadows.

GETTING THERE

From Randle, drive 0.9 mile south on State Route 131 and bear left onto Forest Road 23. After 17.5 miles, bear left onto FR 21. Continue 4.5 miles and then turn right on FR 5601 (near Adams Fork). In 0.5 mile, keep left at the small fork to get onto FR 56 (signed for Keenes Horse Camp). Continue 2.5 miles, then turn right onto an unsigned road (FR 5603, signed for Horseshoe Lake). Proceed on this road for 5.2 miles, then turn right onto FR 2329. In 2.1 miles, turn left toward Muddy Meadows on FR 085. Stay left at the road fork in 0.1 mile to reach the trailhead at the road's end in another 0.2 mile.

ON THE TRAIL

The trailhead is located in the vast Muddy Meadows, with a fantastic view of Mount Adams even before you start your hike. Elk and deer love to graze on the sweet grasses here, so keep your eyes and ears open as you set out. In 0.1 mile, duck into sparse conifers and enter the Mount Adams Wilderness. A

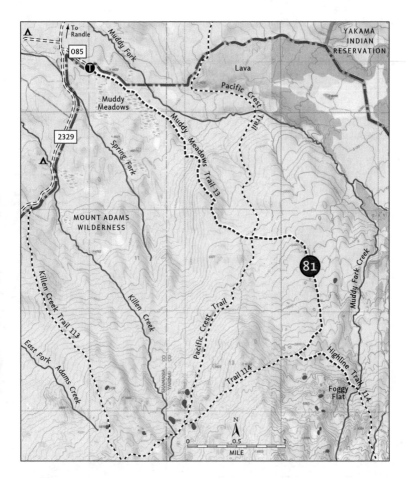

plank-style wooden bridge accompanies you over some wetlands just 0.3 mile from the trailhead and gives you a few last views into Muddy Meadows before it delivers you back to the Douglas firs and lodgepole pines.

The dusty trail poofs as you walk, soiling your shoes and socks with a fine layer of sand, dirt, and old ash from Mount Saint

Helens, still present from the 1980 eruption. The untidy look is fashionable with hikers, so cherish your dirt and wear it proudly! In just over 1 mile from the trailhead, cross another wooden bridge and continue your climb under the forest canopy, while beargrass and huckleberries guide you trailside. One more bridge crosses over a creek at about

2 miles from the trailhead, followed by several gentle switchbacks determined to get you higher into the hills.

At 2.9 miles, arrive at a large trail junction with the Pacific Crest Trail. If you need a break or a snack, several downed logs at the intersection make fine places to park yourself and get refreshed. Signs in the area are weathered and tough to read, so rely on your maps if necessary. Cross the PCT and continue on Muddy Meadows Trail No. 13 as it slides back into the forest. The signs in this direction point to Trail No. 114 (the Highline Trail), which is where you're eventually headed.

About 1.3 miles beyond the PCT, the trail crosses a small meadow and the trees become sparse. Just beyond, to the trail's left (east), is Muddy Fork Creek and an old camp spot turned restoration area in an attempt to revitalize the natural health of the land. In 1.9 miles beyond the PCT junction, arrive at a large meadow and a very confusing trail junction. Only one trail (Highline Trail No. 114) intersects here, but because it turns in two different directions, it can make your head spin. Trail No. 114 travels in a hairpin turn back to the left (east) and also straight ahead to the southwest.

To get to Foggy Flat, your final destination, turn to the left (east) at the hairpin and follow the gently rolling grade as it alternates between timber and open lands. In 1 mile from the last junction, arrive at Foggy Flat, a rather large flat meadow with a good view of the north flanks of Mount Adams. A pretty little trailside camp complete with logs for sitting makes a fine destination for a picnic or a packs-off rest. A small bootpath behind the camp leads to distant views of Goat Rocks and even Mount Rainier through the trees on a clear day. When you've enjoyed the view, head back to the trailhead the way you arrived.

A 60-foot veil of whitewater splits and drops over the dark stone at Langfield Falls.

Appendix I
Permits and Land Management Agencies

Northwest Forest Pass and Other Federal Passes
www.fs.usda.gov

Washington State Discover Pass
www.discoverpass.wa.gov

Cowiche Canyon Conservancy
PO Box 877
Yakima, WA 98907
(509) 248-5065
www.cowichecanyon.org

Gifford Pinchot National Forest
Cowlitz Valley Ranger District
10024 US Highway 12
Randle, Washington 98377
(360) 497-1100
www.fs.usda.gov/giffordpinchot

Mount Adams Ranger District
2455 Highway 141
Trout Lake, WA 98650
(509) 395-3400
www.fs.usda.gov/giffordpinchot

Okanogan-Wenatchee National Forest
Naches Ranger District
10237 US Highway 12
Naches, WA 98937
(509) 653-1401
www.fs.usda.gov/okawen

Washington Department of Fish and Wildlife
Oak Creek Wildlife Area
16601 US Highway 12
Naches, WA 98937
(509) 653-2390
http://wdfw.wa.gov/lands/wildlife_areas/oak_creek

Wenas Wildlife Area
312 Mountain Vale Road
Selah, WA 98942
(509) 697-4503
http://wdfw.wa.gov/lands/wildlife_areas/wenas

Yakama Tribe
4690 State Route 22
Toppenish, WA 98948
(509) 865-5121
www.ynwildlife.org/recreation

Appendix II
Conservation and Trail Organizations

The Cascadians
www.cascadians.org
Cowiche Canyon Conservancy
www.cowichecanyon.org
Forterra
www.forterra.org
Friends of Mount Adams
http://mtadamsfriends.org
The Kinnikinnicks Hikers
kinnihikers@yahoo.com

Mount Adams Institute
www.mtadamsinstitute.com
The Mountaineers
www.mountaineers.org
The Nature Conservancy
www.nature.org
The Pacific Crest Trail Association
www.pcta.org
Washington Trails Association
www.wta.org

Appendix III
Recommended Reading

Bentley, Judy. *Hiking Washington's History.* Seattle: University of Washington Press, 2010.

Fleming, June. *Staying Found: The Complete Map and Compass Book.* 3rd ed. Seattle: Mountaineers Books, 2001.

Grubbs, Bruce. *Desert Sense.* Seattle: Mountaineers Books, 2005.

Lanza, Michael. *Day Hiker's Handbook: Get Started with the Experts.* Seattle: Mountaineers Books, 2003.

Lyons, C. P. *Wildflowers of Washington.* Auburn, WA: Lone Pine Publishing, 1999.

Renner, Jeff. *Lightning Strikes: Staying Safe Under Stormy Skies.* Seattle: Mountaineers Books, 2004.

Romano, Craig. *Day Hiking Columbia River Gorge.* Seattle: Mountaineers Books, 2011.

Sibley, David Allen. *The Sibley Field Guide to Birds of Western North America.* New York: Knopf Doubleday, 2003.

Turner, Mark, and Phyllis Gustafson. *Wildflowers of the Pacific Northwest.* Portland, OR: Timber Press, 2006.

Whitney, Stephen R., and Rob Sandelin. *Field Guide to the Cascades and Olympics, 2nd ed.* Seattle: Mountaineers Books, 2004.

Index

1% for Trails & Washington Trails Association

Your favorite Washington hikes, such as those in this book, are made possible by the efforts of thousands of volunteers keeping our trails in great shape, and by hikers like you advocating for the protection of trails and wild lands. As budget cuts reduce funding for trail maintenance, Washington Trails Association's volunteer trail maintenance program fills this void and is ever more important for the future of Washington's hiking. Our mountains and forests can provide us with a lifetime of adventure and exploration—but we need trails to get us there. One percent of the sales of this guidebook goes to support WTA's efforts.

Spend a day on the trail with Washington Trails Association, and give back to the trails you love. WTA hosts over 750 work parties throughout Washington's Cascades and Olympics each year. Volunteers remove downed logs after spring snowmelt, cut away brush, retread worn stretches of trail, and build bridges and turnpikes. Find the volunteer schedule, check current conditions of the trails in this guidebook, and become a member of WTA at www.wta.org or 206-625-1367.

About the Author

Tami Asars is an outdoor writer and nature photographer living in the Cascades foothills of Washington State with her husband, Vilnis, and her German shepherd, Summit. She is a contributor and columnist for *Washington Trails* magazine and is the author of *Hiking the Wonderland Trail* (Mountaineers Books, 2012). She is almost as passionate about nature photography as she is about hiking, and her photos have appeared in *City Dog*, *Washington Trails*, *Washington Magazine*, and other publications. A former employee of REI (Recreational Equipment Inc.), she taught classes for nearly nine years on outdoor pursuits like the where-to's and how-to's of backpacking. She has also served as a professional guide, teaching folks of all skill levels the wonders of backpacking in the Pacific Northwest. These days, when she's not parked in a chair crunching on deadlines, her feet are parked firmly on trails—she has hiked most of Washington State, from the rugged coastline of Olympic National Park to the remote Pasayten Wilderness. For more information or to drop her a line, please visit www.tamiasars.com.